PRIMAL SHOPPER

About the Author

Eric Bowe has helped clients develop marketing communication programs in a rapidly evolving marketplace over the past two decades. His passion is to uncover what makes shoppers tick and design brand experiences to convert shoppers to buyers. For the past decade, he has actively researched shopper behavior in multiple product categories. Eric's research uncovered something provocative—we all have primal motivations driving our purchase decisions. These motivations predict how shoppers act within the marketplace. Eric derived shopper principles from the research to create effective marketing for clients. Over his career, Eric has worked with a wide array of brands in automotive, travel, retail, restaurant, financial, and healthcare. You can connect with Eric at www.PrimalShopper.com where he offers a regular podcast expanding on the ideas covered in this book.

www.PrimalShopper.com

PRIMAL SHOPPER

Eric Bowe

Rock's Mills Press
Oakville, Ontario
2019

Published by
Rock's Mills Press
www. rocksmillspress.com

Library and Archives Canada Cataloguing in Publication data is available from the publisher on request.

For information about this book and other Rock's Mills Press titles, please contact us at customer.service@rocksmillspress.com.

DEDICATION

To my lovely wife Karen,
My spirited son Matthew,
And my caring daughter Nicole.
You provide the everyday inspiration that keeps me going.

Contents

Contents

Preface

Timing is everything in marketing.

When I began my career in the mid-1980s it was a different world. I was just out of ad school from Michigan State University. My first job was in media research at Ross Roy Advertising in Detroit. Little did I know I had entered advertising just as a monumental shift in the industry was taking place.

The business was simpler back in the 1980s than it is today. Advertising was still dominated by the big three TV networks although cable had a foothold and was growing rapidly. Planning advertising focused on the five traditional media: television, radio, newspapers, magazines, and outdoor (i.e., billboards). Anything else—like direct marketing—was "below the line", which is a nice way of saying non-traditional media was an afterthought. Shopper data analysis was in its infancy. The first PCs were being integrated into agencies with a smattering of Macs for the creative department. If you wanted to do any serious data crunching you needed a mainframe computer. Oh yeah, and the internet was about a decade away.

If someone had decoded Shopper DNA in the mid-1980s I don't know how useful it would have been. Discovering the DNA would have been interesting, but the ability to apply the insights outlined in this book would be extremely limited. So let's fast forward three decades.

Today's marketplace is driven by various trends that don't appear to be subsiding any time soon. We are a highly connected society. People are digitally tethered to each other—and to the world. Connectivity is not limited to a person's phone. Nope, connectivity is reaching all aspects of our life. We live in the era of the Internet of Things (IoT) where it seems like every area of our life is digitally connected, from what we wear to our home to our vehicles. Smart home devices help us control our environment both safely and efficiently. The first connected driverless vehicles are hitting our roads. Industry experts believe we are on the cusp of a major shift in transportation bigger than when we moved from the horse and buggy to the first automobiles.

Connectivity is not just growing, it's exploding. With this explosion of connected devices comes a tsunami of data—data collected in every aspect of our lives, from the minute we wake up to when we go to sleep (and even while we sleep). The Big Data trend has been around awhile and will continue to build as the data mountains increase. There is so much data that people are overwhelmed—they just want a simple view. They prefer easily digestible bits of data. Usually this results in some type of data dashboard. However, while dashboards provide the *what* (e.g., what are the sales, what is our profit, what is the customer trend?), business decisions should be based on the *why*. While some marketers have found shopper insights drive their business, most are still trying to uncover their *why*.

As a society we are in information overload and it will only continue to grow. Content comes from an overwhelming number of sources. Professional sources like networks and on-demand channels continue to create new content to attract viewers (and maintain their existence). Different ways to share within the social environment continue to evolve, including different video formats (e.g. Vine, virtual reality [VR], YouTube) and social platforms (e.g., Snapchat, Facebook, Instagram). If you have a phone, you can be a source for content for your social network and/or the world. Marketers are creating content too, as they try to elbow into a person's life to get attention and get their business.

As the world continues to evolve at a rapid pace, it can become overwhelming to keep up with change, the data—and the insights. One result is that marketers begin chasing the newest trend. They want to use the latest and greatest. They want to be associated with what is cool in the industry. Trying to be part of cool trends may be fun, but it is unlikely going to drive sales.

An old adage holds that the more things change the more they stay the same. I would argue this is true today. As humans we do not move at the speed of technology. For most of us it takes a lot to change behaviors—to adopt new ways of doing things. And even when we do, that does not mean our motivations change. If someone is motivated to save money, they may have been clipping coupons a decade ago. Today, they may be digitally loading coupons on their phone and surfing manufacturers' sites for additional coupons. And they are attracted to other people with the same motivation. They probably belong to a deal-seeker community where they can share their finds and take advantage of those found by others. Nope, the person driven to save money has not changed. Today's digitally connected environment just amplifies their motivations.

My intention in this book is to challenge your current perception of marketing. My journey in advertising and marketing has spanned over three decades. The constant over this period has been to challenge myself to find a better way to market to shoppers—to constantly question conventional wisdom. Where I found a better way I made it a part of my marketing philosophy. Luckily, I had the pleasure of working with many bright people who influenced both this philosophy and the best practices stemming from it (many of which I discuss in this book). I am not a fan of the status quo. I believe there always can be a better way to persuade shoppers by understanding why they behave in a certain way. This book just marks one milestone in my ever-evolving marketing philosophy.

You may agree with the content in this book—you may not. I certainly don't think I have uncovered the only way to market to shoppers. No, there are many different "right ways." What this book is about is one "shopper truth" worth telling. A truth that gets at the core reasons why some shoppers are passionate deal-seekers while others are passionate about their brands. The truth about why some shoppers detest shopping while others can't stop. My hope is that this book will convince you to stop and think about your own beliefs about marketing and advertising. If I do that, then I will consider this book a success.

Acknowledgements

A wise person once told me, "Your career goal should be to gather all the people you enjoyed working with and find a place to work together." Well, this book is my place where we all worked together. As I worked through this book and the ideas, I enjoyed the collaboration on content solutions; the never-ending debates; and most of all, the inspirational conversations. To these people I say thanks, and I look forward to our future collaborations, debates, and conversations.

I owe a special shout out to two people who truly guided me through idea behind Primal Shopper and the creation of this book.

Sue Larue from The Insight Scout was instrumental in working with me to uncover Shopper DNA. Her intelligence and insight constantly challenged my perspective, which turned a concept into a reality. Sue's infectious enthusiasm kept me moving through the discovery and the many surveys to come.

Merrill Pierce from The Pierce Group helped me find the book within me. Her advice guided me in finding my voice, my personality within my writing. Her constant encouragement turned a kernel of an idea into this book.

INTRODUCTION
Primal Shopper

"People's behavior makes sense if you think about it in terms of their goals, needs, and motives."
—Thomas Mann,
German author and Nobel Prize winner for Literature

The idea for the title of this book came from a late-night experience while working at Team Detroit on the Ford account. We were sifting through mountains of data to identify the path shoppers were taking to purchase a new vehicle. I was working with some brilliant analytics people attempting to find the answers—any answers.

As the night progressed, analysis turned into guessing—trying to find the Holy Grail that would unlock the shopper's journey. The guesses came from attempting to view the problem, the data, from a different perspective. Some analytics people focused on trying to find patterns in the digital data. Others analysts extrapolated insights from the response rates within the direct marketing data. And some attempted to reverse-engineer insights from shoppers who bought a vehicle. It was a lot of guessing with very little progress.

The reality that night was we were reading the data tea leaves to try to answer a human behavioral question—an answer rooted in why shoppers act the way they do. This point occurred to me somewhere between hour four and five. Instead of reading the data tea leaves, why not start with the shopper's motivations? This made sense. In many respects, however, our approach was flawed. The data we were analyzing told us what the shopper did. It was the *what*—a historical record of the past. And it was an aggregation of what *all* shoppers did. There are many different motivations driving behavior and they get lost when you look at the entire population. The aggregation of data hid the insights.

In order to affect the future we need to understand *why* shoppers act the way they do. The *why* allows us to predict future behavior based on the environment and marketing stimuli. The Holy Grail was not decoding the shopper journey; rather it is decoding the shopper DNA.

This book will look into the motivational soul of the shopper. The window into the shopper soul is through their behaviors. In reading these behavioral tea leaves you will find something startling: nature has encoded us with shopper instincts governing how we shop, instincts I call shopper DNA. This DNA is predictable and consistent from shopper to shopper and lies within you.

The book is designed to walk the reader through the subject of shopper DNA from discovery through application. I begin with the inspiration that led me to discover shopper DNA. The focus of this section is on the identification of the DNA strands and how the tension between those strands leads to our natural shopper behaviors.

While the first section is about identifying the primal shopper (the *what*), the second section is an introspective look into the principles behind the shopper motivations (the *why*). The principles are motivational layers describing why we shop a certain way, and what our natural shopping preferences really mean. In a perfect retail environment we would default to our preferred DNA, but we are not always in control of our shopping scenario. By uncovering different shopping scenarios you will see why a scenario may be in conflict with our DNA, causing internal tension and stress. The last part of this section will expand the idea of a shopper's journey (or "path to purchase" if you like). The idea is simple: a shopper's journey is made up of a series of decisions. By isolating these decisions and combining them with the shopper's motivations and sources of influence, we shed a whole new light on the shopper journey and why shoppers act the way they do.

The third section places shopper DNA within the context of the marketing world. There are many tried and true ways to market to shoppers—some work, some do not. This is the basis of the discussion. By understanding dominant motivations within a marketplace, we can better understand why some marketing stimuli are able to move a shopper closer to purchase and others are just white noise, having no effect on the shopper.

The final section is about applying the learnings of the book. I cover three topics, and they all deal with movement. The first two are related to the shopper. A marketer needs first to move the mind of the shopper before they can move them behaviorally. Attitudinal movement is changing a shopper's perspective on a brand. Secondly, a marketer needs to advertise to the shopper's DNA in order to redirect their path to purchase. Lastly, I briefly discuss organizational movement. It's one thing to believe in concepts that drive shopper behavior. It's a completely different (and difficult) exercise to integrate this thought process into the creation of marketing processes and collateral, either in a business or at an advertising agency.

PART ONE
Identifying the Primal Shopper

"There's two possible outcomes: if the result confirms the hypothesis, then you've made a discovery. If the result is contrary to the hypothesis, then you've made a discovery."
—Enrico Fermi

I did not set out on a journey to discover shopper DNA. In retrospect I played around the periphery of the idea for over a decade. There was a lot going on in the world—in my life. There was the dotcom boom which energized the advertising industry. Anything seemed possible—it was as if we were inventing a new paradigm to do business, or so we thought. This was followed by the dotcom bust. The new paradigm turned to dust, or so it seemed at the time, but in the ashes there was a continual stream of new digital channels: YouTube launched the video revolution; Facebook took social media to another level; and mobile tech meant we were always connected.

The digital wave swept through our lives and I rode a lot of the wave throughout the 2000s. But something nagged at me both from a personal and business perspective. You see, I have two passions in business: shopper behavior and organizational behavior. The dotcom wave was a series of shiny objects—some succeeded, many failed. At the center of success or failure lies the ability of the inventor to interpret the psyche of the individual. If the inventor understood individuals' behaviors, the digital experience amplified human nature and was a success. On the other hand, tech innovations frequently overestimated people's ability for people to change their behaviors and as a result fell by the wayside. Regardless of outcome, understanding human behavior and adaptation were a critical aspect of the digital wave.

At times during this decade-long wave I saw glimpses of behavior patterns—consistencies in how people behaved. There was something there, but I didn't know how far reaching these patterns were. Then through a period of trial and error, I came to the concept of shopper DNA. It didn't happen overnight. Some hypotheses led to a blind alley, others brought positive results. This section discusses in detail the discovery of shopper DNA: the inspiration, the hypothesis, the blind alleys, and the final results.

ONE
A Shopper Epiphany

*"Look deep into nature, and then
you will understand everything better"*
—Albert Einstein

I am a restless individual. I resist the status quo and am always looking to create something new—invent something that hasn't been done before. Looking back on my career, it explains why I was pretty bored for the first decade out of school. I spent this time in media, researching and planning media campaigns. Back then it was pretty basic stuff: television, magazine, radio, newspaper and outdoor. I worked for two different agencies during this time and I felt there had to be something more.

The next decade was very different. It was the decade the Internet took off. Over the next twelve years I worked for nine different companies. During this time I worked on all aspects of digital—web, CRM, social. The variety of work forced me to look at the business from many different angles, to analyze the work from different perspectives to determine what was successful and why. Probably most importantly it gave me an in-depth perspective into what motivated people to behave the way they do. Decrypting their motivations to understand what made them tick. This meant searching for patterns in their behaviors—better yet, identifying repeatable patterns in how shoppers acted.

At the crux of these insights was data—a lot of data. Like many people in the business I was looking at mountains of data before the term "Big Data" became the norm. The mountain of data rarely relinquished the insights willingly. There was many late nights working with teams to sift through the data to find the "ah-ha!", the actionable insight that would unlock the secret behind the shopper.

During the twelve-year journey a number of different events informed my thinking; two, however, stand out. One was a Myers-Briggs workshop and the other a project for Shell Oil.

It wasn't the first time I took the Myers-Briggs test. Early in my career I had taken it several times. It seemed as though the human resource person had a new tool and they were eager to use it. I would take the test and then the person would score it, proclaiming "You are an ENTP!" At the time the exercise was not inspiring, and I had a negative reaction partly due to aversion to being labeled so early in my career.

While I can't remember the first few times I took the test, the memory of the Myers-Briggs test that inspired me is very clear. It was August 2000 and at the time I was working at the ad agency Organic. I was attending a senior leadership offsite at the St. Clair Inn (a quaint hotel just south of Port Huron, Michigan). During the afternoon session on the second day I took the test, but this time it was different. Instead of just labeling people, Organic brought in a professor from Oakland University to coach the team and interpret the results.

Many people have taken the Myers-Briggs test (MBTI for short). If you're not familiar with it, the MBTI evaluates your preferences in interacting with the world. Based on research by Carl Jung and others, the MBTI measures your preferences based on four different dichotomies. I won't bore you with the details. You can look it up online, if you're interested in learning more.

Anyway, back to the workshop. The professor began to dissect the test results. He began with the first strand, which evaluates your communication preference. To our surprise many of the account people were "Introverts." This was baffling, since the account folk are responsible for client interaction. The professor clarified. He said the communication preference is not an indication of whether you are gregarious or not; rather, it is about how you "recharge your batterie." Extroverts, like me, prefer to recharge their batteries by being around others. Introverts, on the other hand, withdraw from others and prefer to recharge alone.

He proceeded to go through the next several strands, but what struck me most strongly was the discussion of the last strand, which deals with reactions to structure in the outside world. People are classified as either Judging (J) or Perceiving (P). Judging individuals like structure in their world. They tend to be list-makers and prefer their world be orderly. Perceiving individuals prefer to function in less structured environments.

At this point the conversation took an interesting turn. The professor did marriage counseling on the side and stated that when a Judging (J) person marries a Perceiving (P) person it often ends in divorce due to the polarity in dealing with structure. While this was not inspirational, it did hit home: I am a P and my wife is a J. Let's just say he got my attention.

He proceeded to tell that a P or J could operate in the other person's world, at least for a while. The long-term issue in operating outside their preference is that doing so works against a person's internal inertia. It is unnatural. The person would get fatigued and possibly frustrated. Eventually, the person will most likely revert back to their preferred state. In other words, we all have a natural state which guides our behaviors.

This comment struck me both personally and professionally. Personally, it explained why I had difficulty focusing on processing mounds of data. It takes a lot of effort for me to maintain focus. Over a period of time I would become mentally exhausted, often resulting in headaches. As far as list-making was concerned, for years I tried to be more structured in my personal and professional life. I always had the best intentions and would create detailed lists; however, inevitably the lists would fall by the wayside and rarely be completed.

From a marketing perspective, this comment heavily influenced my views of shopper behavior. To this point my perspective tended to be externally focused—a stimulus-response approach. You run an ad and this many shoppers respond. You run a promotion and this many shoppers take advantage of the promotion. This event shifted my perspective from external to internal—not only why shoppers act the way they do, but also whether there are macro preferences driving those actions consistently across shopper and product categories.

The second influential event occurred while working on a project for a major fueling company. The purpose of the project was pretty straightforward: increase the number of customers who fuel at their stations. The client had no shortage of data on the fueling habits of people by demographic, day of the week, vehicle type, the competition, and many other attributes. They used the research in many different ways, and a foundational element from the research was a segmentation they used to drive their marketing decisions.

After reviewing the mounds of research I had a conundrum: the research told me what people were doing, but it didn't get into why a shopper acted the way they did. To develop a solution I would need to go beyond the *what*. I would need additional research to fill in the gaps—to find the *why*. The client questioned doing additional research because of the amount of investment they had already made in the research. One representative of the client stated they already knew the answer, so he felt they didn't need any additional research. I never want a client to spend money they don't feel is worthwhile, so I asked him what the "answer" was that he had gleaned from the research. He said, "It's simple. People make a choice based on three factors: price, convenience, and quality."

His answer highlighted the problem with the research. Price, convenience, and quality are "whats." They are an answer to a question on a survey. They didn't tell "why" someone behaved as they did in a particular station when fueling. It's obvious price is important to many customers, but the research failed to uncover why one person will drive 10 miles out of their way to save ten cents per gallon, while another person will not deviate from their current route. Yet both are looking for a deal. Convenience is important, but the research failed to illustrate why one person would refuse to take a left turn into a station, while another customer has no problem with the left turn. And quality is important to a certain group of fuelers, but it didn't explain why an unbranded gas sold at Costco was perceived by customers as being of higher quality than Shell's fuel.

After completing the research, we developed insights and a three-year marketing plan on how to drive their business based on shopper motivations. A key insight in driving the plan was an analysis combining their segmentation with high-level behavioral findings. The "ah-ha" moment for the client (and myself) was that the chart looked like a DNA strand. To illustrate the findings, I created a diagram for each of their segments displaying the behavioral data which drove action (below you'll see a mock-up of what the output looked like).

The visual showed the strength of each behavioral strand by segment. While there was a segment motivated by price, the diagram showed price was influential for every segment, as were convenience, loyalty, and quality. This was powerful, because there was now an understanding of the multiple motivations influencing the decision. By marketing to each motivation we could move shoppers across multiple segments.

Segmentation Example

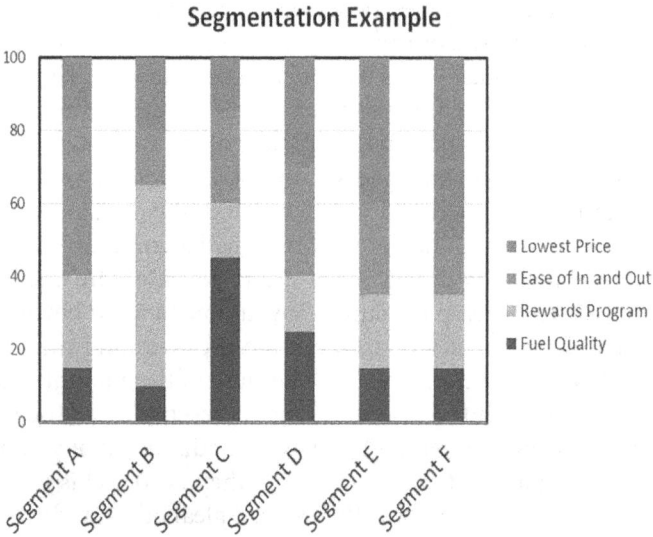

This experience made me reflect on Myers-Briggs results and how the test indicated there were four different dichotomies, each describing someone's preference for dealing with the world. The Shell work and the example of Myers-Briggs would inspire me to search for a universal shopper DNA. The result of this search was a foundational survey called Primal Shopper. The Primal Shopper survey is able to type shoppers consistently across product categories. In the next several chapters I will go into detail about the creation of this survey.

TWO
Nature versus Nurture

*"I'm frugal. I've always been this way. When I was young, my mom
would give me my allowance, and I'd peel off a little each week and have
some to spare."*
—Tyra Banks

The first time I met Monica there was no doubt deal-seeking was in her DNA.
You see, I had talked to many, many people since coming up with the idea of
shopper DNA and as a part of writing this book. The majority of interviewees
were deal-seekers. They were attracted to deals like moths to a flame. They
used many different tools to save money, including coupons, apps and loyalty
programs. While there were varying degrees of effort, they all were willing to
spend their time to save money.

In all the interviews I did, Monica was the most profound Deal Seeker
I found. Within ten minutes of talking to her it became apparent her shopping philosophy was entirely about saving money. Monica saw savings in everything she did. She saw savings in finding the deal before going to the store.
She shopped to find the deal in the store, and she even got deals *after* purchase.
Yep, post-purchase deals. An example of this was a trip to Old Navy, where she
bought herself and her husband, Joe, some summer clothing. She spent $55.
On Monday she received an email from Old Navy promoting savings of $20
on purchases of $50 or more. She did not hesitate to visit the store the next day
and get $20.

The fluid nature of her savings was inherent in all her shopping activities.
I could go on and on about her behaviors (and I will touch on some of these
throughout the book), but the reason I bring up Monica in this chapter is her
curiosity as to whether her deal-seeking was inherited. Monica wondered why
she shopped the way she did. Was it nature or a byproduct of her upbringing?

We discussed her parents' and siblings' shopping characteristics. It was
clear Monica and her father shared a lot of the same motivations. On the surface they both are consummate deal-seekers; however, there is more when you
start peeling back personal characteristics. Both Monica and her father are
very detail-oriented. Monica's shopping approach was all about buying what
she needed. In grocery shopping, there is always a list of necessary items and
you stick to the list (as her husband Joe learned several times over). Monica's
father, too, was very meticulous, in everything from his approach to shopping
down to recording every transaction in a journal.

Comparing Monica to her two sisters was a different story. While Monica was a proficient deal-seeker, her two sisters did not share the same savings motivation. All three children were raised the same way. The same economic conditions existed in the household. Nor did Monica receive "savings training" from her father.

So why the difference? Where did Monica get her acute motivation to save?

You can look at shopping behavior in several ways: is it something we learn through a series of situations, or is it an innate way someone feels about a shopping scenario? We are always learning in the retail environment—constantly adding to our shopping knowledge. Over a period of time, a shopper is able to make decisions quicker based on the heuristics gained through these experiences.

Feelings (or emotive responses) are more natural. They aren't learned; they are part of who we are. The emotion becomes a lens on how the shopper views the retail environment. They don't see prices, they see deals (or not). Their behaviors are governed by fulfilling their inner emotional needs, and abstaining from behaviors that cause angst (like paying full price).

It is hard to assess if Monica's acute motivation to save is innate to her personality or a byproduct of her upbringing. In a way it doesn't matter. The fact is, frugality is ingrained into Monica. It is a persistent preference which guides the majority of her purchase behaviors. If we broaden the conversation beyond frugality, you begin to wonder what other persistent preferences drive purchase decisions. You wonder if these preferences are exhibited by all shoppers, and whether they can be measured. This is the challenge I eagerly tried to decipher.

As you can imagine, finding the key to shoppers' motivations took a lot of research and effort. I did exhaustive research into human behavior analysis, starting with Myers-Briggs theory and diving into shopper behavior research. From there the group I led used shopper interviews, diaries, and surveys to prove (or disprove) our hypothesis about what we believed the shopper DNA to be. While I am sure some of you may get into the geeky research stuff, the majority probably just want to get to the results. So, let me cut to the chase to give you an idea what we discovered.

As we proceeded through a series of tests, certain preferences were discarded, while others were honed to increase predictability. We looked at value, loyalty, and passion among many others (in the chapter titled "Blind Alleys," I describe the rejected DNA strands and why they were rejected). The result was a survey called Primal Shopper. At the core of Primal Shopper are four DNA strands: Brand, Wallet, Time, and Social. The first three are split into a dichotomy or two polarizing mindsets, the fourth is a matrix. The tables on the next two pages provide a high-level overview of each strand.

BRAND	
BRAND CITIZEN (B)	**FREE AGENT (F)**
The brand matters and influences the shopper's purchase. The shopper may have a brand(s) at the start or discover a brand(s) on their journey.	Brand is less important to the shopper relative to other factors in their decision process.
WALLET	
DEAL SEEKER (D)	**PRICE BLIND (P)**
These Shoppers are highly motivated to save money by finding the best deal when shopping.	Price is not a primary influencer for these shoppers.
TIME	
MISSION (M)	**JOURNEY (J)**
For the most part, these shoppers don't like shopping—they prefer to buy and get on with their life.	These shoppers enjoy the retail experience. They may see shopping as a form of entertainment.

The Brand strand is about the importance of brand within the shopper's decision process. Don't confuse this with loyalty. Think of this more as an indication that a shopper *needs* to purchase a brand they recognize, and are willing to forgo other brands with which they are unfamiliar. Keep in mind there are some instances where brand may be irrelevant, especially in commodity categories like milk, produce, and meat.

The Wallet strand is split between Deal Seeker and Price Blind. This strand tests the importance of price in the decision process. It is important to note that the Deal Seeker characteristic is measured by effort or time put into getting the best deal. While attitudinally many shoppers consider themselves to be deal seekers, there is a significant difference in the effort exerted by a true Deal Seeker in finding the *best* deal.

The Time strand compares the approach to shopping and is divided into Mission versus Journey. A Mission shopper is focused on buying—getting in the store and out as quickly as possible to get on with their life. The Journey shopper, well, likes to shop. The emotional perspective of shopping is an important distinction within the Time strand. In most product categories, a Mission shopper does not enjoy shopping. They see it as a chore and prefer to minimize the experience. Conversely, Journey shoppers enjoy shopping and they embrace the experience.

The manner in which Social, the fourth component, is measured is different from the dichotomy of the first three strands. Social is defined in a matrix measuring social influence prior to purchase and social discussion post-purchase. It is worth noting the use of the word "social" in this book corresponds to word-of-mouth, not just social media.

SOCIAL MATRIX		GENERATING (Post-Purchase)	
		NO SOCIAL	*GENERATE SOCIAL*
SEEKING (Pre-Purchase)	*SEEK SOCIAL*	**FOLLOWER** Seeks out recommendations prior to purchase.	**SOCIAL SHOPPER** Socially active engaging others in their shopping experience.
	NO SOCIAL	**LONE WOLF** Does not see the value of social in their purchase process.	**DIRECTOR** Knowledgeable about category therefore likely to offer advice.

The Social matrix measures the willingness of someone to engage their social network within their shopping journey. Social reliance before shopping is a perspective on a shopper's reliance to do it themselves (DIY: Do It Yourself) versus DIFM (Do It for Me). Some shoppers prefer to find the answer on their own, while others rely on others, for various reasons I will discuss in detail in later in this chapter.

Post-purchase sharing is part human nature (a willingness to help others) and part social recognition. There is a myriad of reasons why people share. In the chapter titled "Shopper Bragging Rights," I will get into these different nuances of sharing.

Critical to our research was identifying the true shopper, not the aspirational shopper. A potential flaw with research in general lies in the fact many people hold an aspirational view of themselves. In the fuel study we asked people whether they got the best price. Many responded in the affirmative. As a part of the study we also asked where they fueled, and were able to compare nearby prices. Of those who thought they got the best price, about one-third over-paid relative to nearby stations—*one-third!* The reality is different than the aspiration. So we needed to get past the perception and hone in on the reality that is embedded in shoppers' behaviors.

The behavioral self can't lie. It is truly who we are. While situational context may impede natural behaviors in the short term, our persistent behaviors will surface in the long term. An example of aspiration versus behavior can be found in something as simple as recycling. The aspirational self may want to recycle more in the future, because it feels like the right thing to do. However, the motivational self decides how much to recycle based on the effort the person is willing to exert. The person may fill three recycling bins every week or the behavior may be limited to just the bottles and cans with a deposit. The behavioral self is an insight into our DNA. It is also the best predictor of our future behaviors, which in turn provide insight into our preferred state.

A shopper's preferences can change from product category to product category. Some frugal shoppers may be consistently seeking deals in a majority of product categories; however, there may be products where they "splurge" or forgo the deal. I interviewed a couple as a part of my research. The bottom line was that they spent time to save money. In their deal-seeking tool kit, they used coupons, loyalty programs and a membership to Sam's Club. They would minimize their expenses on necessities including driving out of their way (about 8 miles) to fuel their vehicles at Sam's. However, there was one staple they splurged on: coffee. They were coffee connoisseurs and spent time to find the best coffee blend. They lit up as they talked about the blend of coffee they searched high-and-low for. They found their favorite blend in a small grocer in northern Michigan, and purchase it online.

The story is common. A shopper may be a Deal Seeker for the majority of items they purchase, but will become Price Blind because of emotive factors like passion for a product category. This is the reason a person may have different shopping preferences in different categories. Emotion is an inherent catalyst for behaviors and determines the strength of behaviors. In almost every product category there is passionate shopper. The passion creates a tension between the brand and wallet preferences of a shopper.

Another example of passion creating tension in a purchase is automotive fuel. While "gas is gas" to many people, there still is a passion within the category and it begins with the car. If someone views their vehicle as basic transportation, they typically view gas as a means to an end. They will most likely fuel at the station with the cheapest price on their route or, if they are motivated to get a better deal, they will go out of their way to find the best deal. These shoppers driving out of their way to get the best deal are destination fuelers. They will use pricing apps like Gas Buddy to check prices nearby to get the best deal. There is a heightened desire to reduce the amount paid for fuel on an ongoing basis. The emotion lies in the deal.

Then there are those people who love their car. It's their baby. They pamper it. They follow their scheduled maintenance (or maybe even go above and beyond). And when it comes to fueling, the brands of fuel matter. They perceive a difference in the quality of fuel. They are willing to pay more for what they perceive as a higher-quality brand of fuel because of the passion for their vehicle.

Incidentally, habit can be misleading. A shopper's habits can cloud the results, because if a shopper is operating on habit they are not thinking—they are shopping on autopilot. Think about grocery shopping. How many items do you just toss in the cart because you always buy them? You're not alone. The majority of what a typical shopper buys is based on habit.

Habits may have been established long ago as a result of purchasing the same products or brands again and again. Over time we stop thinking and just subconsciously purchase the same product. In shopper DNA research, the effects of habit are normally removed from the results (or at least treated as a separate segment) because when following habit, shoppers are not actively assessing their product options. They have locked into a product (or brand) and just buy it. Also, from a marketer's perspective, trying to disrupt a shopper operating on habit can be very challenging (not, however, impossible, and I will discuss this matter later in the book).

Screening for habit was critical in uncovering DNA preferences. Did the shopper truly make a decision, or were they operating on habit? In low-consideration purchases, habit is prevalent. However, a shopper may be unaware they are shopping on habit, and therefore respond to the survey as if they are making a decision every time they purchase.

I started this chapter by discussing Monica's savings motivation, and whether it was the result of nature or nurture. Look, I am not a geneticist. I can't tell you that the Deal Seeker gene is found on a certain chromosome, and drives extreme deal-seeking in some shoppers while lying dormant in others. What I can tell you is that there is an inherent, consistent behavior driving our decisions. It's fascinating and manifests itself in different ways—ways I will describe throughout this book.

THREE

The Tiebreaker Moment

*"I know what's best for me, and I want to do things my way. So, now
I listen to my inner voice and my heart—and that's how I make my
decisions."*
—Nina Hagen, singer

There are many different shopping trips a person makes, but none is more enlightening than a stock-up trip to the grocery store. The grocery trip can provide a glimpse into the shopper's psyche and consists of different decision layers that affect what is motivating the shopper.

The first decision is where to shop. While some shoppers go to a single store, many go to multiple stores for groceries. The reasoning varies. Some people prefer the convenience of one store to get staple items, and prefer a different store for a higher quality meat or produce. Another reason is the deal. Some shoppers will survey the retail landscape to determine their best deals, lay out a plan and then execute it.

The second decision layer consists of the various brand decisions a shopper makes within the store. Many of the purchases are habitual, with a shopper retrieving the product from the shelf and placing it in the cart without thinking.

There are other products the shopper deliberates over. They pause to determine which brand to buy. Different factors could weigh in their decision. The shopper looks at the different national brands, trying to decide which to buy. They notice the private label brand; it's less expensive but what about the quality? Maybe check out the ingredients and the nutritional label. Wait a second, this product is on sale—5 for $5 if they buy five participating items. The shopper's eyes scan back and forth on the shelf. Maybe they pick up each product to help them decide. This decision dance could go on for a moment or minutes.

These decision scenarios can be referred to as tiebreaker moments. A tiebreaker moment is triggered by the internal DNA of the shopper trying to reconcile what product to purchase. The shopper is trying to decide which brand is right based on the perceived quality relative to the price. Sometimes price wins out because the cognitive quality difference between products was insignificant to the shopper. Other times the shopper will choose a brand even though it was not the cheapest alternative. The choice could be based on a quality cue or just brand recognition (buying an unknown brand wasn't worth the risk).

Time is a factor in the tiebreaker moment. Some shoppers are willing to spend the time, while others prefer to limit their time within the retail environment. A Mission Shopper prefers to operate with a plan and normally sticks to it. Their tiebreaker moments may occur prior to arriving at the store as they build their list at home. In the grocery aisle the shopper's internal clock limits the amount of time spent deciding in order to minimize the time in the store.

These tiebreaker moments allow a true glimpse into the shopper's psyche and behaviorally define the shopper. They illustrate the tension within the shopper and how they make a purchase decision. A critical part in the creation of Primal Shopper was comparing the survey to the shoppers' actual behaviors in the retail environment. To do this, we had respondents complete a diary capturing their retail experience. Specifically, we asked them to highlight tiebreaker moments.

As an example of a tiebreaker moment, consider John and his choice of salsa. Some people buy the same salsa every time. Not John. He likes variety and will try different types of fresh and canned salsa—mainly different styles. Whether it is salsa made with black beans, pineapples, or peaches, John prefers his salsa have a kick to it; mild salsa just won't do.

At the store this week John's tiebreaker moment involved which salsa to purchase. He was debating between several brands and flavors: Arriba Roasted Red Salsa, Mrs. Renfro's Hot Hobanero Salsa, and Mrs. Renfro's Hot Green Salsa. John's preference was with the premium brands and not the mainstream national brands or store brands. Price really didn't influence his decision. John was willing to spend more (as long as it was under $5). He weighed options for a few minutes and ended up selecting Mrs. Renfro's Hot Green Salsa. John's choice had more to do with the type of salsa than brand.

Another tiebreaker moment—one of several during Jennifer's grocery trip—involved coffee. You see, Jennifer had recently bought a new Keurig and was shifting her home coffee habits from a French press. She preferred premium brands of coffee, but was still getting used to the price per serving (she felt she was paying too much). While she liked the convenience of the Keurig, she still hadn't adjusted to the increased price, so she found herself searching for a deal on premium coffee.

On this day she was debating between two breakfast blends: Peete's and Green Mountain. They were both on sale. Lately, she had been buying Peete's, but was also familiar with Green Mountain. Peete's was regularly $8.99 with a sale price of $6.99. The Green Mountain was on sale plus there was a buy 3 and save an additional $3 offer, which (based on coffee math) dropped the price below the Peete's. So based on past experience and the better deal this week, Jennifer purchased the Green Mountain.

As you can see, each tiebreaker moment can be different. However, there is consistent tension between Brand and Wallet. As you might imagine, a Deal Seeker will spend more time to find the deal—they have no problem spending time to save money. Sometimes the Deal Seeker is looking for the best deal on a type of product (e.g., strawberries, milk, boneless chicken breasts), while at other times they are trying to find the best deal on their preferred brand. Time (and effort) is a function that when combined with Brand and Wallet amplifies the preference. Time tells us the strength of the deal desire within a shopper.

The tension of the tiebreaker moment is reflective of the tension between Brand, Wallet, and Time. Grouping Brand, Wallet, and Time together, we end up with eight typologies. Each typology illustrates an acute behavior. For example, if you combine Brand: *Free Agent*, Wallet: *Deal Seeker* and Time: *Mission* you get the typology Deal Surgeon. Think of the Deal Surgeon as a Black Friday shopper.

Primal Typologies

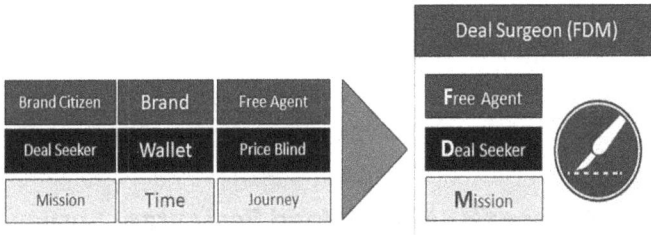

Brand Citizen	Brand	Free Agent
Deal Seeker	Wallet	Price Blind
Mission	Time	Journey

Deal Surgeon (FDM)

Free Agent
Deal Seeker
Mission

The Deal Surgeon's tendency is to get the deal and get out. They can be hyper-focused on the best deal and extracting it. The Deal Surgeon normally has a list—a plan—and will stick to it. This type of shopper is less likely to be up-sold or cross-sold in the store because of their fixation on their deal—on their plan.

An opposing typology is less influenced by Brands, Deals, and Timeliness. This typology is focused on the project: the Solution Shopper. These shoppers are Free Agents, Price Blind and Journey Shoppers. They are motivated to get the best solution for their purchase scenario. A good example of this typology is someone remodeling their kitchen. It is rare for this kind of shopper to be a Brand Citizen for several reasons. One is the infrequent nature of remodeling. Very rarely does a homeowner remodel their kitchen. A shopper may discover brands as a part of the process of designing their remodelled kitchen, but they probably didn't begin the process with those brands in mind. Also, there are many different product decisions—cabinets, counters, flooring and appliances. Some shoppers may have ideas about appliances (which are higher frequency purchases) but probably are open to a wide range of cabinet, flooring, and counter brands.

Remodeling a kitchen can be a pricey endeavor. However, many price-conscious shoppers are more interested in meeting an overall budget than deal-seeking on every aspect of the kitchen. Such projects are often carried out by a general contractor, who will present the homeowner with options. Unless the homeowner is a Do-It-Yourselfer, the ability to nickel-and-dime every decision does not really exist with a contractor. The deal-seeking happens when choosing the contractor, if at all.

Finally, Time is about the Journey—about the homeowner discovering the right options. This is characteristic of high-consideration purchases; the shopper spends the time necessary to learn about different options and combinations in order to make their decision.

As I discussed in the previous chapter, a shopper's preferences can shift from one product category to the next. Obviously, if preferences can change, so will the shopper's typology. To bring this point home, I have included a simplified version of the Primal Shopper fast food survey for you to take. I have also included four more surveys in the appendix so you can compare your preferences from one category to the next.

Keep in mind the surveys are meant to be based on a recent purchase. In deciding which survey to take (in this chapter or the appendix), choose a product based on your recent purchase history. I have also included the results from these surveys so you can compare yourself to all respondents who took the survey.

What's Your Shopper DNA? Fast Food Restaurant Survey

Note: The Fast Food Survey is screened based on visiting a fast food restaurant in the last two weeks. You can still take the survey if your most recent visit is beyond two weeks. The purpose for a recent visit in the past two weeks is remember-ability—memory will fade the further your trip is in the past.

Please circle the appropriate answers to the following questions based on your most recent trip to a fast food restaurant.

BRAND

1.	When it comes to fast food restaurants, I would describe myself as "brand loyal."	Agree	Disagree
2.	When it comes to fast food restaurants, I don't patronize brands, I just buy something to eat.	Agree	Disagree
3.	When it comes to fast food restaurants, I always choose the lower price over brand name.	Agree	Disagree
4.	When purchasing fast food, the restaurant name:	Is very important	Is not very important
5.	When I shop for fast food, if a brand I prefer is unavailable, I:	Buy another brand	Wait and buy the brand I want at another time.

WALLET

1.	When it comes to choosing a fast food restaurant, I usually:	Spend time to save money	Spend money to save time
2.	I often price out items or meals at more than one place, and then I buy it where it's cheapest.	Agree	Disagree
3.	I am not really satisfied with a fast food restaurant purchase unless I feel I've gotten a good deal.	Agree	Disagree
4.	If I want to eat out at a fast food restaurant, I usually look for a promotion.	Agree	Disagree
5.	When choosing fast food, I actively use tools that save me money (e.g., coupons, deal websites, or pricing applications).	Agree	Disagree

TIME

1.	Choosing a fast food restaurant is a task that I check off of my "to-do" list.	Agree	Disagree
2.	I usually put off choosing a restaurant until I absolutely have to eat.	Agree	Disagree
3.	When I choose a restaurant, it is usually:	Like a mission—there is a very specific goal and plan of action	Like a journey — there is a process of discovery and evaluation
4.	When I choose a restaurant, I usually:	Want to spend as little time as possible	Enjoy it and like to browse around to see what's available
5.	When I choose a restaurant, I usually:	Have a plan for what I need and stick to it	Know what I need, but I'm open to other products and services

Scoring your Survey

Based on your results on the previous page, give yourself a point for each of your answers that match the answers below:

BRAND	Answer	Score
1. When it comes to fast food restaurants, I would describe myself as "brand loyal."	Agree	
2. When it comes to fast food restaurants, I don't patronize brands, I just buy something to eat.	Disagree	
3. When it comes to fast food restaurants, I always choose the lower price over brand name.	Disagree	
4. When purchasing fast food, the restaurant name:	Is very important	
5. When I shop for fast food, if a brand I prefer is unavailable, I:	Wait and buy the brand I want at another time.	
Total Score for Brand		

If you have three or more answers that match the above give yourself a "B" (meaning Brand Citizen) in the Brand typology box below; if you have less than three give yourself an "F" (meaning Free Agent).

WALLET	Answer	Score
1. When it comes to choosing a fast food restaurant, I usually:	Spend time to save money	
2. I often price out items or meals at more than one place, and then I buy it where it's cheapest.	Agree	
3. I am not really satisfied with a fast food restaurant purchase unless I feel I've gotten a good deal.	Agree	
4. If I want to eat out at a fast food restaurant, I usually look for a promotion.	Agree	
5. When choosing fast food, I actively use tools that save me money (eg., coupons, deal websites, or pricing applications).	Agree	
Total Score for Wallet		

If you have three or more answers that match the above give yourself a "D" (meaning Deal Seeker) in the Wallet typology box below; if you have less than three give yourself an "P" (meaning Price Blind).

TIME	Answer	Score
1. Choosing a fast food restaurant is a task that I check off my "to-do" list.	Agree	
2. I usually put off choosing a restaurant until I absolutely have to eat.	Agree	
3. When I choose a restaurant, it is usually:	Like a mission: there is a very specific goal and plan of action	
4. When I choose a restaurant, I usually:	Want to spend as little time as possible	
5. When I choose a restaurant, I usually:	Have a plan for what I need and stick to it	
Total Score for Time		

If you have three or more answers that match the above give yourself a "M" (meaning Mission) in the Time typology box below; if you have less than three give yourself an "J" (meaning Journey).

My Fast Food Restaurant Typology

BRAND	WALLET	TIME

To determine your typology combine your three letters together and find your typology in the table below. I have included a brief description for each typology. For an extended explanation of each typology, please refer to "Typology Overview" later in this chapter. For reference purposes I have also included the results of the Fast Food Restaurant survey.

Compare Your Results to Other Fast Food Restaurant Consumers

Typology	Typology Name	% of Fast Food Survey Respondents	Typology Description
BDM	Brand Tracker	9%	These shoppers prefer specific brands, want a deal, and do not want to waste time shopping for it.

Typology	Typology Name	% of Fast Food Survey Respondents	Typology Description
BPM	Loyalty Lasers	16%	Shopping is quick and easy for these people because they simply buy brands they know.
BDJ	Fanatical Finders	12%	These shoppers shop the same brands on a consistent basis; therefore they are knowledgeable about pricing and know when a brand is a deal.
BPJ	Comfort Zoners	18%	They limit their selection within a product category to brands they know and brands they have tried.
FDM	Deal Surgeon	12%	Saving money and efficiency are priorities. These shoppers identify what they need and which brands have the best deals.
FDJ	Bargainista	12%	Deal trumps brand, and these shoppers are willing to try different brands in order to save money.
FPM	Shopping Minimalists	11%	The goal in for these shoppers is to spend the least amount of time shopping.
FPJ	Solution Shoppers	11%	These shoppers are goal based and have a higher-level intent when they shop, which supersedes brand and price.

Shopper Typology Overview

Following is a brief overview of each shopper typology. A typology is created by combining the three primary shopper DNA strands (Brand, Wallet, and Time). The result is an acute motivation driving the shopper's behavior. Keep in mind as you read these that your typology may change based on different product categories or retail environment. As you read through these typologies, think of products or services where you may act like the description of the typology.

BRAND TRACKER
Shopper DNA

Brand	**Wallet**	**Time**
Brand Citizen	**D**eal Seeker	**M**ission

The Brand Tracker prefers specific brands, wants a deal and doesn't want to waste time shopping for it. Brands influence these shoppers; however, they are not willing to pay full price. The Brand Tracker gravitates toward the deal for their brand(s). They will spend time finding the best price/deal prior to going into the store. They pre-plan because they do not enjoy shopping. Their preference is to get a deal on their brand as quickly as possible.

This typology relies on past experience with the brand when purchasing. This fact limits the influence of many sources on their decision, except when it comes to price. Sources influencing their decision tend to be brand sources like a web site, television, or email. Keep in mind, the source isn't influencing what brand to buy but, rather, what price to pay. The Brand Tracker is trying to find the best deal on the brand.

Categories where Brand Trackers are prevalent tend to be frequent purchases where the shopper has developed a brand relationship (for instance, many consumer packaged goods). A category with the promise of a quick deal is attractive to this typology. Such is the case with auto insurance and the promise that a better rate is only a web site visit away.

FANATICAL FINDERS
Shopper DNA

Brand	**Wallet**	**Time**
Brand Citizen	**D**eal Seeker	**J**ourney

The Fanatical Finders (like Brand Trackers) buy their brands on a consistent basis and are looking for the best price. The difference, though, is that this shopper enjoys shopping. They are willing to spend to time get the best deal. They are always looking for the "find", especially on the brand they love. They are shopping savvy and knowledgeable about what their brands cost, and therefore can spot a deal when they see it.

Think of this shopper as "always on" for their brand deals. They seem to be sensitized to communication about the best deal on their brands. For high-consideration purchases, Fanatical Finders are consistently influenced by television—more so than any other typology. This shopper enjoys shopping and it shows when analyzing the sources influencing them. They are on a deal quest, looking at many different sources to find the best deal on their brand.

The Fanatical Finder tends to over-index in high-consideration categories where they have a brand relationship. An example of this can be found in hotels where they are a repeat guest (or have a preferred hotel chain) and try to get the best deal for their stay.

LOYALTY LASERS
Shopper DNA

Brand	**Wallet**	**Time**
Brand Citizen	**P**rice Blind	**M**ission

The Loyalty Laser sees shopping as quick and easy. There is very little to decide for these shoppers since they know their brand, they are not looking for a deal, and they do not enjoy shopping. So, they just buy. There is a very good chance many of these shoppers are operating on habit.

The Loyalty Lasers are focused on the buy, so very few sources influence their purchase decision. They rely on past experience for future purchases.

Like Brand Trackers, Loyalty Lasers index higher in high-frequency product categories like consumer packaged goods. Dog food is a category where shoppers tend to purchase the same brand on a regular basis, and one out of three of these shoppers is a Loyalty Laser.

COMFORT ZONERS
Shopper DNA

Brand	**Wallet**	**Time**
Brand Citizen	**P**rice Blind	**J**ourney

The Comfort Zoners are called that because they operate in a brand comfort zone. They limit their selection within a product category to brands they know and brands they have tried. While they enjoy shopping, they stick to brands they know.

Comfort Zoners are influenced little by most sources since they operate based mostly on past experience. One source which stands out for them is in-person conversation, especially when it comes to the restaurant category. Word-of-mouth may be a function of the group decision to determine where to dine.

The Comfort Zoners are prevalent in high-frequency retail categories. As stated above, an interesting nuance to this typology is the fact that they over-index for group decision purchases, especially in choosing a restaurant. Comfort Zoners are the largest typology found in studies of fast food, fast-casual and family-style restaurants.

BARGAINISTA
Shopper DNA

Brand	Wallet	Time
Free Agent	**D**eal Seeker	**J**ourney

Bargainistas enjoy shopping for the "find". They are motivated to find the best deal on products. They will spend the time necessary to find the deal, especially in the retail environment. The deal trumps brand, and these shoppers are willing to try brands they don't know in order to save money. They tend to view products more as commodities and will switch brands for a better deal. This limits their brand loyalty, since the brand with the best price wins.

If there is a deal to be had, the Bargainista is sure to find it. They are influenced by many sources due to the time they commit to shopping. There are also socially active—sharing their purchases and finding deals through social media. In their deal journey the Bargainista will tend to use brand agnostic sources rather than brand sources. In hotel shopping, for instance, this typology is influenced more by online travel agents (e.g., Expedia, Kayak, Hotels.com) than any other shopper.

You can find Bargainistas in most retail categories that are driven by the deal. This would include grocery shopping, apparel, and outlet malls. Since this type of shopper is less about having a plan, they gravitate to retail environments where there are deals on a variety of products.

SHOPPING MINIMALISTS
Shopper DNA

Brand	Wallet	Time
Free Agent	**P**rice Blind	**M**ission

The name of the Shopping Minimalist is self-explanatory. They want to spend the least amount of time shopping. Period. This affects their choice in stores—they choose stores they are familiar with and that are convenient for the products they need to buy. This typology is prone to surfacing during times of duress, for instance, when an appliance or device unexpectedly fails (like a cell phone, refrigerator or garage door opener). The motivation of the shopper is to get the product replaced as soon as possible, which results in a quick shopper journey.

The Shopping Minimalist is on a mission, but rarely does his/her homework. This typology uses sources within the retail environment as much, if not more, than any other typology. They rely on in-person conversations and sales personnel to complete their journey.

Category convenience is a key indicator for this shopper, especially since they do not enjoy shopping. First of all, their motivation makes ecommerce options very desirable. In categories like grocery shopping, using Amazon Prime Pantry or a store's ecommerce delivery service would appeal to this typology. Also, Shopping Minimalists are common in appliance and device categories where a product can unexpectedly fail, leaving the customer in a bind.

DEAL SURGEON
Shopper DNA

Brand	Wallet	Time
Free Agent	**D**eal Seeker	**M**ission

The best way of explaining the Deal Surgeon is to consider Black Friday. Black Friday is a competition to save the most on limited deals—shoppers better have a plan or they will lose out. The Deal Surgeon thrives in this environment. This typology has an acute desire to save money and they do not leave anything to chance—identifying what they need and who has the best deals. Ironically, as much as the Deal Surgeon enjoys saving money, they view shopping as a chore.

The Deal Surgeon spends the time needed to effectively plan their shopping trip. No one source has a dominant influence since they use multiple sources in planning. Also, since this typology is highly influenced by saving money, and hyper-sensitive to deal communication. The Deal Surgeon can be prompted to get a better deal by a television ad or an email from a retailer promising a better deal than they already have.

The Deal Surgeon and Bargainista are commonly found in many of the same categories. They both love the deal, but hold contrasting attitudes toward shopping. The Deal Surgeon is often found in deal-driven categories lacking an emotive connection to the shopper. These might include everyday shopping experiences (like grocery shopping or buying gas), and considered purchases like mobile phones and auto insurance.

SOLUTION SHOPPERS
Shopper DNA

Brand	Wallet	Time
Free Agent	**P**rice Blind	**J**ourney

Solution Shoppers are goal-oriented. They have a higher-level intent when they shop which supersedes brand and price. One way to think of this shopper is as someone who has a desire to complete a home project like remodeling the kitchen or landscaping their yard. The project mindset often means they are open to brands based on their goal. They also enjoy the shopping experience, and are motivated to achieve their goal.

The Solution Shopper is more influenced by sources they seek out (as opposed to those that interrupt their day). While they may be influenced by brand sources, they tend to be more influenced by brand-agnostic sources. Interestingly, Solution Shoppers tend to over-index within the restaurant category. One reason for this is the group decision involved in deciding where to go out for lunch or dinner. Going out with friends or family is an enjoyable experience (for most) and the decision begins usually with the question "What does everyone want to eat?" Then the dinner party settles on where to eat, and, if there is a deal seeker in the lot—"Who has a coupon?"

FOUR
Blind Alleys

"Art and science have so much in common—the process of trial and error, finding something new and innovative, and to experiment and succeed in a breakthrough."
—Peter M. Brant, American businessman

A few years back I was presenting Primal Shopper in a new business pitch. The prospective client was very curious, asking why we hadn't considered different areas—specifically "value". This is a very good question. Value is often brought up when discussing Primal Shopper. The concept of value is frequently used to describe why a shopper chose one product over another. Also, a great value is often referred to as a deal. In the simplest terms, a person is triangulating value based on cost, perceived quality, and convenience. Perceived quality is from their perspective (not the brand's), and this could include many different variables like reliability, dependability, or safety.

The problem with value is that it is too generic and subjective. Does value mean importance? Does value mean deal? Does value mean quality? Value can mean any or all of the above, depending on the individual shopper. Value is a subjective word, the interpretation of which is up to the shopper and therefore difficult to measure. This is why we abandoned the concept of value early in the exploration process.

I spent the first few chapters discussing what DNA is used to evaluate a shopper's behavior. I find it just as an interesting to discuss the rejected DNA—the DNA that did not make the cut. In exploring plausible ways to predict shopper behavior there turned out to be some dead ends. That's fine. Blind alleys are a part of exploration, and help make the final result more powerful.

One potential strand of shopper DNA we rejected was personal passion. We know passion is a factor that influences shopper behavior. Indeed, passion can be so strong that it will alter a shopper's behavior from one product category to the next. Take a look at a tech enthusiast. They have a passion for technology and will spend their discretionary time reading up on the latest and greatest tech innovations. This passion can also influence their tech purchase behavior. It is not uncommon for a "tech-thusiast" to be frugal in all other categories; however, when it comes to tech, they become Price Blind. They will forgo the deal in order to get the latest and greatest.

So it seems like passion should be a DNA strand, right? Not so fast. Passion can exist in every product category. In fact as a part of Primal Shopper, we tried to find a category that had zero passion (and still had brands). We triaged products like toilet paper, paper towel, and butter to find a passionless product category. We failed to find one—inevitably some shoppers had a passion for one brand over another. I am not suggesting some people are "toilet paper-thusiasts," but I am suggesting there is still some emotion attached.

Passion also differs from other DNA strands in being timeless, not timely. Passion persists from one purchase to the next and is a part of the shopper's overall brand relationship. In fact, while passion is not a DNA strand, we do measure the strength of passion within the relationship in every study.

An interesting aspect of passion is that it is not a dichotomy. There are layers to passion: it can range from unemotional attachment (e.g., commodities) to category passion (e.g. tech-thusiast, foodie, car-thusiast). Brand advocacy is a layer of passion, too. Passion is a derivative of the shopper's ego—passion defines "me". It can be how we define ourselves—how we live out life. A tech-thusiast defines themselves through their passion for technology and invests discretionary resources like time and money in that passion. There are many different passion derivatives such as pets, health, fashion, or automotive, just to name a few. Passion is an emotional trigger inherent within shoppers and while not a part of the DNA it does affect many purchases. I will spend time talking about the different levels of passion in the chapter titled "The Passion Alter-Ego."

Loyalty is another factor in a shopper's decision process. More specifically I am talking about loyalty programs. Initially I described this potential strand of shopper DNA this way: "I Belong: This person's thought process centers on a membership to a brand or service. Costco, BJs and Sam's Club members are the most obvious examples; however, there are many other loyalty programs, like Speedy Rewards, Delta Miles, or Best Buy Rewards."

While it's true that belonging to a brand can alter one's behavior, that "belonging" does not need to involve a loyalty program. In fact, many loyalty programs appeal more to the Deal Seeker in the shopper than they do to the advocate. The critical factor in separating loyalty from advocacy is seeing what happens if the stimulus (the loyalty program) is removed. Would the person still continue to be loyal, or would they buy a different brand if the Pavlovian response were removed?

One retail example is Kohl's department store. Kohl's is mastering Pavlovian marketing through the use of a Kohl's loyalty program, percentage coupons for their credit card holders, and through a rebate program called Kohl's Cash. But if a shopper were not incentivized to shop at Kohl's by these programs, would they still go there? We may never know because the Kohl's business model is so ingrained with deal-seeker tactics that they would be foolish to end the promotions.

In the end, I handled the potential "I Belong" strand by breaking it into different means of belonging to a brand: advocacy, loyalty programs, and habit. I will discuss these throughout the book.

This brings me to my last blind alley: Social. Yes, I know Social is a part of the DNA discussion, but originally it was a DNA strand itself. We split social between active and inactive. This made sense at first. But we ran several surveys and something was not jibing, especially when we merged Social into the typologies. The more we analyzed Social, the more it became clear that Social was an influential outlier, but not part of the typologies.

So, two things happened. The first was that I created a matrix out of Social, between prior-to-purchase (seeking input) and post-purchase (sharing the experience). And, second, Social was removed from the typologies.

Currently there are eight typologies. Originally, however, there were sixteen. As we researched the acute behaviors in each typology, in some cases we could not identify a meaningful difference. Let's take Deal Surgeon as an example. We applied the two Social states (active and inactive) to Deal Surgeon. The results seemed simplistic; just because you can apply something doesn't mean you should.

The studies we completed did show a strong correlation in considered-purchased categories between Deal Seekers and Social (both before and prior). In fact, many Deal Seekers love to brag, as they are looking for social recognition. Sharing may occur offline or online. Social media is a catalyst for spreading the word in the deal community. A good deal will "catch fire" and spread, due to an altruistic desire to share the deal and social recognition in finding it.

We also know there is a strong correlation between passion and Social. This makes sense given the time invested by the person in their passion and their likelihood of sharing. This sharing can be unsolicited. Some people will steer conversations to their passion. My favorite is the bait-and-switch, where an enthusiast asks someone else a question about the enthusiast's own passion in order to change the subject, then proceeds to take over the conversation.

Skepticism drives innovation. Through the building and then breaking of Primal Shopper, I got to the findings in this book. Through healthy team debates and constructive criticism from shopper strategists, concepts matured. The survey became more robust, and the results became more insightful. While there has been considerable progress developing Primal Shopper, I still think there are territories we do not fully understand. One such territory is group decision making, which is the subject of the next chapter.

FIVE

Use with Caution

"Every problem can be solved as long as they use common sense and apply the right research and techniques."
—Daymond John

In a perfect world a shopper makes a decision on their own. They shop at their own pace, choose their brands, and decide how much to pay. The only problem with this scenario is that we don't always shop in a perfect world, especially if you share the responsibility for purchases with your significant other.

I have entitled this chapter "Use with Caution," because a large portion of our research is premised on a single shopper making all the decisions. The cautionary note is, of course, to remember those occasions when shopping includes multiple decision makers. And we have only scratched the surface in how personality, conviction and passion play out in a group environment.

Let's start out with something simple to explain this concept: lunch at work. I am not talking about the person who bags their own lunch and eats at their desk or in the office cafeteria. Rather, I am referring to the group lunch of three or more people, which requires a group consensus on where to eat. As we analyze this situation certain roles emerge:

ROLE	MOTIVATION
The Project Manager	Makes sure everyone is punctual and returns to work on time.
The Foodie	Presses the group to go to fashionable or trendy restaurants.
The Deal Seeker	Focused on saving the group money through coupons or promotions.
The Pleaser	Agreeable group member who blows with group consensus.
My Food History	Person who trumps options based on where they ate recently.

These roles are not mutually exclusive. One person could be both the Project Manager and the Foodie, driving the group's decision according to time, distance and food appeal. And everyone probably has a food history that may restrict the restaurants they will go to, perhaps because of a bad experience or recency ("I was just there yesterday").

You can see the complexity of the dynamics in a group decision. What I have not covered is what happens when there is a redundancy within the decision. If you bring two Foodies together they could be at odds as they look for social recognition as the expert within the group (decision paralysis), or they could agree on a choice and trump anyone who objects (decision bullying). If you end up with two project managers they, too, could find themselves at odds as they both try to project manage the logistics. Or they might agree and the group has the most anal retentive lunch possible.

Multi-decision-maker shopper journeys are common for couples and/or families, especially for high-consideration purchases. New vehicle purchases involve multiple decision-makers about fifty percent of the time—for instance, a couple deciding on a vehicle, or a parent making the purchase with a child. Rarely are these decisions truly joint decisions. Normally, there is a dominant person involved in the decision-making. That dominance could be based on many factors. It could be personality. It could be expertise. It could be based on past history within the relationship where one person typically gets their way.

My wife and I share in vehicle-purchase decisions. Group decisions can be stressful, especially if the parties are motivated differently, and this is true for my wife and me. There are different psychographic profiles for drivers. My wife would be classified as an autophobe. Autophobes are afraid of driving. This does not mean she is a bad driver. Just the opposite—she is an excellent driver. Her fear is of the other drivers on the road. Therefore she wants to be prepared for encounters with less skilled drivers by driving a larger vehicle like an SUV. This emphasis on driver safety also makes her hypersensitive to vehicle safety features.

This safety obsession often conflicts with my core DNA: the Deal Seeker. Let's just say safety options are not cheap. I remember buying our first minivan. At the time Ford had discontinued their minivan, the Windstar, and was pretty much giving them away at the end of the model year, offering the base model for about $18,000 or so. But my wife noticed they had a family safety package to the tune of an additional $8,000. What was I to do? How could I argue that an autophobe should forgo safety so I could get a better deal on the vehicle?

Grocery shopping can be frequent friction point for household purchases, because there are two levels of decision-making involved: the products purchased and the total amount spent. In interviews over the years I have heard many stories of grocery decisions gone awry. A commonly heard story is when the husband is supposed to stick to a list the significant other put together, but deviated from the plan. In one instance the husband lived in an Oreo family (I realize this is a new definition of a "brand family"), but decided to purchase the store brand of cookies. His motivation was to save a few bucks. The next day his daughter tried the brand imposter, and summarily threw the entire package in the trash. No words. No conversation. Just threw them in the trash.

Other stories could be classified as sticker or receipt shock. This normally entails the non-Deal Seeker shopping and spending over the expectations of the Deal Seeker. The Deal Seeker sees the receipt and is shocked by the amount of money their significant other spent on groceries. In one interview, a Deal Seeker described how her husband spent $100 more than was necessary. She proceeded to audit each bag and inform him where he had overspent or could have saved money.

Since I am talking about families, let me wrap up this chapter by talking about family dining decision making. The angst of deciding where to eat can lead to decision paralysis in a family. As a part of a casual dining study we identified two core players in the decision process: The Me and The We. The Me is the self-centered perspective of each individual on what type of food they would like to eat and/or the restaurant they want to visit. The We is the consensus builder. The We is the normally the matron of the family. Her motivation is less about where she wants to eat and more toward having her family at the same dinner table to enjoy the meal. The We acts as the reconciler in getting the group to a decision. If there is no We, and everyone is a Me, the decision process could spiral out of control and become heated as people get hungrier.

The complicated dynamics of group decisions is just one reason why I caution you to be cautious in understanding why shoppers behave as they do. Personal, physical, and environmental barriers all may influence a person's shopping behaviors. The best way to uncover those motivations is to understand the shopper principles and interpret accordingly.

PART TWO
Eighteen Primal Principles

"One can't predict the weather more than a few days in advance."
—Stephen Hawking, English physicist

Where do you go to find out what the weather will be like tomorrow? There are many sources for weather forecasts. You could go online to weather.com. Check the weather app on your mobile phone. Tune into the weather report on your local news channel. Or maybe check the geeky weather station you installed in the back yard. All are valid sources of information to assist you in figuring out what the weather will be tomorrow.

Now, where do you go to change the weather? That's right, where can you go to change the weather? Seems improbable, and maybe it is—for the weather, that is. However, in marketing we create stimuli to change the "shopper weather." We believe we can market to the shopper and increase our revenue by getting them to buy our product rather than the competition's. We believe we can affect the future in a positive manner. We believe we are rainmakers.

If you are going to be a rainmaker, you need to go beyond the "what" and understand the "why." Rainmakers are able to take the pulse of their targets' motivations—their desires. The rainmaker is constantly learning why something works (as opposed to what worked in the past). In the first section of the book, I focused on the preferences of shoppers (the "what"). In this section I take an in-depth look at the "why."

Why does the brand matter at some times and not at others?
Why is the deal more than a price, but actually a physiological stimulus?
Why is there a love or hate relationship with the retail environment?
Why does word of mouth drive some purchases and has no effect on others?

While the "what" is interesting, the "why" is much more important. It is actionable insight that can be leveraged in designing successful marketing campaigns and tactics.

The "why" is also bigger than just exploring the shopper DNA discussed in Part I. There are other facets governing shopper behavior. One of these is decoding the shopper journey. The path to purchase is not a series of sources; rather, it is a series of decisions. This shopper-centric perspective provides an insightful method to understand the journey and why a product is purchased or not.

Another topic I will discuss in detail is passion, which I touched on earlier. A shopper's passion can change their preferences depending on their emotional bond with a product, brand, or lifestyle interest.

Finally, I will look at a series of environmental forces affecting shopper preferences. In a perfect world, a shopper's default preferences will guide their purchase decision, but since we don't live in a perfect world it is worth reviewing different environmental stimuli. These stimuli force shoppers to shop against their preferences—increasing stress and anxiety.

SIX
It's a Matter of Brand

"The most dangerous thing for a branded product is low interest."
—Dietrich Mateschitz,
Australian businessman and co-founder of Red Bull

Shopping for a new mobile phone can be emotional. For most people their mobile phone is their connection to the world. It connects them in real time to their social network through texting, chatting or FaceTiming. The phone is also an information pipeline. It is their weatherman, their newscaster, their restaurant critic, and their traffic guide. Finally, the phone is their retail portal. It can seek out deals, allow them to shop anywhere, and has the capability of paying the resulting bill.

Obviously a mobile phone is a critical component of many people's lives. It also provides an interesting window into the shopper's psyche. The emotional connection to the device creates tension between brand affinity and deal seeking. For some shoppers in this category brand is paramount, while for others not so much. Let me explain.

Most people purchase a new mobile phone every two years or so. In between these purchase cycles, smart phones are evolving: new cell technology, new phone features, new models introduced. When a person buys a new phone, they often need to rediscover which phone is right for them. Most people who purchase smart phones are *Free Agents*. A Free Agent is more focused on the phone than the brand.

During the Free Agent's journey of discovery they have a heightened awareness to phone advertising. They will absorb what is new and different since the last time they purchased a phone. They may ask their friends for advice, especially people who recently purchased a phone. Many will go online to sites like CNET, Tech Radar or other tech sites. For most phone purchasers their journey will lead them back to their current cellular provider. They will try different phones. Eventually they will purchase a phone based on features or a cost that is suitable to their needs.

While the majority of the category behaves in the aforementioned manner, iPhone owners behave differently. They are *Brand Citizens*. To them brand does matter. Indeed, they can be a bit extreme in their passion for the brand. I work in advertising, where Apple is the brand of choice. For some advertising people, Apple is at the center of their tech life. They use a Mac at work and probably own one too. They probably use AppleTV and own the obligatory iPod. Oh yes, they own the latest iPhone too. Many iPhone evangelists will make the pilgrimage to the Apple Store to purchase their phone. To them it's not a phone, it's an Apple.

This example illustrates the dichotomy in a category as to when brand matters and when it does not. The strength of brand is measured in behaviors or effort. When does a shopper not only prefer a brand, but will go out of their way to obtain a particular brand? Conversely, when is brand irrelevant to a shopper? When the brand is irrelevant, pretty much every product within the category is viewed as being the same and shoppers view the category as a commodity. These shoppers will not exert extra effort for a brand.

As you'll recall from Part I, the shopper-DNA strand called Brand is divided into Brand Citizens and Free Agents. For Brand Citizens, brand matters; however, this fact doesn't necessarily entail loyalty (or borderline evangelism in the case of Apple). Rather, Brand Citizens will seek out brands they recognize within their purchase process. Free Agents, on the other hand, are open to most brands because they see them all as pretty much the same, or are driven by some other factor in their decision.

Shoppers can switch between being Brand Citizens and Free Agents depending on category, and sometimes within the same retail environment. Think about your most recent grocery stock-up trip. How many nationally branded products did you purchase? How many private label products (or store brands) did you buy? And for how many products was brand irrelevant because another factor like price or deal was driving your decision?

In the past I tested brand sensitivity in the grocery aisle. The results are not earth shattering. There are some national brands which dominate a category—for instance, laundry detergent and cereal. There are also categories where private label products dominate, like milk and beef. Then there are the "tweeners," where shoppers can go either way, such as cheese, pasta, and canned vegetables.

I probably didn't need to reference a study to tell you this. Envision the shelf space in a grocery store as a voting booth. In the laundry aisle the shoppers have voted and the aisle is dominated by national brands (particularly Tide). The voting in the cheese aisle is a split decision between a mix of national and store brands. And the results from the cereal aisle lean toward national brands.

In many respects the brands available to the shopper could be considered a *Brand Democracy*. Shoppers vote every time they make a purchase. In a perfect store-shelf scenario, brands with a higher purchase frequency would have more shelf space, and products with lower frequency would have less shelf space or be discontinued all together.

When presenting the concept of Brand Democracy, shopper marketers in the audience bring up how consumer packaged goods manufacturers pay for shelf space or how some grocers are increasing their private label offerings. Their point is that the grocer is in charge of selection, not the shopper. To a certain extent this is true. In the shelving democracy, a retailer can try to persuade the shopper by limiting alternatives. They can reduce the national brand options and/or force store brands into the mix. It's no secret private label products offer a grocery store a higher profit margin, so not surprisingly shoppers are seeing more shelf space taken up by private labels.

But we need to remember that the grocer is in charge of the shelf space, not the Brand Democracy. Shoppers are in charge of that. A key factor to consider is that the majority of grocery shoppers shop at more than one grocery store. In other words, a grocery shopper is a Free Agent when choosing a grocery store, and views stores in terms of an open relationship: *they are not married to any one store*. Free Agent grocery shoppers typically category shop, buying certain products at different stores. They may stock up on paper products from Costco once a month; purchase dairy, bakery, and meat from Kroger; and buy their produce from a higher-end grocer.

Given this behavior, the shopper has multiple stores where they can buy what they need. So if a grocer decides to fill their shelves with private labels instead of a shopper's preferred national brand, the shopper will just purchase their national brand at another store.

Worth noting is a product which has very high Brand Citizenship: dog food. Dog food is an example of when brand dominates a category. In fact, in studies completed to date, dog food shoppers have the highest brand citizenship. What this tells us is that brand dominates the decision process compared to other factors. Is this a surprise? Not really. Most dog owners will tell you that once you find a dog food your dog eats, you stick with it.

Just because a shopper is a Brand Citizen does not mean they are locked into a brand when they begin shopping. Brand discovery can be a fluid process in the Brand Citizen's shopper journey. A shopper may begin the journey knowing what brand(s) they want to buy, and then discover another brand during the journey. Just because a brand is not in a shopper's consideration set at the beginning of the journey doesn't mean it won't be purchased. Since brand matters to a Brand Citizen, they need to become familiar with the brand. This takes time, and too little time can be the Achilles' heel of brand discovery.

Consider this example of brand discovery from some work I did on a pitch for Chamberlain garage door openers. It was an interesting category, because the lifespan of a garage door opener is about 15 to 20 years. That's a long time between purchases and the category seemed primed for brand discovery. But the results were split. I found shoppers for a new garage door fell into two divergent journeys: "*Replace it immediately!*" or "*Let me research what's out there before I decide.*" The "replace it" target generally bought a Genie. This was not a surprise, since Genie had dominated the category in awareness for decades. The "research it" target was more likely to buy a Chamberlain. In fact, the likelihood of purchasing a Chamberlain garage door opener increased with the length of the journey, primarily because of glowing online reviews from consumer experts and owner reviews.

In your next shopper's journey think about when brand matters to you, and also about when brand does not matter. A trick to help you determine your perspective is to ask yourself the commodity question: "For me, is all [insert name of product you're buying] pretty much the same?" For example, if you are buying fuel for your vehicle, you would ask yourself: "For me, is all gas pretty much the same?" If you answer in the affirmative, you are most likely a Free Agent. If not, then brand matters—you are a Brand Citizen (at least in that category).

It's a Matter of Brand Principle
Brand influence is about emotional attachment. If brand does not matter, the shopper views the product category as a commodity.

SEVEN

The Brand Rotation

"Variety's the very spice of life,
That gives it all its flavor."
—William Cowper, English poet

Sometimes one brand is not enough.

Think about your restaurant choices. How many different restaurants do you typically visit in a given month? I will venture to guess that if you eat out regularly you don't go to the same restaurant every time. Your restaurant rotation probably combines different types of restaurants including fast food places like McDonalds, Subway or Taco Bell; fast casual restaurants like Panera, Chipotle or Panda Express; casual dining establishments like Applebees, Fridays, or the local family diner; and there may be upscale restaurants thrown into the mix too.

In 2015 for the first time the amount Americans spent eating out surpassed what was spent on eating at home, and there are a plethora of choices available. While there are patrons who go to the same restaurant every time, most customers will rotate through a group of restaurants. The desire for variety motivates people to choose from a short (or long) list based on their preference on any given day.

Results from a fast casual restaurant study provide an example of such brand rotation. Over the past decade fast casual restaurants have grown in popularity as an alternative to fast food restaurants. Panera leads the category and was also the most popular restaurant in the study in question. The top diagram on the following page displays the rotation pattern of customers who went to Panera in the previous two weeks.

The first thing worth noting is that about a third (36 percent) of people went exclusively to Panera. The majority of customers visited at least one other fast casual restaurant. Chipotle was the most popular choice for Panera respondents in the study. But what if we focused on another restaurant, say Five Guys Burgers? How many Five Guys customers are exclusive? How much does the Five Guys customer brand rotation vary from the Panera rotation?

As you can see from the second chart, only one about in five respondents (21 percent) were exclusive to Five Guys, with the largest amount of overlap with Panda Express. The variety of restaurants available to customers is obvious, but is there something deeper going on here?

No matter what restaurant was studied, customers exclusive to that restaurant were a minority of respondents (Panera had the highest exclusivity at 36

Panera Brand Rotation

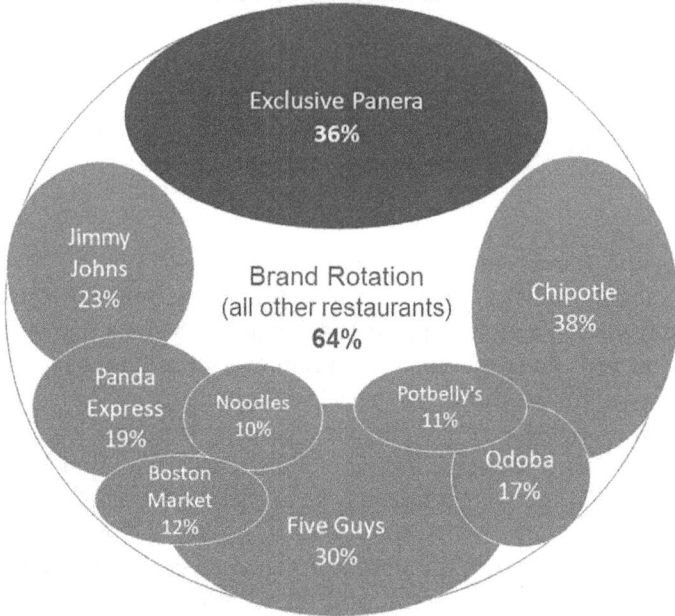

Exclusive Panera
36%

Brand Rotation
(all other restaurants)
64%

Jimmy Johns
23%

Chipotle
38%

Panda Express
19%

Noodles
10%

Potbelly's
11%

Qdoba
17%

Boston Market
12%

Five Guys
30%

Five Guys Brand Rotation

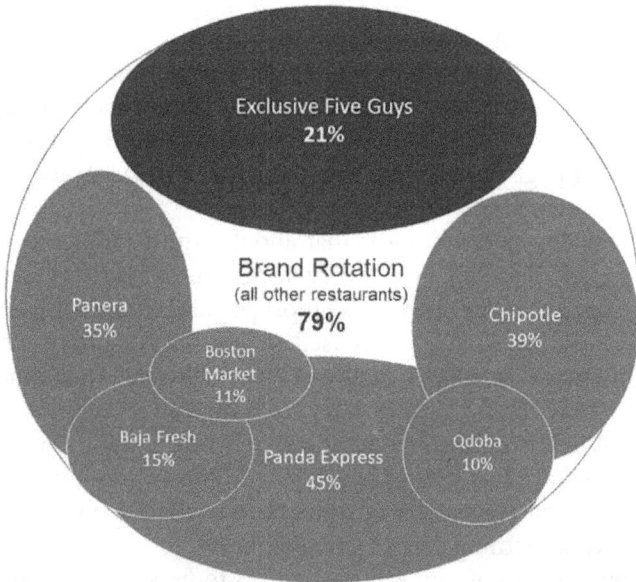

Exclusive Five Guys
21%

Brand Rotation
(all other restaurants)
79%

Panera
35%

Chipotle
39%

Boston Market
11%

Baja Fresh
15%

Panda Express
45%

Qdoba
10%

percent). Clearly there is a desire for variety—for a change of pace. The available variety of cuisines indicates that an intent exists (whether conscious or subconscious) for people to try something different each time they eat out. This makes for an interesting tension between the restaurant and customer: a particular restaurant wants to get as many as possible (if not all) of the customer's visits, while the customer desires variety.

One danger from a marketing perspective is to think customers restrict their choices to marketing groupings like fast casual. The fast casual study focused only on the restaurants in the category, as defined by the restaurant industry. This is an industry classification, not a shopper restaurant rotation. A shopper's restaurant rotation will not align with industry classifications. For example, consider the 36 percent of respondents who were exclusive to Panera. While they did not go to another fast casual restaurant, 18 percent went to Subway, 26 percent went to Starbucks, and 30 percent went to McDonalds during the previous two weeks.

One other factor in analyzing restaurant choice is to look at decisions by time of day. By isolating restaurant choice by breakfast, lunch, and dinner, we can extrapolate different factors driving the shopper's decision. The following diagram displays several factors, including time available and the make-up of the dining party.

Restaurant Daypart Dynamics

Breakfast: On my way	Time: Very Limited	Party: Just Me
Lunch: Within our time	Time: Lunch Hour	Party: Friends, Coworkers, Alone
Dinner: Make everyone happy	Time: Plenty of Time	Party: Friends or Family Members

Morning is normally about picking up something on the way. Time is a factor for many people in the morning—they are on the way to work and often act habitually. Taking the same route … fueling at the same gas station … and getting their coffee or breakfast from the same location. These factors often result in a person using a drive-thru to get what they need in the morning. It also may result in frequenting the same restaurant each morning.

At lunch, the amount of time available increases slightly; however, most working people are restricted to eating lunch within the span of an hour. Secondly, many people dine with friends or co-workers, so the decision changes from an individual to a group decision. These factors may broaden choices, but travel time will limit how far afield person or group will go. Proximity matters for those with one hour for lunch, so the rotation is primarily defined by conveniently located restaurants.

In the evening, there is more time to eat so you could possibly travel further to your restaurant of choice. An important factor in the evening, especially with family choices, is recent restaurant history. The evening rotation is more about friends and family, while the lunchtime rotation is more about individual choice or co-workers.

The evening or dinner rotation is intriguing because there is a dual decision process occurring: the "Me" and the "We." The "Me" represents what each individual in the dining party wants to eat (and where to eat). The "We" is the consensus builder attempting to get everyone to agree on where to eat.

In a study of family style restaurants (e.g. Bob Evans, Denny's, iHop) one of the dominant typologies was the Solution Shopper (Free Agent, Price Blind, Journey). What solution could this decision maker be solving for? If you are deciding on dinner for yourself, you would act more like a Comfort Zoner (Brand Citizen, Price Blind, Journey), basically deciding on a preferred set of restaurants you enjoy. The Solution Shopper is the "We", and their role is to get people to agree on one restaurant.

Sometimes the motivation of the "We" is less about the brand of the restaurant and more about getting a group of people together. Think of a mother trying to get her children to agree on a restaurant. Sure, she may have a preference on where to go, but her primary motivation is to get everyone to eat dinner together.

Restaurants are not the only variety category. Exclusivity levels for beer and wine are similar to those for restaurants. In a study by Nielsen, 67 percent of wine drinkers consumed four or more brands in the previous year with 33 percent trying at least seven brands. Fifty-two percent of beer drinkers tried four or more brands over the past year with 26 percent trying at least seven brands.

Wine drinking grew significantly in popularity over the last decade and a half. Frequent wine drinkers (those who drink wine several times per week or daily) increased from 7.6 percent of respondents in 2000 to 13 percent in 2015. The proportion of occasional drinkers also grew during the same time period. Millennials fueled a lot of the growth, drinking 42 percent of all wine sold in the U.S. in 2015.

There is no shortage of wines in most retail stores. It is estimated that there are well over 7,000 brands of wine, but this doesn't account for the true number of wine labels. The highly regarded wine industry statistical research firm, Gomberg, Fredrikson & Associates, notes that it tracks over 15,000 wine stock keeping units (SKUs). Combine this fact with another: there are over 7,500 wineries in the U.S., each with its own selection of wines.

Wine drinkers are prompted to try different wines in a variety of ways. Wine tasting is a core activity within the industry, and occurs in many different venues. Wine tasting can happen at a vineyard, in a restaurant or at a social gathering at home. This activity introduces wine drinkers to an array of wine styles and brands. Some brands the shopper may add to their rotation, others they will never try again.

A wine drinker's brand rotation can be very fluid. The number of wines available and locations where wine is served create a complex decision making process. If a person is ordering in a restaurant, the restaurant may carry a favorite brand in their rotation. If not, the person will most likely select a brand that complements the meal.

The evolving beer category is seeing a continued increase in the number of craft beer drinkers with about 23 percent of total sales volume coming from craft beer. In a craft beer study Nielsen carried out with the Brewers Association, respondents purchased an average of 3.6 different brands in a month. If the person drinks craft beer at least weekly, the number of different brands increased to 4.4.

The beer industry coined a term for shoppers who seek variety: *flavor seekers*. The flavor seeker is interested in trying different flavors and willing to pay a premium. With the persistent growth of microbrews around the country, there is no shortage of different flavors to sample (the only shortage is shelf space in the grocery store to accommodate the burgeoning number of brand choices).

In addition to the proliferation of microbrews, the craft brew industry has a seasonal flavor rotation. Most (if not all) craft brewers rotate their beers by season, creating a cycle of choice. Many brewers will create a special winter brew followed by a lighter summer ale or shandy for the warmer months. The fall normally welcomes in an Oktoberfest brew and the year finishes with holiday specialty beers. Many flavor seekers are like kids in a candy store as they survey current options in the beer aisle, contemplating which brew to buy.

The grocery category also boasts a significant number of shoppers who follow a rotation of their own. The majority of grocery shoppers go to more than one store for groceries. A typical rotation will include one store for shelf-stable items, another for meat and or produce, and finally a store or two may be the "go-to" for fill-in shopping between stock-up trips. Many people also throw a warehouse club into the mix to do a monthly stock-up on various products that may be otherwise purchased at the weekly stock-up store.

Getting a deal may also drive brand rotation for a Deal Seeker. In order to maximize savings, that rotation would include stores where a person would find the best deals. According to Ipsos Research, 75 percent of grocery shoppers shop at more than one store. Why? For a Deal Seeker it is about saving money. In order to save money, the Deal Seeker shopper creates a "deal rotation" which may be driven by heuristic knowledge or the weekly circulars.

So, how or why does a brand get added into a person's rotation? There are various reasons, ranging from the motivation of self-discovery (think early adopters) to environmental factors which disrupt a person's current rotations.

The early adopter is driven to be the first to find and first to share. This desire can be across multiple product categories or within one category. Early adopters are motivated to explore. A secondary motivation is to share their experience with their social network. Their egos respond to social recognition. As you might imagine, the early adopter's rotation is very fluid, with restaurants added (and removed) on a continuous basis.

The early adopter is a catalyst to disrupt the rotation of others. They introduce new brands into their social circle. Sometimes it is passive ("Hey, you should try this …") and sometimes it is interruptive ("Let's all go eat at the new restaurant that just opened"). This social influence may cause the other person to revisit their rotation and either accept or reject the suggestion based on their own shopper motivations. If the person is motivated by variety, they may add the new brand to the list. If the person already has a brand for that particular brand's genre, they may either replace the old brand with the new one (e.g., Jimmy Johns replacing Subway) or reject the new brand as a substandard alternative, keeping the current brand in their rotation.

Advertising may serve as a stimulus to alter a person's rotation. However, this may be a difficult "sell" for shoppers with a set rotation. The ad must get the shopper to rethink a brand's place within their rotation. This can be a daunting task; most shoppers are not continuously rethinking their rotation, so the ad must be attention-grabbing and provocative. I will discuss at length the influence (or lack thereof) of marketing when I discuss how marketing affects motivation in the next section.

The Brand Rotation Principle
In some product categories shoppers prefer a brand variety. Uncovering the reason for a shopper's desire for variety will also uncover the role of Brand in the shopper's decision process.

EIGHT
The Life Stage Eraser

"Right now I'm having amnesia and deja vu at the same time."
—Steven Wright

What if you awoke tomorrow with brand amnesia? You would just see products with different logos and package designs. To further confuse the issue, each brand carries a different price. At first you might want to choose the cheapest product, but you hesitate and wonder if price is an indicator of quality. You contemplate the most expensive brand, and hesitate again. This time your Deal Seeker DNA kicks in, making you feel like you are overpaying. The internal struggle between price and quality rages as your Mission DNA gets more and more frustrated, wishing you would just make a decision.

We take for granted our internal Brand Citizen, which guides us through many purchase decisions. We take it for granted until one day it is gone. Several times in my life I had brand amnesia. One bout occurred in Sweden in 2010. You may or may not remember the infamous Icelandic volcano, Eyjafjallajökull, spewing ash into the air and grounding all flights over the Atlantic. I still remember hearing about the flight cancellations because of the volcano. At first I thought it was a joke, but it became less funny as my flights kept getting cancelled and I found myself stranded in Trollhattan, Sweden.

Trollhattan is a sleepy manufacturing town in Sweden that is home to the headquarters for Saab. Saab was the reason I was there. It was for the brand's re-launch after General Motors had spun them off. Anyway, I was stranded in Sweden not speaking a word of Swedish. Luckily I was stranded with two other people who did speak the language. We killed time by taking daily excursions to different locations. One such trip was to the local Trollhattan Mall. I figured that while we were there I would pick up some running gear so I could at least exercise while the blasted volcano spewed invisible ash into the air.

My first reaction to the mall was a bit of brand shock. There was no shortage of running apparel; however, I did not recognize many of the brands. So, I found myself immediately evaluating brand quality based on price. Hey, I didn't know any better. After a while this became frustrating because I felt I was overpaying for products. I then found myself observing other people who were like me (or seemed relatable). I looked at what they were wearing and which brands they were buying. In the end I became exasperated, and just bought something in the middle price range.

Branding helps us navigate the retail world, probably more than we realize. We default to our Brand Citizen DNA to guide our decisions. We become acutely aware of our dependency on brands when all the brands are new to us. This "new brand" phenomenon is called a *life stage eraser*.

I first heard this term when I was working on a shopper strategy for Chevrolet. The customer relationship team identified this phenomenon when looking at owner life stages. Major life stages, such as the first time living on our own or when we become new parents, introduce the shopper to a new set of brands. Since brand adoption is usually so gradual, we don't notice the gradual adoption and acceptance of new brands. However, when we enter a new life stage we may feel lost in the brand world. I still remember when my wife and I were expecting our first child. We made the inaugural trip to Babies "R" Us. It felt like Trollhatten. I was overwhelmed with the brands, the variety, the choices. Seriously, how many different baby bottles do you need?

Now think of a life stage eraser in your life. How did you handle it? Who (or what) did you rely on to assist you through the brand confusion? In the Babies "R" Us case, my wife and I relied heavily on the sales associate and I also phoned my brother who coincidentally had also had his first child at the time. He walked me through some choices by referencing personal experience and researching products through *Consumer Reports*.

Earlier, we discussed minivans and cross-utility vehicles (CUVs). These vehicles are often associated with new parents. Imagine the vehicle purchase history of a new parent. Up to this point, they probably bought several compact cars, and maybe a sedan or two. Now they are looking at minivans, a vehicle class they know very little about. There is a good chance the shopper will increase the number brands they consider to better understand the category. They may also consider more vehicles than normal to figure out what model is right for them.

Another example is the first time you grocery shopped on your own. You may have spent an inordinate amount of time on that shopping trip. Some purchases were easier, because you were buying brands you already preferred. With others, you had to make first-time decisions. Over time as you become a more experienced shopper you begin to operate on habit, making decisions easier. While your experience may vary, current grocery research estimates shoppers put no less than two-thirds of products into their carts without thinking.

The grocery example demonstrates how we progress through life stages. We begin to establish brand habits. The interesting part is how our brains process this information. In his book *Habit: 95% of Behaviors Marketers Ignore*, Neale Martin does a wonderful job of illustrating how our minds work. As Martin explains, customers have two minds: the conscious brain (or executive mind) and the subconscious mind (or habitual mind). The executive mind likes a challenge and is fully engaged when something is novel. However, over time, repeated, once novel situations become routines and are etched into the subconscious mind. In other words, we come to operate on habit. For example, when you arrived at work today you may not even remember the drive. Your executive mind was probably focused on something novel so your subconscious mind took over—your trip into work was accomplished through habit.

All of this also applies to our shopping. If the shopping journey is new or novel, they executive brain is engaged. If you buy the same product repeatedly, the subconscious takes over. Think back to the scenario of the first child. New parents need to make initial decisions about everything their child needs. Some are one-time decisions (e.g., baby crib, stroller) and others are ongoing (e.g., baby formula, diapers).

The thought process involved in one-time purchases may be more exhaustive because of lack of knowledge and perceived risk. For instance, parents may fear buying the wrong crib, which could be harmful to the child. So what is a parent to do? Probably rely on sources who are deemed expert (like my brother referring to *Consumer Reports*), on experienced parents with babies, or on the sales associate. These one-time purchases will always be novel, and therefore not habit forming.

Ongoing purchases are another story. The first such purchases may be trial and error. Take diapers. New parents may initially buy a brand they know, say Huggies or Pampers. If the product performs according to expectations, they may continue to buy that brand and not change. The habit is formed. Unless other factors creep into the shoppers' decision process—like price—they go on "diaper autopilot" and just keep buying the same diapers until their child is potty trained.

Can you change a shopper's habit? Sure, but subtlety probably won't work. The first step in changing a habit, whether it is your own or someone else's, is to engage the executive mind. If there is nothing interesting about the purchase, the shopper will keep operating on habit. There must be something different, something novel to shake that habit.

This is why many brands see trials as a means to develop brand loyalty. If their product meets the customer's expectations, for future purchases the shopper shifts to autopilot. The typology for this is the Loyalty Laser (Brand Citizen, Price Blind, Mission). The Loyalty Laser is a brand's dream typology, because they are not looking at other brands. They know what they want and just buy it, as though they are on autopilot.

The Life Stage Eraser Principle
Shoppers experience brand amnesia as they move through different life stages, causing them to (re)discover brands.

NINE

The Brand Tattoo

"Brand is not a product, that's for sure; it's not one item. It's an idea, it's a theory, it's a meaning, it's how you carry yourself. It's aspirational, it's inspirational."
—Kevin Plank

Tattoos. Love them or hate them, they are a sign of personal expression. Sometimes the decision to get a tattoo is regrettably made in haste (or inebriation), but most times considerable thought goes into the decision. The tattoo becomes a part of a person's branding. The tattoo is a statement.

A brand tattoo is an advocate's statement, both literally and figuratively. For instance, a Harley Davidson tattoo has for decades been a biker's statement—a brand tattoo that is a biker's signature even when they are not cruising down the Interstate on their Harley. Similar to the Harley tattoo are tattoos for many classic automotive brands like Corvette, Camaro, and Mustang.

Yep, there are many brand tattoos, some you would expect and others not so much. By searching Google, you can get a feel for them. Where there is a passion for a category you will most often find brand tattoos. Take music, for example; you will find tattoos for Gibson guitars, Fender guitars, and ZIldjian cymbals. The tech world is a holy war between Mac and PC and you will also find tattoos for Apple and Microsoft advocating for their brands. The list goes on and on including power brands like Budweiser, Starbucks, and Coca-Cola.

There are also instances of tattoos for more obscure brands. In the fast food category it makes sense that you will find Taco Bell tattoos, given the appeal to the tattoo generation. You will find tattoos for classic fast food icons like the Whopper, Big Mac, and KFC Colonel. Then there is a smattering of tattoos for Wendy's, White Castle, and A&W. While there are a number of tattoos in the fast food category, there are very few tattoos of other restaurant brands outside of fast food.

Now, while some people proudly display a tattoo of their favorite brand, the vast majority of us don't have a brand tattoo. But the funny thing is that most of the rest of us do, in a different way, display brand tattoos. They may not be permanently etched on our bodies for all to observe; however, they are still there. They signify something more than loyalty. They signify a commitment to the brand.

Maslow knew something about this. I doubt he wore a tattoo of his favorite brand, but in his famous hierarchy of needs the third level is a sense of belonging—the human need to identify with others. The tattoo is an external expression of how a person would like to be perceived. Belonging, though, is not limited to an external projection—it is an emotive connection bonding a person to a brand—and to a brand community.

Loyalty can be non-emotional, too. Our loyalty to brands can be analyzed based on whether the loyalty is based on functional components or an emotional attachment. The functional components are related to the shopper's motivations and brand loyalty is created by reinforcing those motivations on a regular basis. The emotional attachment is based on brand motivations and how a customer feels about the brand. The following diagram breaks down these aspects of functional and emotional loyalty.

Loyalty Spectrum

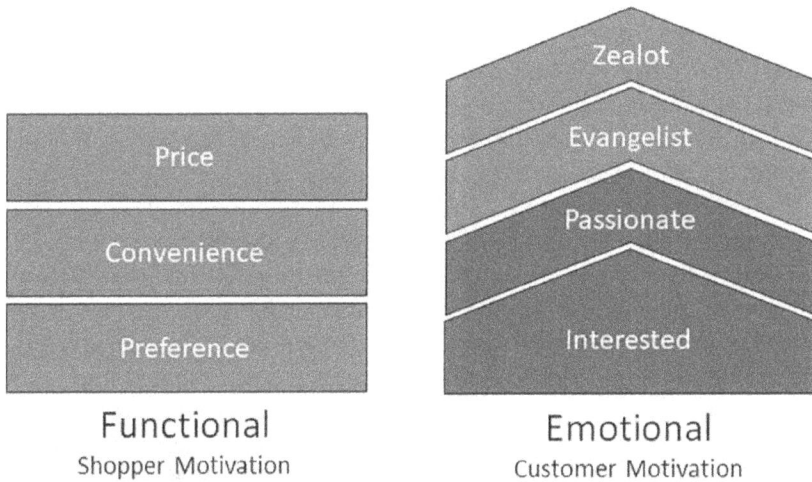

Price

Convenience

Preference

Functional
Shopper Motivation

Zealot

Evangelist

Passionate

Interested

Emotional
Customer Motivation

On the functional side, the shopper motivations are based on getting a deal, delivering on a shopper's retail motivation (i.e., Mission or Journey), or providing a preferred product type. This can be as simple as buying the store-brand pasta because the price is the cheapest (and the shopper views all pasta as pretty much the same). Over time the shopper will continue buying the store brand. Their emotional attachment is to the price, not the product.

Similarly, a shopper can buy fuel from a gas station along their route to work. They are not price sensitive, and pretty much view gas as gas. They will inevitably create a habit of going to the same station because of the convenience. This scenario obviously leans into the Mission Shopper's preferences. However, the Journey Shopper can also exhibit the same tendencies. Think about a nearby mall. The Journey Shopper will prefer to go there because it is convenient. Their favorite mall may be 30 miles away, and they can only afford (from a time perspective) to go there a few times per year. In between those trips, the local mall will do just fine.

Preference is related to product type. A trendy example is gluten-free food. Many people are on a gluten-free diet (some because they have celiac disease and have to be, others by choice). They will obviously gravitate to gluten-free options. This is less about the brand and more about the gluten-free option. Could they create an emotive attachment to a gluten-free brand over time? Possibly. More likely, though, they will be loyal to the actual gluten-free offering. If a given brand were to stop carrying a gluten-free option, the shopper would easily move onto another brand.

By contrast, on the emotional side, customer motivations are rooted in the emotional attachment a person has with their brand. The various levels define loyalty in terms of purchase behavior and strength of brand advocacy. The emotional spectrum runs from Interested (I like this *brand*) to Zealot (My brand is the only *brand* worth buying). With each emotional level the passion increases and the ability to have an open mind toward other brands decreases. A person who is interested in the brand will recommend it to others but honestly doesn't care what others buy. As you climb the ladder to Evangelist and Zealot, you find they are passionate about their brand and see their brand as pretty much the only choice in the market.

There is a fine line between an Evangelist and a Zealot. The evangelist is an advocate for their brand and believes everyone should buy it, but does not make a big stink about it. A Zealot is a different story. A Zealot believes there is only one brand, their brand, and if you don't buy it, well, you're wasting your money. They will let you know it, too. Their passion can be very convincing and if you don't buy their brand, well, you will most likely hear about it.

Apple products provide a good example of such zealousness. Some customers love Apple, and they are all in. They have Apple products integrated into their lives: Apple TV, iPhone, Mac, Apple Watch. Their love affair most likely began with a Mac. Some Mac customers can be Evangelists or Zealots when it comes to comparing the Mac with a PC. They believe the Mac is a superior product, with a superior operating system totally integrated into their life. In an office environment, a Mac Evangelist will balk at the idea of having to use a PC and may resist doing so at all costs (again, I come from an ad agency; many agencies are all Mac or give employees the option of a Mac or PC).

Advice or recommendations can come from either functional shoppers or emotional customers. A noticeable difference between the two is whether the advice is unsolicited or solicited. If solicited for their opinions, both types of customers will offer advice. However, the emotional customer will more likely bring up their brand even if unsolicited, especially if the customer is higher on the emotional spectrum (i.e., an Evangelist or Zealot).

The nature of the responses will also be different. The functional shopper will mention the brand but their own motivations will be presented as the reason to choose it: "Just go to the local mall and shop there; it's very handy" or "I find brand X gluten-free is pretty good."

The emotional customers will more likely begin with the brand and tell you why that brand is better. For example, "You should buy a Mac because it is easier to use, more reliable, and brings out the creativity in you." Often their emotions will lead them to bring personal examples into the recommendation. This is a side-effect of their emotional connection with the brand. In many respects the brand is a part of them—a piece of who they are—sort of like a brand tattoo.

The Brand Tattoo Principle
Loyalty is a generalization better defined through a functional relationship (shopper motivations) or an emotional relationship (customer motivations).

TEN
The Deal Effort

"The efforts you make will surely be rewarded. If not, then you are simply not ready to call them efforts."
—Sadaharu Oh, Japanese-Chinese baseball player

Effort defines a Deal Seeker. If a shopper walks into a store and finds a deal on something they need, I doubt they would refuse the discount and insist on paying full price. Everyone wants a deal; however, not everyone will exert the effort to get the best deal.

Remember Monica, our deal seeking heroine? She not only exerts the effort to get the deal, I don't believe she knows any other way. She saves on groceries, clothing for her family, and appliances. Even their home was a deal, as they saved a massive amount of money by buying during the Great Recession (and looking at more than 65 houses before finding their ideal home). Also worth noting is the fact that Monica purchases quality products. It's not about getting the cheapest price; rather, when Monica is buying quality products she strives for a great price.

Her deal seeking seemed so pervasive I had to ask if there was any major purchase in the household where she had to pay full price. Monica and her husband Joe thought about the question for a while. After about five minutes, Joe brought up the Weber grill that Monica had bought him for his birthday. Joe's response made sense since Weber Grills are consistently priced across retail stores and never seem to be on sale. You would think Joe was right, but Monica quickly corrected him. She had saved $100 on the grill Joe wanted. How did she do it? Well, by playing Home Depot against Lowe's. She knew Lowe's had a sale and told the Home Depot sales associate she could get the same grill at Lowe's for $100 less. After some deliberation, he conceded and reduced the price by $100 at check-out.

Do you spend time to save money? Or do you spend money to save money? This is a foundational question that speaks to whether you are a true Deal Seeker. Most people believe themselves to be Deal Seekers. Seriously, who doesn't want a deal? The difference between a true Deal Seeker and a faux Deal Seeker is one word: effort.

Effort is critical to gauging the level of commitment of a Deal Seeker. I often classify myself as a lazy Deal Seeker. Sure, I want a deal; better yet, I want a great deal; but I rarely exert the effort to get the best deal. A recurring example is my weekly trip to Kroger for groceries. As I shop from aisle to aisle I gravitate to the products on sale, the "Buy 6, get $6 off your bill," the BOGO opportunities. And when I check out the cashier politely informs me I saved something like $25 and I now have seventy-cents in fuel points. I feel like I got a deal (and possibly a bit of an adrenalin rush), but I applied minimal effort—I spent perhaps an extra 15 minutes in the store on my deal-seeking quest.

Comparing my grocery shopping behaviors with those of a true Deal Seeker, a Monica, shows how I didn't spend nearly enough time to save the most on my groceries. The true Deal Seeker preps for the trip, spending at least half an hour making a list and finding out where they can save the most money at local grocery stores. They will regularly take time to find coupons on the items they need this week or to find stock-up deals on shelf-stable products and add them to their list. Their journey normally includes more than one store, where they will cherry pick items based on the best deal. While I spent 15 minutes more on my trip, the true Deal Seeker will spend hours more getting the best deals.

The initial Primal Shopper benchmark study was product agnostic. In that study, 83 percent of respondents were classified as Deal Seekers. But in reality, after carrying out more than ten different studies, we found that in only one product category did the percentage of Deal Seekers even come close to the 83 percent mark (I will discuss this category later in the chapter). One way of interpreting the results of the product agnostic study is to suggest that people *believe* they always shopped for a deal. However, if I ask this question about a specific, recent purchase, the shopper's actual behaviors reveal their true level of deal seeking. This is an important point: while attitudinally a shopper may believe they are a Deal Seeker, behaviorally they may not act like one.

Assessing your own Deal Seeker quotient, you will probably discover that you may function as a Deal Seeker in some product categories, while you are Price Blind in others. For example, when buying this book did you look for the best price across multiple stores or websites or just buy the first copy you came across? Did you look for promotional codes from the publisher? Did you wait until the book was discounted? Or were you Price Blind, figuring it was not worth your effort to save a buck or two? Compare this behavior to the last time you bought a household appliance or major electronic device. Did you exhibit the same deal behavior, or did you exert more effort because the product price point was much higher? While spending time to save money isn't the only issue, it does provide a key insight into a shopper's commitment to getting the best deal.

A person's Deal Seeker quotient represents how much people value time relative to saving money. In other words, how much of a deal would it take to give up a certain amount of time? A way to demonstrate this point is to ask the following question to a large group of people: *If gas were 50 cents per gallon, how long would you be willing to wait in a line to fill up your car?* (Let me get the one question out of the way that someone invariably asks: Your car is nearly empty but you have enough fuel left to wait in line.) I proceed to ask people to raise their hand if they are willing to wait one hour. Typically about ten percent of people raise their hands. An interesting aspect of the exercise is that the people who raised their hands are amazed at those who wouldn't wait an hour, while those who didn't raise their hands can't believe these people have nothing better to do but wait in line for gas. I continue this line of questioning, changing the wait time from an hour to thirty minutes to fifteen minutes and then finally to no waiting time at all. The ensuing group discussion centered on each person's tolerance to exert effort to save (or not save) money.

The previous example is an attitudinal projection of what people would do in a hypothetical situation (i.e., if they could purchase fuel for 50 cents a gallon). People react behaviorally to fuel prices on a regular basis. Take Costco members as an example. Costco typically sells fuel for 6 cents to 12 cents less than nearby stations. However, many people who buy gas at Costco are destination fuelers, making a special trip to fuel up with the expectation of waiting in line (a wait that could be as much as 30 minutes).

In Primal Shopper we use the Wallet strand to assess how important a deal is to a shoppers' purchase. The DNA strand is split between Deal Seeker and Price Blind. Deal Seekers exert time and effort to get the best deal. Some of the behaviors a Deal Seeker would exhibit include:

- They review deals at multiple stores and buy where a product is the cheapest.
- They hold off purchases until a product is on sale.
- They actively use various tools, including web sites, to find the best deal.

The category with the highest proportion of Deal Seekers is auto insurance at 84 percent (the same level as that found in the product agnostic study). No other category comes close. You might wonder why auto insurance boasts so many Deal Seekers. The answer is no further than the next commercial break on television. Usually, at least one auto insurance ad can be found in every commercial break. The category spends billions of dollars per year to let people know they can get a better deal—and it works. According to J.D. Power, about 39 percent of people shop for auto insurance each year; however, only about 12 percent actually switch insurance companies. There are several reasons why so many people shop for auto insurance each year. A primary factor is the legal requirement for a driver to have auto insurance—it is not a want, it is a need. Given this, many people show an aversion to overpaying for required purchases (in addition to auto insurance, think about fuel for your car, utilities, or cellular service as other examples). So there is a general desire to try to get a better deal, especially when the brands in the category are all promising shoppers that there is indeed a better deal out there.

By contrast, one of the categories with the lowest proportion of Deal Seekers is fast casual restaurants. Only 14 percent of fast casual restaurant patrons are Deal Seekers. For comparison purposes, consider quick serve or fast food restaurants, where Deal Seekers account for 44 percent of all customers. If you look at the marketing efforts in the two categories, you see this fact played out: fast food restaurants are constantly promoting the deal, with dollar menus, value menus, 3 for $5, 4 for $5, 5 for $5—it seems as though there is always one competitor upping the ante on a "multiples" promotion.

Fast casual advertising, however, centers on product quality. Panera is one example: their mantra since 2005 has been "Food as it should be." Since 2014 Panera's mission has been to clean up its food and remove artificial flavors, sweeteners, preservatives, and colors. Panera successfully met that objective in 2017 and began a new campaign centered around their food being 100 percent "clean." Panera is not about the deal; rather, they are about creating a brand worth a premium price.

At the core of every Deal Seeker is a common thread—a fixation on the lowest price. Extreme couponers are a dramatic example of this concept. If you haven't watched the show *Extreme Couponing*, I highly recommend watching at least one episode. It gives you a perspective on how the adrenalin of the deal affects people. Extreme couponers have gamified their shopping experience so they get an adrenalin rush throughout their journey, culminating at the cash register when ringing up their extreme savings.

A few years back I read a *Wired* article on extreme couponing. In the article the author followed various extreme couponers on their quest to get as many products for as little money as possible. After one successful quest, where the shopper purchased over $1,000 in groceries for some ridiculous amount like $1.50, the author asked the person why they purchased so many products they didn't need. The response was simple and impactful: "In the store I see price, I don't see product until I leave the store."

"Price before product" is the human truth in every Deal Seeker. A shopper may be looking for a specific product type or brand, but at the point they switch from product to price the Deal Seeker DNA takes over. I believe we all have a little extreme couponer inside ourselves when we believe we get a great deal. A great deal is accompanied by an adrenalin rush that provides a sense of accomplishment: we were successful shoppers.

A common misconception is that a deal is the cheapest price. This is not entirely true. A deal is based on getting a perceived quality product at an unbelievable price. In coming up with the Primal Shopper questionnaire, we had respondents fill out diaries in addition to taking the test to validate results. One woman was going through her diary describing a recent trip to the mall where she got a great deal on a pair of boots—they only cost her $300. While that did not seem like a deal to me, the shoe brand, Jimmy Choo, elevated the quality perception and validated the deal.

To sum up, deal seeking is about the effort to get the best deal. On your next shopper journey, pay attention to the time and effort you invest in deal seeking activities to gauge the influence of the Deal Seeker within you.

The Deal Effort Principle

The propensity for a shopper to be a Deal Seeker is directly correlated to the effort they exert in getting the "deal." Effort is measured in their willingness to use discretionary time to seek out the deal.

ELEVEN
Feel the Deal

*"Nice 34 cents a gallon. Love #CheapGas thanks @WinnDixie
#FuelPerks."*
—Jason K on Twitter

Deal Seekers feel the deal and they are inclined to share it. A simple proof point is to search Twitter or Instagram for #FuelPerks. You'll see many pictures of the price at the pump after the shopper's fuel perks were deducted. These shoppers feel the deal, so much so that they wanted to share their deal with the world. As you review the pictures, you will likely be impressed with the low price per gallon people paid. You recognize they got a great deal. Why? You probably remember the price of gas because you fueled your vehicle in the past week or drove by numerous gas stations during your daily commute.

For most people it is not difficult to determine when there's a deal on gas, as it is a regularly purchased commodity. Sometimes to feel the deal on a less frequent purchase you need a quality anchoring point. Let's say I told you I bought a quart of ice cream for $1. What would be your immediate reaction? Would you think I got found a great deal or I think I purchased a cheap brand? When I pose this question to a group, most people will claim that the ice cream is not good (especially when the retail price for a premium brand of ice cream is about $5 for a quart). Now, if I revealed that I bought a quart of Breyer's Oreo Cookie and Cream for a dollar, most people's reactions would be: *How did you get a great deal?*

The anatomy of a deal is simple: it combines a product's perceived quality with an unexpectedly low purchase price. The combination of product quality and price dictate the deal energy of a purchase. The higher the perceived savings on a specific product, the higher the deal energy. The diagram on the next page depicts the anatomy of a deal.

A product's quality can be defined through multiple factors. Product type is the base comparison of quality. If the product is considered a commodity, no additional comparison is needed to assess the quality. So if a shopper is sharing a deal on gallon of milk, gallon of gas or a pound of bananas, the product description is enough. Most shoppers think milk is milk, gas is gas and a banana is a banana.

A second factor is an attribute qualifying the product that increases the quality perception. There is a perceived quality difference between a pound of ground beef and a pound of grass-fed ground beef or between red delicious apples and organic red delicious apples. The premium qualifier of "grass fed" or

Deal Equation

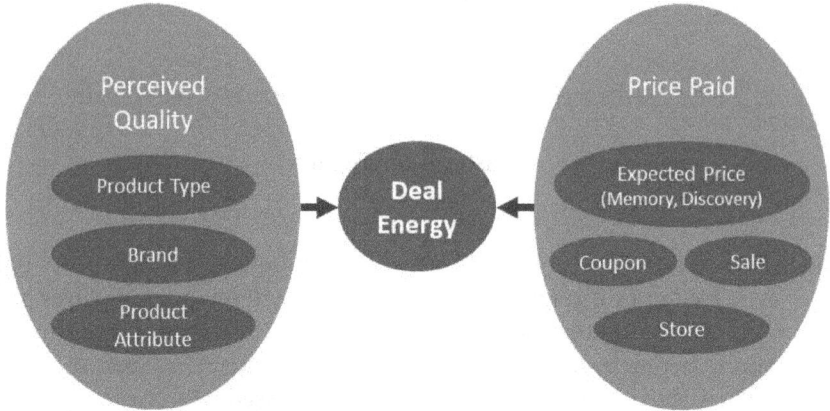

"organic" elevates the product to a premium level.

Finally, a brand can elevate the quality perception of a product. Saying "I bought ice cream" as opposed to "I bought Breyer's" or "I bought Ben & Jerry's" immediately changes the quality perception of the product that has been purchased.

The other half of the deal equation is the price paid. The first aspect of price is recognition. There are two primary methods by which people process prices: memory and discovery. Most people (and especially Deal Seekers) remember prices for products they buy on a frequent basis. A Deal Seeker can rattle off prices for commonly bought grocery items, fuel, or clothing. The stronger the price memory the easier it is for a Deal Seeker to spot a deal (and react).

On less frequent purchases, a shopper relies on discovery to determine prices. Discovery can be a point in time or occur during a journey. Buying batteries is a simple but infrequent purchase, and many shoppers don't recall the price of a prior purchase. So, whether they are in a hardware or department store, the shopper is comparing prices in the moment to determine the best deal. The deal tie-breaker moment for batteries will bounce between the packaging volume (four batteries versus 20 batteries) and brand (generic store brand versus Energizer or Duracell).

Getting a discovery deal while in the moment is difficult, because the shopper is looking at just one location—one store. They don't know if the store has the lowest price for batteries of all the stores nearby, or if there were available promotions they could have utilized. They can only choose from the options presented at the store. They may feel satisfied with their purchase, but probably not exhilarated at finding the best deal.

Discovering the price during the shopper journey is something that happens in the case of many high-consideration purchases. I once did some work for a garage door opener company. Garage door openers fall into this category because they are low frequency purchases (normally every 15 to 20 years) and relatively expensive, ranging from $125 to $300 in price before installation. The initial reaction of many shoppers is to wonder why prices differ, even within one brand offering several different models. The major factor at this point is less about finding a deal than it is about determining what the shopper is willing to pay.

The shopper will continue to evaluate the different garage door openers until they settle on the brand or model which will meet their needs. Once they focus on one model, they have established a quality price point. Suppose the shopper determined (based on research they carried out) that they wanted a belt drive, three-quarter horsepower garage door opener that is smart phone enabled. At this point the Deal Seeker has a benchmark price to get the best deal through promotions, shopping different stores, or waiting for a sale.

Part of deal energy is believability. Many shoppers are skeptical of cheap prices. Just because you bought ice cream for $1 does not make it a great deal—it may just be cheap ice cream made with substandard ingredients and pumped up with air to increase the volume. The low price begs the question of how a shopper was savvy enough to get the deal.

Just as there are quality qualifiers for products, there also need to be price qualifiers to explain how the price came to be so unbelievably low. This is where coupons, sales or the store itself come into play. A low price can be explained through a sale and/or a coupon. Just as the extreme couponer got $1,000 of groceries for pennies, the savvy Deal Seeker is smart enough to work the system to get a great deal. In addition to coupons or sales, some stores, such as dollar stores or warehouse stores, are synonymous with deals.

A shopper won't necessarily always feel they got a great deal, even if they did. In some situations the effort invested corresponds to the adrenalin rush one receives. Think about couponing. The avid couponer will invest significant time in finding, clipping, and using coupons to reduce their grocery bill. The couponing effort is driven by the desire to save, and the reward is literally itemized on the grocery receipt. The reward reinforces the behavior—the couponing effort.

One way to look at effort is the amount of time spent finding the deal. A shopper can go to multiple stores to price check certain items and then buy where it is cheapest, or they can research the stores through circulars or websites and then visit the store with the best deal. They feel the deal because they know the prices—they did their homework.

If a shopper is a single-store shopper, they may have a difficult time discerning whether they got a deal. Think of the person who does their monthly stock-up trip at Costco. Their general belief is they are getting a great deal on what they purchase. It may be true—it may not. It depends on the savviness of the shopper in doing their homework ahead of time or remembering the price they paid for the product at another store. Determining whether you got a deal at a warehouse club can be difficult due to the simple fact that many items are sold in bulk.

The single-store shopper may only feel the deal if the store itself informs them they got a deal. A store that does this well is T.J. Maxx, which helps the shopper "remember" the price by showing the original price and the deal price. T.J. Maxx uses this tactic on their clothes tags. This tactic brings the deal front and center on all branded goods. The Deal Seeker need look no further.

Another factor in deal energy involves need vs. want for a product. A needed product will normally amplify a Deal Seeker's effort more than a product they want. Take, for example, purchases of gluten-free products by someone who sees them as part of healthy living, as opposed to someone suffering from celiac disease, which requires a gluten-free diet. The first shopper resigns themselves to the need to spend more. In effect the shopper becomes price blind, because past experience tells them that if they want to be on a healthy diet there is a premium to be paid. The healthy shopper would welcome a deal, but they are *choosing* to spend more. If they were serious about saving money, they would swap organic products for less expensive, non-organic products.

The person with celiac disease, on the other hand, *must* buy gluten-free products. The gluten-free Deal Seeker will be hypersensitive to saving money and take the effort to research brands and stores to determine where the deal is.

In Primal Shopper studies we see this dichotomy between needs and wants. When a person chooses to buy a type of product based on a "want," there is very little difference in deal-seeking behavior between that person and others in the study. But a person who has to shop for a need will be more likely to be a Deal Seeker. Needs-based decisions tend to increase the desire for the deal— the desire to reduce the cost of life's required items, so a person can spend more on their desires.

Why have I spent so much time talking about feeling the deal? Well, the degree to which a person feels they got a deal affects their propensity to share that deal within their social circle or on social media. The more a person feels they got a great deal, the more likely they will share it with others. If multiple people find the deal and pass it along on social media, the result could be a "deal wildfire." One such example involves the ALDI grocery store. ALDI cycles in special-buy products on a regular basis. One week the store's special buy was gluten-free products, which were priced well below what other stores were charging. The prices were so unbelievable that the word spread through the gluten-free community and the store quickly sold out of the products. Many people need to purchase gluten-free products and feel they are forced to pay a premium. When this grocery store offered an inexpensive alternative, the desire to buy (and stock up) was strong. The desire to share was just as strong.

The desire to share a deal is a powerful impulse I will discuss further in an upcoming chapter.

Feel the Deal Principle
Deal perception is a combination of brand value and getting a great price, as defined by shopper experience, shopping situation, and/or the shopper's social circle. The deal strength drives the likelihood of sharing it with others.

TWELVE
The Final Number

"I want a car that will last 10 years or longer because I totally hate the process of researching, shopping for a new car, and then haggling for the price. I wish I could just snap my fingers and my car is there."
—Kiran Ahluwalia, singer

You would think buying a new car would be exciting. The idea of a new set of wheels with the odometer set to (almost) zero and that new car smell permeating the vehicle sounds exciting. Sometimes just sitting in a new car can excite the senses. The feel of the leather as you firmly grip the steering wheel. The new gadgetry integrated into the vehicle to accentuate the driving experience. The rumble of the engine as you put the vehicle through its paces during the test drive. Ah yes, did I mention the new car smell?

Yep, you would think buying a new car would be a bit of an adrenalin rush. Many aspects of the shopping experience are exhilarating: test driving the car, looking at different models, finding the perfect vehicle. However, there are aspects of the car buying process that are highly stressful for most people. At the core of that stress you normally find money—the price of the vehicle. While there are some people out there who live for negotiating, many people find it stressful and feel they are being taken for a ride (sorry, I couldn't resist).

Over my career I worked with different car companies to rethink the car buying process and make it more positive. The goal was to rethink the entire process, both online and offline. We left no stone unturned. We looked at every aspect of the shopping process: online, word-of-mouth, the dealership, accessories, financing, trade-ins. We spoke to innovative dealers in the field who were not only surviving but thriving during the recession. We spoke to salespeople about what worked and what didn't. The most popular approach during this time period (this was during the Great Recession of 2008–09) was the full-court press, as I liked to call it. If a shopper inquired about a vehicle, dealers would consider this a hot lead and over the next two weeks would email the shopper seven times and call three times, regardless of whether the shopper reciprocated the communication. Not the best method, but it was in the middle of a recession and a lead is a lead.

In the course of designing a new approach we reviewed the mountains of shopper research that Ford had accumulated over the years: research surveying shoppers on customer satisfaction, sources of influence, and pricing. The pricing research was probably most disturbing, as it identified a gap in expectations. First off, shoppers believed there was only one true price and that wasn't at the dealership. So all of the "price-vertising" was largely ineffective in persuading shoppers, mainly because of ingrained skepticism of advertising and the gigantic disclaimers at the end of every car commercial. This identified gap was not in the shopper's favor, meaning the shopper expected a lower price than the dealer was willing to offer. This disconnect in pricing led to a lot of consternation and tension in the dealership.

My client realized this and asked what could be done about it. Transparency was an option—in fact, the industry had tried it before. Years prior, the industry introduced "employee pricing," which was a fixed price discount on the vehicle—non-negotiable pricing. The initial reaction to employee pricing was very positive; however, over time it waned and the pricing expectation gap persisted.

The reason for the expectation gap involves how a person typically pays for a car. The price is more complicated than just the price of the vehicle. More often than not, the car is financed, which makes the monthly payment the "final number" (only about one in ten new vehicles are purchased with cash). This means a shopper is thinking of a monthly payment when they enter the dealership. Whether it is $250 or $400 per month, the shopper has a bogey in mind. The best salespeople realize this and they start the conversation by listening to why the shopper is buying a new vehicle now, what the most important features in a new vehicle are for them, and the amount of the monthly payment they are willing to spend.

The monthly payment calculation is normally based on the result of three mini-negotiations: the price of the vehicle, the financing rate and the trade-in value. Often shoppers feel they got a great deal if they walked out of the dealership paying less per month than they expected to (regardless of how the deal was arrived at).

Leasing a vehicle is growing in popularity. Reasons include rapid advances in technology (similar to mobile phones) and people's desire to continually have the latest and greatest. Also, a lease can result in a significantly cheaper monthly payment than buying the vehicle outright. Leasing is also simpler, since the person buys into a monthly payment based on miles driven annually and a down payment. But whether a person is leasing or buying a car, the monthly payment is the final deal number.

This complex equation isn't unique to buying a car. Home buying or refinancing operate the same way. A combination of the price of the home for sale, the financing rate, mortgage insurance premium (PMI), and equity in the previous home determine the mortgage payment. This purchase scenario is typically far more complicated than buying a car due to the number of parties involved, including (most likely) multiple financing institutions. But whether it is a home or car, most shoppers look at the transaction straightforwardly. They can get frustrated with the manipulations of facts and figures. They just want to know what their bottom line is—their monthly payment.

Or consider mobile phones. About one in four people purchase prepaid mobile contracts, which means that the majority of mobile phone users are concerned about their monthly payments. For an individual shopper, getting a deal on phone service depends on the plan, the devices (e.g., phone, tablet), and the accessories. If shopping for a family plan the dynamics can get more complicated.

A quick survey of the brands in the industry reveals two distinct groups organized along the lines of quality versus price. Verizon has long since hung its hat on the quality of its signal (brought to life in its iconic campaign "Can you hear me now?"). For years Verizon and AT&T battled over signal quality, making the shopper's choice one that was about the better signal, not the better deal.

In 2015, Sprint made it about the deal by attempting to commoditize mobile phone service. In a series of ads they offered 50 percent off to anyone who switched to Sprint, and oh, by the way, their coverage is within 1 percent of Verizon's. Sprint's ads cleverly used the "Can you hear me now" guy, Paul Marcarelli, from the original Verizon ads.

A second step in commoditizing the category was establishing a single price for unlimited data. T-Mobile was one carrier that decided to make a big deal out of unlimited data. The idea was simple: while other carriers advertise a low price, that price is normally accompanied by hidden fees. For example, T-Mobile publicized a direct comparison between themselves and AT&T. On the face of things, AT&T looked like the better deal at $110 per month versus T-Mobile at $160 per month for four phone lines. However, after doing some phone math, the AT&T price skyrocketed to $222 per month versus $160 per month. Also, AT&T provided 25 gigabytes worth of data versus unlimited for T-Mobile.

The final number is what a shopper wants to see, and what they want to pay. They do not want to see a price advertised in a commercial with an ominous paragraph of legal copy filling the bottom of the screen. The shopper wants transparency—a price they can trust. The attack on AT&T led to a change in its marketing strategy. Within a year or so, AT&T and Verizon were both advertising unlimited data for a set price.

A deal on the mobile monthly payment is relative. Normally, the deal begins with what the shopper may be already paying—this sets a baseline or expectation. The Deal Seeker operates from this vantage point and wants to reduce their payment while retaining the same coverage, or to add coverage and features for the price they are currently paying. The lower the amount they negotiate, the more they can feel the deal.

Another factor in mobile monthly payments is the phone. Currently people are replacing their cell phones every two to 2½ years, and carriers discourage the shopper from purchasing a new phone outright. If the shopper is thinking about getting a new phone, the provider gives the shopper several options: pay for a new phone upfront, or add the cost of the phone to the monthly payment for a period of time. A shopper may be looking at an unlimited plan for two people at $115 on AT&T; however, throw in two new iPhones (paid for over 30 months) and the monthly payment jumps an average of another $50.

The Deal Seeker would normally do their homework and find the best deal; however, their strategy may change based on the brand DNA. If the deal-seeking shopper is a Free Agent too, then they are willing to go to whichever carrier has the best deal. For these shoppers, the carrier and the phone are interchangeable. On the other hand, if the shopper is tied to a particular type of phone—say an iPhone—then they are locked into the phone (and the cost to purchase it). They may take their time and shop competitive carriers until one offers free iPhones for new customers. Finally, if the shopper is tied into one carrier and one type of phone, then they are limited in the deal they can get. They would probably be hyper-sensitive to the carrier's promotions and upgrade when a good deal comes along.

I have discussed several industries here, but other industries also wage war over the monthly deal. Cable companies are notorious for offering limited time deals and then increasing the price after the promotional time period elapsed. They continue to increase their bundling efforts. Most offer cable television, internet access, and a phone land line. They are expanding into home security and smart home services. Yep, all for one low price—or not.

I've spent the better part of this chapter discussing different industries and how they approach getting to the final number on a complex purchase. If you are a marketer and you've figured this out, why not just promote the lower number to shoppers? Well, many marketers do. You frequently see promotions for automotive lease rates, mobile phone service rates, and monthly bundled rates from cable providers.

From the Deal Seeker's perspective their deal soon becomes obsolete. Very few shoppers in these categories get the best deal ever. It seems like the week after they make their purchase, yet another "best deal we have ever done" comes along. Soon the adrenalin rush of the deal wears off and the customer just sees their monthly payment. Inevitably, they will be sitting on their couch watching television or surfing the internet and they will come across a new and better deal. This is the premise of the next chapter, "The Ghosts of Purchases Past."

The Final Number Principle

For complex purchases, the deal is not the price of the product; rather, the shopper's deal perception is based on the price they expect to pay each month.

THIRTEEN
The Ghosts of Purchases Past

"With three kids, it was always very, very tight, and it was always a scramble for what was my next job. So I learned never to go into debt because I don't want those monthly payments to preoccupy my thoughts."
—William Shatner, actor

Every month people are haunted by the ghosts of purchases past. There is the cable bill which seems to get bigger every month, making you question whether you really need all the pay channels. Of course you bundled it with internet service and you cannot tell where one service begins and the other ends. Sure, you can change it, but is it worth the effort and for how much savings?

Then there's the cellular bill. The mobile bill can be a confusing compilation of costs and fees (especially for a family). There is an intricate mishmash of services and devices all bundled together. It seemed like a smart idea at the time to bundle two new iPhones into the bill for several years, but now the bill is a monthly reminder that your old phone may have been good enough. And, oh yeah, how come unlimited seems to be so expensive?

Auto insurance is yet another ghostly reminder—a mandatory payment for the privilege to drive. It doesn't seem to reward you if you are a good driver, and if you get a ticket or (God forbid) end up in an accident, it seems to rocket out of control. The higher premium sucks up a larger portion of your paycheck that you'd originally tagged for something good—something you wanted or would like to do. Not anymore, gotta pay the insurance bill. Gotta live with it. Unless you can do something about it.…

Life is often lived through a series of monthly payments. Sometimes we pay the bills without thinking twice. Other times, we wish we could reduce the cost of necessities in order to spend money on something we want. Rarely does a person take action; it's too much effort. Rather the payments haunt the person each month, building up in their minds until they can finally muster the energy to take action and reduce them.

Advertisers hope a person will take action. Hope is built into every commercial break. A promise to reduce your cell phone bill in half. A promise to cut your cable bill AND give you more to choose from. A promise to lower your auto insurance payment, if you can just carve 15 minutes out of your life.… You get the idea.

Payments are a result of past transactions lingering into the present. For some people, the resulting behavior is to try to reduce those payments. It's like a *necessity reduction principle*—I need to reduce the amount I pay for "needs" to increase the amount of money I can spend on "wants." This is a different form of Deal Seeker—a person who is trying to get the best deal on monthly payments by constantly shopping for them.

People take action at different thresholds. A person may be agitated with their cable bill month after month and, each time they pay it, they vow this is the month they will do something about it. However, that desire may remain dormant unless there is a secondary trigger. For example, I moved from Comcast (or Infinity) to AT&T. I had been fed up with Comcast for years as I watched my bill increase 50 cents a month. AT&T came along and promised a great deal, AND they would switch my cable in just a few hours.

It worked that time for me. But then again I am a lazy Deal Seeker. My friends Monica and Joe are active Deal Seekers—they spend time to save money. They act far more quickly and abruptly. I recall a lunch conversation with Joe. I had been complaining about my cable bill. Joe told how Monica will pay attention to commercials, and if their current cable provider is offering a better deal than the one they have, she will get them on the phone right then and there and negotiate a better deal—lowering their monthly bill.

While I wanted to switch, Monica *had* to switch—it is in her DNA. In fact, many Deal Seekers would be haunted until they took action. They know (or believe) they can get a better deal. Monica told me in her interview how she would either switch providers or renegotiate her bill when her contract was up. Her logical argument with the cable company was "Why do they offer new customers a better deal than their loyal ones?" In the five years I contemplated switching my cable bill, Monica switched or renegotiated three times.

The payment ghost is strong in necessity categories. Necessity categories are the basic amenities we purchase to live our lives. Some come in the form of a monthly payments (e.g., mortgage/rent, car payments, utility bills), while others are ongoing expenses (e.g., groceries, gasoline, prescriptions). Sure, the person is getting value in exchange for their payments; however, a Deal Seeker will constantly try to get these necessity payments as low as possible.

So, necessity categories with monthly payments are ripe for such action, especially if they are perceived as commodities. This reminds me of a conversation I had with a health insurance client a few years after Obamacare (the Affordable Care Act) was enacted. Health insurers could charge different rates and in health insurance surveys "price" was the number one factor in choosing a plan. I asked the client a simple question: "Is health care being commoditized?" Her response was an emphatic "yes." Then I posed the question, "What is preventing one health care provider from changing their marketing strategy and Geico-ing the category?" "Nothing" was her reply.

Like auto insurance, many people see little to no difference in health insurance offerings, making price the deciding factor for many enrollees. And a person typically enrols through some website or call center. There is no face-to-face conversation, no relationship, just a faceless entity providing a service and sending a monthly bill. The necessity reduction principle is evident in research in which the majority of people state that the monthly premium drives their decision—their decision to choose a provider, and their decision to switch providers.

This commodity perspective drives action for the Deal Seeker. Consider the following table and how different each brand is within a category. If brands cannot convince the shopper there is a discernable difference between themselves and the competition, the category runs the risk of being commoditized.

Category	Major Players	Difference
Cable	AT&T, xfinity, Dish, Direct TV	Price, Variety, Reception
Cell Service	AT&T, Verizon, Sprint, T-Mobile	Price, Coverage, Phones
Auto Insurance	Geico, Progressive, State Farm	Price, Service
Health Insurance	United Healthcare, Blue Cross	Price, Coverage, Services
Mortgage	Quicken, Ally, Local Brokers	Interest Rates, Service

Worth noting is the fact that brand differentiation is not the same as personal differentiation. Take mobile phone service. Let's say Verizon covers 98 percent of the United States. That's fine, but if a person spends all their time in Dayton, Ohio, many providers with more limited coverage areas nonetheless offer enough coverage to meet their needs. From the Daytonian's perspective all the brands are the same; therefore, the category is commoditized.

From a customer perspective you need to ask what is stronger: the perceived difference of the service or the monthly cost savings. If a brand offers a 50 percent discount on the same or similar service, the Deal Seeker gene kicks in and the person considers changing providers. The key word here is "considers." "Considers" does not mean the person is going to switch, because switching takes effort. Whether a person is changing their mobile phone service, cable provider or refinancing a mortgage, there is a time commitment to make a switch. And if you are normally Price Blind (i.e., you spend money to save time), you are less likely to exert the effort to switch because of the fact this is not a typical behavior. Sure, down the road either the persistent reminder may finally drive you to action or a deal comes along you just can't pass up, but the threshold to action is far higher than for a typical Deal Seeker.

Some ghosts haunt us on a daily basis. Fueling your vehicle is a great example. The price of fuel will drive different actions, and the higher the price the more people will act. The primary reason is that most people believe "gas is gas," and therefore want to minimize their expenditure. Some people will take basic actions and fuel at the station with the lowest price. Others will use a fuel perks program or visit a warehouse club, where they are guaranteed a lower price than at the average station.

Grocery shopping is a weekly haunting for most people. An interesting fact worth noting is that most grocery shoppers are Free Agents when it comes to grocery store brands. This means the store brand is not as important in their decision on where to shop as other factors. If you think about it, this is not surprising. Many shoppers shop for the brands on the shelf, and most grocery stores carry the same brands: the same brands of cereal, same brands of orange juice, same brands of toilet paper. The difference for Deal Seekers is in the price they pay for those brands. For a Deal Seeker, it all depends on the total amount on the receipt at check-out. This is why the Deal Seeker will exert effort to lower their grocery bill as much as possible—even if it means shopping at multiple stores, using coupons, and/or buying private label products.

The ghosts of purchases past live on through the promise of a cheaper payment. It seems simple from a marketer's perspective to get people to rethink their current situation and opt for a lower rate. Not so fast. Having the lower promised payment is key to getting a shopper to take action, and most marketers know it. This is why the categories I discussed in this chapter flood their marketing with a promise of a better deal.

This isn't a case of one marketer offering a better rate and everyone else talking about how much better their service is than the competition's. Rather, shopper action is dependent on several factors, including the number of Deal Seekers in the category and the timing to switch. If a person is six months into a two-year contract they are going to be haunted for a long time.

The Ghosts of Purchases Past Principle
There is a natural desire to reduce necessity payments; however, action only occurs at a point where the effort is worth the reward to switch.

FOURTEEN
For the Love of Brick and Mortar

"Why do you go into Target for just a couple of things and ALWAYS spend $100?! Why??????"
—Steve M. on Twitter

There is a one hundred dollar question for many Target shoppers. Can you get in and out of Target and spend less than $100? It is a recurring question I have seen in researching shopper DNA, conversations with friends, and on social media.

You probably believe me; however, if you don't, just search for "Target spend $100" on Twitter and read the posts. While some posts are from shoppers exasperated they spent so much, in most posts you can feel the "love" for Target. And the $100 serves as a badge, an expression of how much the shopper enjoys shopping at Target.

Do you love shopping? Do you go up and down every aisle wondering what is around the corner? Is it something novel? A deal? Or something you forgot you "needed"? Are you a shopper who looks forward to a trip to the store or a person who can't wait to get in and out of the store?

My family avoids shopping with me at Lowe's or Home Depot. Regardless of what I am going into the home improvement store to get, I will wander up and down every aisle. Check out the seasonal decorations. Look at the tools (and dream about the next tool I will buy). Check out the lawn tractors or snow blowers. And maybe check out the latest yard tools to see if there is something I need to add to a garage stuffed with yard gadgets. A ten-minute trip to get light bulbs and salt for our water softener quickly turns into a one-hour browsing adventure—every time.

Okay, I may be atypical. Let me offer another extreme. While building the shopper DNA, we had people complete diaries and then compared their survey results to their diaries to ensure we were getting an accurate read for the survey. Linda was one of our respondents. Linda didn't care to shop—in fact, she hated it. She minimized the time she spent in the store. For example, when we asked her about her grocery trip, she produced a receipt from Rite Aid. She had done her grocery trip for the week by going to Rite Aid. She found Rite Aid an expeditious solution to the grocery store.

Time is polarizing. Within Time DNA we classify shoppers as either Journey or Mission. Mission shoppers limit their shopping experience. They typically have a list and more likely than not they get in, get out, and get on with life. Journey shoppers are the opposite. They are likely to go down most of the aisles. They are exploratory, as opposed to Mission shoppers who are more surgical in their approach.

An interesting aspect of Time DNA is that it doesn't change much from study to study. While we can assess polarization in the Brand DNA (e.g., dog food) and Wallet DNA (e.g., auto insurance), Time DNA is typically split equally between Mission and Journey. The reason for this lies in a shopper's emotive connection to shopping. It is no surprise that Journey shoppers are more likely to enjoy shopping, while Mission shoppers—well, not so much. For example, in grocery shopping the majority of Journey shoppers refer to grocery shopping as "fun time" or "me time." The majority of Mission shoppers stated they felt shopping was a chore.

A shopper may shift from Journey to Mission depending on retail category. This is not surprising. You may find yourself enjoying shopping for tech equipment or pet supplies, and loathing shopping for groceries. The reaction is partly based on a shopper's personal perspective on shopping, but passion for a product category could also sway someone who exhibits the traits of a Mission shopper in most of their shopping to act like a Journey shopper when shopping for products (or brands) they are passionate about.

This is also where Time blends with the other two DNA strands: Brand and Wallet. Let's go back to the Apple advocate. While they could buy their iPhone at AT&T or Verizon, they prefer an excursion to the Apple store in order to enjoy the entire brand experience. There may be several different emotions triggering this behavior, such as brand advocacy (always needing to go back to the Apple Motherland), brand assistance (only Apple employees know Apple products), or brand exploration ("I would also like to see what other new Apple products are available").

Deal seeking is also a catalyst for Journey shopping. If a shopper enjoys the hunt for the deal, they will have an expansive shopping experience searching high and low for that deal and gladly doing so. Therefore they are Journey shoppers.

A twist within this DNA strand involves online shopping vs. offline shopping. Every year there is a lot of buzz around the growth of online shopping. Brick and mortar retail is dead or dying. There is proof of this trend within the retail category as certain types of stores got "Amazoned" (e.g., books, video). And it seems like it will be only a matter of time until we will do the majority of shopping online.

Well, not so fast. There is probably an ecommerce ceiling. Why? Well, if everyone hated shopping or was a Mission shopper, ecommerce would inevitably come to dominate many retail categories. But the Journey shoppers are not going away. They love the experience of shopping. For some people shopping is entertainment. For others it is a passion. And for some it is an addiction.

Many such shoppers rationalize why they go to the store instead of buying online. The top five reasons from a survey by BigCommerce on why a person shops brick and mortar stores include not wanting to pay shipping costs (58 percent), wanting to touch and feel the product (49 percent), not wanting to wait for delivery (34 percent), difficult online return policies (34 percent), and privacy concerns (29 percent).

Ecommerce will continue to grow in prominence and scale. There is an emerging concept of an omnichannel shopper, a shopper who will seamlessly buy from whichever channel they find beneficial in the context of a particular purchase. Sometimes convenience will be paramount and they will opt for ecommerce. Other times they will prefer the shopping experience and go to a brick and mortar store.

There is a middle ground, too, where a shopper may blend both online and brick and mortar shopping experiences together. For example, showrooming is a situation in which a shopper first goes to a store and then checks online for a better price. The tactile shopper likes to personally view and touch the product before making a purchase; however, the showroomer also want the best price. Showrooming poses a major problem for many brick and mortar electronic stores.

Best Buy, for instance, has struggled with showrooming. In 2013 Best Buy estimated about 40 percent of shoppers who came in its stores had no intent of buying. To survive Best Buy embraced an omnichannel approach that integrated online and offline efforts. Subsequently it saw growth in both online and brick and mortar sales.

Best Buy has avoided becoming "Amazoned," at least for the time being. However, many other retailers are feeling the pinch. Department stores have been particularly hard hit in recent years, with J.C. Penney, Sears, Kmart, and Macy's closing large numbers of stores. Is this a sign of a shift in shopping preferences to online? The result of an over-saturation of retail stores? Or is there another reason?

It's too easy to declare the demise of retail. Based on shoppers' love and hate of the retail environment there exists an equilibrium point for retail stores, both online and offline. Many times a retailer struggling with brick and mortar will decide the solution is to add an online presence. This may help if the retailer has a unique niche in the retail space they can exploit online. If not, they are just creating another channel, not a solution.

For any given retail category or brand you need to take an introspective look at the type of shoppers they are attracting. In the mobile phone category, 59 percent of shoppers are Mission shoppers and 41 percent Journey. This means that to satisfy Mission shoppers' needs the retail experience needs to be expeditious. Whether online, offline or both, the goal is to get the shopper a new phone and/or cellular plan with as little effort and in as little time as possible. If a retailer fails to meet these needs, shoppers will gravitate to other brands, other channels.

An interesting trend to watch is the growth of ecommerce in the grocery category. Grocery shoppers are roughly a fifty-fifty split between Mission and Journey shoppers. Ecommerce options that either deliver to home or curbside pick-up seem ripe for the Mission shopper, but perhaps not for every Mission shopper. The Deal Surgeon (Free Agent, Deal Seeker, Mission) views grocery shopping as a chore they would like to get done—you know, check the box and move on with life. The one caveat is that they also want a deal. The tension occurs when they order groceries online: are they seeing all the deals? Also, they normally will shop at more than one store, making ecommerce a cumbersome option. Finally, there is normally a surcharge to have someone shop on your behalf, which works against their deal DNA. If the shopper were Mission and Price Blind, they would be more open to using an ecommerce grocery service (this DNA combination represents about one in five shoppers).

There are several reasons shoppers prefer brick and mortar stores. One benefit of brick and mortar is problem solving. With the purchase of a mobile phone there is the need to transition photos, contacts, apps and other content from the old phone to the new phone. Sure, it may be as simple as restoring the phone from the cloud; however, the cloud may be a hard concept to grasp for some people. This is where a person needs human assistance to complete their shopping mission and get on with life.

Another brick and mortar benefit is feeding the "love of the find." Some stores are conducive to the Bargainista's desire to find the deal. Sometimes the deal is on something that's needed, other times it is more about the exhilaration of finding a great deal on something they hadn't actually planned on buying. Some deal searching can be done online and this works well for the Deal Surgeon (Free Agent, Deal Seeker, Mission). But the Bargainista is more about exploration. Sure, they can find some deals online, but they also believe they can get deals instore and will gravitate to outlets that fulfill this desire. Some stores are built for the Deal Seeker; think of TJ Maxx, Home Goods, and Dollar Tree. Their retail approach is designed to feed the impulsive Deal Seeker.

A final brick and mortar benefit involves celebrating the passion. Passion stores cater to the passionate enthusiast. Cabela's and Bass Pro Shops are designed for the outdoor enthusiast. Their stores are more than a retail environment but, rather, a celebration of everything outdoors. There are massive aquariums stocked with fresh water fish, possibly a gun range, product demonstrations, and outdoor gear as far as the eye can see. These passion stores appeal to the Journey shopper. The depth and breadth of the store encourages exploration and browsing.

Claims of the death of the retail environment may at times be over-exaggerated. However, this does not mean all retail stores will succeed. The retail store must feed into different shopper motivations. Some stores thrive by attracting the Deal Seeker, while others suffer because they cannot dislodge the Deal Seeker from the competition. Kmart's history centered on the deal—and on the famous Blue Light Special. Back in the day, the Blue Light signified a deal, and Deal Seekers flocked to it. As time went on, the deal energy at Kmart declined and competitors like Target pulled Deal Seekers away. The question today is: can Kmart recapture the deal energy it once had, or is it too difficult to wrestle Deal Seekers away from the competition?

For the Love of Brick and Mortar Principle
The shopper's Time motivations (those who love shopping versus those who hate it) will heavily influence the number of brick and mortar stores within a retail category.

FIFTEEN

Shopper Bragging Rights

"It's not bragging if you can back it up."
—Muhammad Ali

ALDI can be a polarizing grocery store. Some people find it a quirky because you need to bring your own bags, use a quarter to "rent" a shopping cart, and the store is stocked primarily with private label products. Oh yeah, and there is no Muzak playing in the background while you shop. Other shoppers love the store. They love the deals and, just as importantly, they love telling others about ALDI.

I grew up in Grand Rapids. My belief was that it was one of the most frugal cities in the country—or at least in the top 10. But I did a little research and found out Grand Rapids does not even crack the top 25. The top five frugal cities (based on coupon usage) are Orlando, Florida, Washington, D.C., Charlotte, North Carolina, New York, and Atlanta. The five cities combined clip more than 110 million coupons annually, saving over $200 million.

Anyway, Grand Rapidians are not cheap, they just like to get the most for their money. Enter ALDI. ALDI has been operating stores in Grand Rapids for a while. So when I started working on ALDI I asked my mother if she ever shopped at an ALDI. I assumed she did since she is a self-proclaimed savvy Deal Seeker. However, I found out my mother was in the "ALDI is quirky" category. Her rationale was typical of an ALDI rejecter: "You know, they sell brands I don't recognize. You need a quarter to put in the cart and you have to bag yourself. It's just weird."

Several years went by and I would periodically encourage her to try ALDI, always getting the same response. Then out of the blue she told me she would try ALDI. I was curious why all of a sudden she was willing to try it. She proceeded to tell me a story about her sewing circle (understand this is Grand Rapids and my mother is in her seventies), and how the conversation steered toward the best place to get a deal. Different stores were mentioned but two stores kept coming up: Costco and ALDI. The sewing group was so convincing she was willing to try ALDI.

Why do shoppers share? There are several different motivations that can manifest themselves in various ways.

Sharing is about an emotional connection. A connection with something we are passionate about. A connection with others. A connection with brands. Many times it is egocentric; the sharing is all about social recognition—about getting credit within your social circle.

There is a lot going on here, so let me break it down.

Social sharing varies by category. This is not a surprise. Some categories have few social conversations because there isn't much worth talking about. Most established consumer packaged goods brands fall into this group. Two categories we looked at were dog food and yogurt. Both generated minimal word of mouth due to the lack of novelty. Seriously, what's worth sharing? Pet owners are very brand-centric and therefore there isn't much need to discuss dog food (unless you are a first-time dog owner).

As for yogurt, it generates even less conversation. The Greek yogurt phenomenon might be worth talking about but there is not much reason to discuss any one specific product. There *is* conversation around smoothies. But this has more to do with a passion for fitness or weight loss than for a specific product.

This brings me to an important point: passion. People tend to share when they are passionate about a brand, product, or experience. By the way, they are just as likely (if not more likely) to share a negative product experience as a positive one.

I discussed in the Brand Tattoo chapter the fact there are levels of passion for brand advocacy. Operating at a higher level of passion than the brand advocate is the category enthusiast. These people transcend any one brand, and their passion defines how they see themselves (and want to be seen). A category enthusiast (e.g., auto-enthusiast, tech-enthusiast, foodie) will frequently discuss the object of their passion because it is a part of who they are. They spend discretionary free time invested in their passion. Living in Detroit, you run into many auto-enthusiasts. Some have a forward-looking passion about what's next (e.g., the next Mustang, Corvette, or F-150) while others have a reflective passion based on what was (e.g., classic cars). Normally, this reflective passion is associated with a vehicle they are restoring (or have owned in the past). The reflective enthusiast may have some interest in the future, but they really light up when you ask about their '68 Cutlass Convertible 442.

The passions of these two types of enthusiasts are reflected in two mega-events in the Detroit area: the North American International Auto Show (NAIAS) in January and the Dream Cruise in August. The NAIAS is the ultimate experience for the forward-looking enthusiast. Auto companies from around the world reveal their upcoming line-ups along with a smattering of concept cars, which tease the enthusiast with possible trends in vehicle design, performance, and/or functionality.

The Dream Cruise is an immersion in nostalgic car culture. On the third Saturday in August, classic car enthusiasts motor to Detroit to participate in the largest such cruise in the country. A 16-mile stretch of Woodward Avenue is shut down for the Dream Cruise, which brings to Detroit more than 40,000 classic cars and about one million spectators.

The kind of auto enthusiast that a shopper is impacts the social nature of their shopper journey. The future-focused auto enthusiast functions in a very directed manner. Since they are in tune with the industry and what is coming next, they are far less likely to seek out other people's input when buying their next car. Odds are they have been dreaming about the next vehicle for years, possibly since they purchased their previous vehicle. Conversely, the classic enthusiast may seek out social interaction, since they are more in tune with their classic automobile than what the latest vehicles have to offer.

Tech-thusiasts are similar to auto-enthusiasts. There is exuberance when techies talk about what's next. When I say what's next, I refer not to a future that is years away, but, rather, the next new device they intend to buy. It could be a phone, tablet or gaming system. Whatever the device, they look forward to purchasing with passion and want to share. This is reflected in the long-time trend of "unboxing" on YouTube, in which tech-thusiasts record themselves opening the box of a new device they just purchased. The proud purchaser talks through the different functions and features which motivated them to buy the product, revealing to other techies their passion for the product.

An aspect of post-purchase sharing worth bringing up is post-cognitive dissonance. Often a customer shares their purchase story with others to get confirmation they made the right decision. This can be a sign of buyer's remorse, where the person isn't sure they made the right choice and is using social input to validate their decision. If the product is a socially safe purchase (e.g., buying the latest iPhone) very few people will question the purchase. However, if a shopper bought a niche brand in the eyes of their social group, they may feel they need to justify it or risk being questioned about the purchase. The initial rationalization will lean toward logical reasoning (e.g., "I got a great price" or "My company paid for the phone"). If once in use the product exceeds their expectations, they will evolve into more of an advocate for the brand. They may not overtly tout the brand, but will be passionate about the brand when asked.

Advocacy for a brand also prompts sharing, whether it rises out of true passion for a brand or insecurity as described above. I have discussed Apple advocates throughout this book. Apple has made an emotive connection with many of their customers that transcends the device. Those customers are passionate about the brand and the role it plays in their life. I could speculate about how the brand makes them feel (e.g., creative, progressive), but it does not matter. The emotive connection is all that matters, and this is why they share their passion with others.

There are other brands that have a similar effect. Many automotive brands like Jeep, Ford Mustang or Chevy Camaro have a strong following. The conversation varies slightly by brand. Many Jeep-related conversations center on going off road and delivering on Jeep's brand promise ("Trail Rated"). Online you will find company-sponsored blogs as well as blogs from Jeep Momma, The Orange Jeep Dad and Jeepsies, which is written through the eyes of a Jeep newbie.

The Mustang and Camaro blogs normally fall into two groups: what was and what's next. "What was" blogs and forums are about restoration. The community shares a passion for rebuilding classic cars and taking them to car cruises. The "what's next" conversation is about the manufacturer's planned vehicle enhancements in upcoming years.

If you have time you can search for conversations on any car. That said, the vast majority of vehicle owners are not talking. The reason is they have very little to share. Usually this is because they are not emotionally attached to their vehicle and therefore not compelled to share.

All of this is not unique to automotive. Another example: Weber grills have been around for years and have an avid following. The centerpiece of Weber conversations is Weber Nation—a blog run by the company. Another outdoor cooker, Big Green Egg, has developed an impressive following over the past decade. The enthusiasm for the product is indicated by the number of people who are blogging about their ceramic grill. Owners of the grill also seem to be "Big" and ready to share, like Big Green Joe (BigGreenJoe.com), Big T's Big Green Egg Recipe Blog (bigtsbge.blogspot.com), and Big Green Craig (BigGreenCraig.com). It doesn't matter if it is a Weber or Green Egg, the passion is expressed through appetizing recipes and tips to get the most out of your grill.

An interesting aspect most of these brands have in common is the fact they are Price Blind brands. Rarely, if ever, do the brands go on sale. A commitment to pay more relative to other brands in the category is a sign of advocacy. If shoppers are unwilling to pay a premium for a brand, there is commoditization within the category. In that situation, shoppers tend to be unwilling to brag about their "brand" purchase—instead, you will see more discussion about the deal.

Let's now switch the perspective and talk about how the category enthusiast engages in providing advice to other shoppers. While the tech or auto enthusiast is less likely to ask for advice themselves in buying their next product, they are very willing to assist others in their purchase. This may appear altruistic, but it goes deeper. Their egos are tied to their knowledge, and if they assist others it validates them as experts. An interesting experiment would be to ask two category-enthusiast experts for advice at the same time. Depending on the size of the individuals' egos, the conversation could spiral into "who is right" as opposed to "the right advice for you."

Another aspect of the advocate is how they weave their love of brand into the conversation. Weber advocates don't just grill, they "fire up the Weber." Apple advocates watch "Apple TV."

One distinction between a category enthusiast and a brand advocate is that in the case of the category enthusiast, it's all about the person talking, while in the case of the brand advocate it's about the brand community. Brand advocacy serves as a connection point. Their shared passion is a reason to talk—a reason to discuss why they love a brand. And love for a brand attracts others. Social sites are spawned by advocates and many join in on the conversation. With the advent of Facebook, fans created pages to express their love of a brand.

As much as love of a brand can draw people closer, it can also create an adversarial situation, especially with competitive brands. Like love of sports teams, brands can bind and divide people. The classic campaign by Apple—"Are you a PC or a Mac?"—amplified this love of brand and general distaste for things non-Apple. There are other brand adversaries: Pepsi vs. Coke; Whopper vs. Big Mac; Chevy vs. Ford. If you do a simple search on Facebook you will discover the adversarial tenacity of each group. Both Ford and Chevy have "hate pages." The I Hate Chevy fan page had 230,000 likes when I checked, while the I Hate Ford fan page boasted 476,000 likes.

There are plenty of tech adversaries out there too, especially on Twitter. The nature of the hate varies by context, however. With Apple it is about the device, and more often than not, the device is the iPhone. There is no love lost for Microsoft either, with many people fuming about the latest Windows release or more likely one of the components of Microsoft Office (e.g., Word, Excel, Outlook). There are also hate posts for Samsung centering on its phones. This is a different kind of adversarial relationship than with vehicle brands. Most tech posts are in reaction to the device or software not meeting their expectations, while with vehicles adversarial hatred runs in parallel with love of a different brand.

The brand argument is an egocentric one. It is about bragging rights, especially for Deal Seekers. Grocery shopping is not the province of the category enthusiast. It is not a personal passion like fashion, pets, or fitness. Yet, strange to say, grocery shopping is among the highest social sharing categories we have come across. The answer is simple: shopping is a passion for many people, and for Deal Seekers it is about saving the most at the cash register.

The conversation is often grounded in the question of who is a better shopper. This is less about advice and more about bragging rights. The conversation will evolve from what is right to who is right. It could center on a topic like the best gluten-free or best organic produce, but inevitably shoppers tend to defend their choice, their store.

The internet is littered with grocery shopper ego. Just go to Google, type in "my groceries," and look at the images that pop up. Grocery shoppers like to share their weekly haul and how much they saved (rather like techies unboxing their new acquisitions). They may feel they are sharing their wisdom, and they are. However, they are also looking for social recognition that they are the best at what they do.

I've discussed a lot of different reasons why people share. Summing up, there are four "levels" of sharing. The first level, the simplest and most common, is *novelty*. At this level, the conversation is about the product or store experience, which can be new to everyone or just one shopper. The first time a person ventures into the Apple store, Cabela's, or an American Girl store, they may feel compelled to share, while for many others it's "been there, done that."

Novelty can also come in the form of a product purchased infrequently, like cars, tech products, or household appliances. This novelty lasts a while but not forever. In the automotive category, you could argue novelty subsides when the new car smell fades away.

The second level of sharing is *brand advocacy*. Love of the brand is usually expressed through the owner's use of the product or advice to others on how to get the most out of their product.

The third level is *category expertise*. This desire to share is based on a personal expertise within a product category. Think about a tech-thusiast buying the new device or a fashion-forward person purchasing new shoes or clothing. This can also encompass low-consideration purchases like wine, microbrews, or recipes.

The fourth level involves *shopper expertise*. It can be about a shopper's passion to find unique products on a regular basis (persistent novelty), or may be a case of a Deal Seeker who knows how to beat the system and save the most money.

Regardless of the level, the goal of sharing is social recognition. It's about feeding the ego.

Shopper Bragging Rights Principle
Shopper bragging is a result of an egocentric connection point between people based on novelty, brand, passion, or expertise.

SIXTEEN
Beware of the Brand Governor

"Some said he shouldn't save Detroit. But President Obama made the tough and right call to save more than a million American jobs in an important, iconic industry."
—Harry Reid, retired U.S. Senator from Nevada

In the late 2000s very little was going right for the domestic auto industry. The imports were stealing share from the Detroit Three. I remember seeing a very desperate chart depicting this brand decay. I was working on the Ford account at the time. The chart displayed a one-decade shift in how people went shopping for new cars. In the late nineties, about 50 percent were shopping exclusively for domestics, 30 percent exclusively for imports, and the balance were shopping for both. Fast forward a decade and the situation flipped. About 40 percent were shopping exclusively for imports, 30 percent for domestic and the remainder shopped both. Not a good trend to say the least. The analysts theorized it would take a good decade to shift the trend back to the pre-2000 situation, if it could be done at all.

At the time there was not a lot of good news coming out of Detroit. This was on the cusp of the recession and the infamous bail-out hearings. Detroit auto manufacturers were not doing well, especially in the "smile states" (for the uninitiated, the smile states are all the states outside the heartland). Of course, the domestic manufacturers were still selling cars in those states, but buying a domestic wasn't a socially accepted purchase. If someone bought a Ford Focus in San Diego, it was doubtful that neighbors were flocking to see the vehicle. Instead the driveway conversation went something like this:

Neighbor with a condescending tone: "So you bought a Ford?"
Ford customer responding defensively: "Well, yeah ... but I got a great deal!"

That was the typical response at the time: "I got a great deal." Hardly a ringing endorsement but predictable, given that imports were the socially accepted purchase, not the domestic brands.

To change a social trend, you first need to understand the dynamics powering social energy. There are three roles in the social triangle: owners the shopper knows, experts they trust, and the Brand Governor (see the diagram on the next page).

Owners the shopper knows are customers who bought the same product or a similar competitive product. It doesn't matter if it is a new car, smartphone, appliance, or trip to Disney. The customer can give the shopper a firsthand account of the product experience. The good. The bad. And they typically put

The Social Triangle

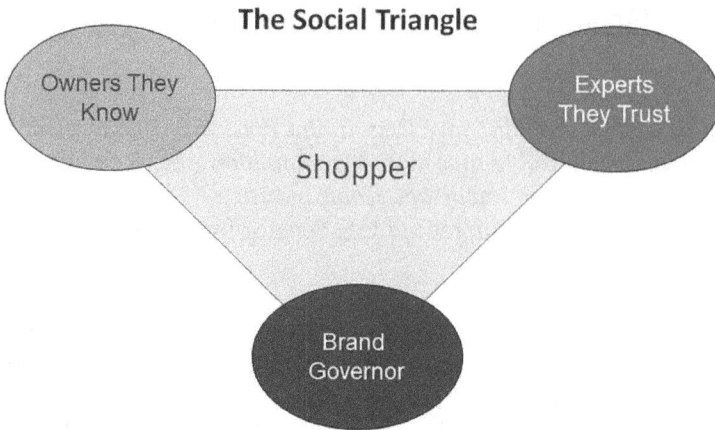

it in the shopper's personal context, because they probably know the shopper's likes and dislikes.

Experts can be a person or a source. *Consumer Reports* is the default expert for some shoppers—the Bible for major purchases. An expert can also be someone in your social circle. If you ever want to find out how many experts are in your social circle, do a shout-out on Facebook asking for assistance with a purchase. A while back I was purchasing an HDTV and needed assistance, so I posted: "I am looking to buy an HDTV for about $700. What are the features I should consider and what features aren't worth having in that price range?" Within the hour I received about ten responses from my social circle. Worth noting is the fact that all the responses were from developer friends. They shared a common tech-love and regularly go to tech sites, like CNET, to see what is the latest and greatest.

Lastly, beware of the *Brand Governor*. The first two sources within the social triangle have firsthand knowledge of the product. The Brand Governor does not. Their views are opinion-based. But don't underestimate the influence of the Brand Governor in expressing social norms. The shopper has a choice: either purchase the product and put up with the Brand Governor's negative attitude, or buy a socially accepted product.

Once when I was presenting this idea, a woman in the audience provided me with an example that was the opposite of the reaction to buying a Ford that I mentioned earlier. Her father worked for decades at General Motors and was very pro-buy American. No one in his family was going to buy an import! While the woman wanted to buy a Honda Civic, she ended up buying a Chevy instead to avoid a reaction from her father, the Brand Governor (and probably a lot of family grief). The zealousness of her father imposed a restriction on her purchase that she accepted.

The Brand Governor is alive and well in many product categories, especially those where there is social input into the purchase (and social acceptance post-purchase). The brand purchased (or the store brand where the product was purchased) can define people within a social circle, and the brand governor rules the roost. Products within categories from cars to clothes, from vacation trips to grocery shopping can all be frowned upon. Think about the following within your social circle:

- Is Trader Joe's or Whole Foods more acceptable than Walmart or Dollar General?
- Is a trip to Las Vegas more acceptable than one to Branson, Missouri?
- Is it more acceptable to purchase a Toyota, Nissan or Chevy?
- Is buying shoes from Zappos, DSW, or Payless more acceptable? Or is the store irrelevant and a shoe brand like Anne Klein or Nine West more important?

The subtext of these questions tell you as much about your social group as the answers. Is your social group driven by brand or the deal? Brand divas are particular about the brands people choose. I couldn't imagine trumpeting the merits of the new Microsoft smartphone to an Apple-zealot at the ad agency. The social circle creates the acceptable norm. Take grocery shopping. One social circle may view Whole Foods as the acceptable choice (and Walmart as the "closet" choice). Conversely, a deal-centric social circle may think Whole Foods is an overpriced, socially unacceptable shopping choice (and then Whole Foods is in the closet).

So can a social circle shift? Yep, and faster than you think.

I began this chapter talking about the Ford dilemma. If you were to look at Ford's social trajectory at the time, it was declining. There were more negative than positive conversations about the brand. However, with one brand action Ford reversed the trend: they didn't take the bail-out money. When Ford did not take the money it shifted the social conversation. That one brand action reversed the trend and began a positive trajectory. Combined with Ford's investment in social programs (most notably the Fiesta Movement), this helped propel Ford into a socially accepted purchase. No longer was the driveway response "I got a great deal"; instead it was "Wow, that's the new Fiesta. Can I go for a spin?"

Brand Governor Principle
There are three primary shopper influencers: owners they know, experts they trust, and the Brand Governor whose opinion may be as powerful (if not more) than the other two influencers.

SEVENTEEN
A Tale of the Lone Wolf

"It is a well-documented fact that guys will not ask for directions. This is a biological thing. This is why it takes several million sperm cells ... to locate a female egg, despite the fact that the egg is, relative to them, the size of Wisconsin."
—Dave Barry, Pulitzer Prize-winning author and columnist

Consider the age-old question: *Why do some people ask for directions, while others refuse?* Many hypotheses are offered. One is that it is a gender thing: specifically, men don't want to ask for directions. The male gender displays characteristics that feed into this notion. You could call it a pride thing. Men want to be seen as strong and feel that asking for directions may be a sign of weakness. More interesting is an insight suggested by Dr. Linda Sapadin: men learn by doing, not by being told what do do. She further claims this is a general reason why boys don't do as well in school. They want to experiment, try things, and draw conclusions themselves. Men don't really grow out of this, and instead of asking for directions, they prefer to figure it out themselves.

So why talk about directions? Well, in shopping some shoppers ask for directions. In other words, they ask others for advice. They ask others about the best place to buy items. What store has the best deals? What brands are worth buying and which ones are worth avoiding? What hotels are worth staying at and which ones should you stay away from?

Then there is the Lone Wolf. I classify a Lone Wolf as a person who does not ask others for advice or input prior to buying and also doesn't discuss their purchase afterward. They prefer an anti-social approach to shopping. They work on their own recognizance. Chart their one path. Go their own way. You get the idea. The question is why. To get to the true reasons we need to peel this back like the many layers of an onion.

On the surface there are some obvious answers. Habit is an obvious reason to shun advice. If you buy a product on a regular basis there isn't much need to ask others their opinion. In many respects the shopper is comfortable with the product or service and just buys. As I stated earlier in regard to grocery stores, about two-thirds of what you buy is based on habit—no thinking required. Just throw it in the cart and move on—also no reason to ask others what they think.

Another reason is that the product may have a low risk. A shopper will be more cautious purchasing a high-consideration product. They will do their research and probably ask others what they think. Low-consideration purchases don't require advice, possibly due to product simplicity and also because the product may have a low personal risk—if the product fails to meet expectations, the person will just buy another brand.

I spent a previous chapter talking about why people share. One of the social targets, the Director, operates similarly to the Lone Wolf prior to purchase—they don't ask for input. But their reasoning is different than the Lone Wolf's. Since they are immersed in the category, they see themselves as experts. Their confidence within the category (and probably ego) prevents them from asking others—they feel they know it all.

However, the ego is a funny thing. If we peel back the motivational layer, we find one of the reasons for the Lone Wolf's ego or pride. Much like the reason why men don't ask for directions, the Lone Wolf shopper feels they need to find things on their own. Ego prevents them from asking for help, because that may be perceived as weakness.

Garage door openers can be an ego category. Many people will just call a service to replace their garage door opener—Do It For Me (DIFM). By comparison, the DIY'er will feel pride in installation and in choosing the brand to install. Of the two types, the DIFM'er tends to be the Lone Wolf. They are on a mission to get it fixed; therefore, they tend to be Free Agent and Price Blind. Since they are fixated on getting it done quickly they are not asking for input from others except for one person, the installer.

The DIY'er is on a journey to replace their door. Factoring into their thinking is a desire to save money on installation, so it is no surprise they are more likely to be a Deal Seeker. In general, Deal Seekers tend to be more socially oriented to finding the best deal, and Deal Seeker garage-door shoppers are no different.

The Shopping Minimalist (Free Agent, Price Blind, Mission) typology normally indexes high for the Lone Wolf. In many respects this is just common sense. The Shopping Minimalist motivation is to just buy the product. They do not want to expend effort in research or asking someone what they think of their purchase (or share their purchase after the fact).

While pride may play a part in some people's journey, enjoyment may be another. Some shoppers enjoy the journey. They enjoy the find. In many respects they are not lost but, rather, prefer to see themselves as on a quest (hey, enjoy the journey).

Many shoppers wander around big box stores looking lost. When a sales associate inquires whether they can help, the shopper responds, "I'm okay, just looking around." Some refuse directions because they feel their "Pride in the Find"; however, others are enjoying discovering what is just around the next aisle.

In the shopper journey, there is enjoyment too. The enjoyment found in researching their impending purchase. This varies depending on the emotional tie to the product purchase. If a shopper is passionate about the product category, it is no surprise they are more social. Keep in mind, category enthusiast shoppers spend their discretionary time keeping up on the category. Therefore they may be a Social Shopper; however, they are more likely to be a Director and not ask for social input prior to purchase, though they will likely share their wisdom to assist others in their purchases.

Connectivity is another layer to consider. Do you really need to ask for directions today? Most people have a smart phone with a GPS that can tell them the way, literally. It doesn't take much effort to plug in the destination and choose a route; the phone does the rest. Similarly, there are many shopping sites and apps to assist shoppers in their quest to find the right product, find the best deal. Why would a shopper need to ask someone else? Just ask Siri.

To wrap up this section, let's circle back to how I began and ask: *Is the Lone Wolf more likely to be male?* The majority of studies show no gender bias. In studies of purchases of mobile phones, garage door openers, and auto insurance, there is no significant difference between the gender of the Lone Wolf and the overall gender composition of the sample group. In one category, hotel shopping, the Lone Wolf is more likely to be male (51 percent male Lone Wolf versus 39 percent for the overall study). The predominant reason is that men were more likely to view hotels as a commodity, with two-thirds of the men in the study agreeing with the statement that "all hotels are all pretty much the same."

Lone Wolf Principle
The Lone Wolf is socially inactive in their purchase, most likely because they are a Shopping Minimalist and they don't shop—they buy.

EIGHTEEN
The Passion Alter-Ego

"I'm very glad to have something to be passionate about. I can't imagine a life without passion."
—Sylvia Kristel, Dutch model and actress

Mark is one of the most frugal people I know. He is always seeking out a bargain to save money. He actively uses coupons, will go out of his way for sales, and will trim costs wherever he can (like bringing his lunch to work).

Mark may be frugal, but I would not call him cheap by any means. Mark does spend money, specifically on his passion: the '68 Mustang convertible he is restoring. Mark will spend hours in his garage working on the vehicle. Like many car enthusiasts, the vehicle is his passion and he will spend whatever it takes to get it into mint condition.

This duality to Mark is representative of how a shopper can be motivated one way in a certain category and shift to a different motivation in a different category. One of the main reasons for the shift is passion. At the core of passion is an emotional attachment. The shopping shifts from purchasing a necessity to purchasing a "want" or something the shopper desires. Sometimes passion is overt and obvious, like my friend Mark and his passion for restoring vehicles. Sometimes it is more subtle—a subconscious passion silently guiding the shopper to a decision.

When I talk about passion, I am referring to an emotional connection which alters a shopper's behavior. People are passionate about many different things; however, not all will alter their shopper motivations. Knowing this, first we need to assess how passionate someone is about a specific activity. To do so, we need to focus on a common denominator—one that is equal regardless of age and income levels. This common denominator is *time*. Time is a limited resource that people decide how to use every day, and their choices many times reflect their passion.

Let's do a simple exercise to prove this point. First jot down three to five activities you are passionate about in your life. Next I would like you to write next to each activity how much time you spent in the past month doing each. Does an activity dominate within your list? Is there an activity that has no time in the past month? Now think about how these passions may (or may not) alter your shopping behaviors.

In general, passion *does* alter a shopper's motivation. Assume a person is a Deal Seeker and Mission Shopper in most categories. In their passion category they could easily shift to Price Blind and Journey. Journey shopping normally occurs because the person is shopping for items where there is more of an emotive connection. The person revels in their passion and therefore will spend more time enjoying the shopping experience. When it comes to Wallet, this connection becomes a catalyst against the Deal Seeker DNA. While it may not outright trump the Deal DNA, it may suppress the importance of getting the best deal on the passion purchase.

There are four different levels of passion to account for in determining whether a shopper will act differently. The first level is looking at the product from a non-emotive or passionless perspective. I call this a commodity test. Does the shopper view the product as a commodity or agree with the statement that *"to me all of _____ is pretty much the same."* A lack of differentiation based on brand or product type provides insight into the emotional investment in the purchase. As you can imagine, there will be a difference in the prevalence of this commodity perspective by product category. The fast food restaurant segment has a relatively high level of commodity perception, with 40 percent of respondents agreeing that "to me all fast food restaurants are pretty much the same." Hotels, on the other hand, are a low commodity-perspective category, with only seven percent of respondents agreeing all hotels are the same.

The commodity question relates strongly (and positively) to certain DNA strands, beginning with the Deal Seeker. If all brands are equal in the eyes of the shopper, then price becomes prominent in deciding which brand to buy. For example, fast food has an elevated commoditization; therefore the deal is at the forefront in a shopper's decision. This is partly due to a perception which is reinforced by category marketing. Fast food advertising is emphasizes the deal. Now is this deal-vertising affecting the commoditization of the category? Maybe.

Compare fast food to family style restaurants, which have a lower commodity perception (30 percent of respondents). However, let's isolate the respondents who agreed with the commodity question. Within this target group there are elevated numbers of Deal Seekers and Free Agents. This makes sense—if all brands are deemed the same (or equal), then the deal or price takes over as the most important factor. In other words, when brands are equalized price becomes a dominant factor.

Within the family style study one brand in particular, Denny's, had a significantly higher commodity perception. This perception can be attributed to their marketing approach. Denny's focused on a deal-centric menu (similar to fast food restaurants) with dishes at $2, $4, $6 and $8.Not surprisingly, Denny's customers also included the highest proportion of Deal Seekers in the category. Denny's approach is not driving the category, because the competition is not promoting the deal. So, while it affects Denny's own brand, it is not impacting the category in the same way as fast food, where many brands are promoting a value menu.

Shifting gears to the opposite end of the spectrum, let's talk about brand passion. Brand passion is about liking particular brands and sharing your passion with others. As I stated above, fast food restaurants attract larger numbers of Deal Seekers, and their customers also show a lower level of brand passion, with only about 20 percent of respondents stating they love their brand and like to share it with others. Compare this to fast casual restaurants. For these restaurants over half the respondents were advocates for their brands, and only 18 percent of respondents viewed fast casual restaurants as pretty much the same. This divergence between commodity and brand advocacy is consistent across all restaurant brands within the category.

If you keep looking at different categories you begin to see a correlation between high brand advocacy scores and low commodity perception. The hotel category has a very high brand advocacy score with 73 percent of respondents stating an affinity for their brands and likelihood of sharing. Also, very few respondents (only seven percent) viewed a hotel as a commodity. Mobile phone purchasers can be passionate and many are also ambivalent. Both brand advocacy and commodity perception are about 37 percent in this category. This is not a surprise. There are people who love their iPhone or Galaxy phone, and yet about one-fourth of the category uses a non-contract phone. The pay-as-you-go-shopper is looking to minimize their cost—they just need a phone.

Inherent in the brand advocacy question is the desire to share. Advocacy translates into more than just willingness to share their brand—these shoppers have elevated social shopping behaviors. For example, the hotel brand advocate is more likely to follow brands on social media, use word-of-mouth advice to make a hotel choice, and is more likely to share their hotel experience. While these hotel shoppers have an affinity for their brand(s), it doesn't mean they don't want a deal. The Deal Seeker mindset is consistent with the category (54 percent brand advocate Deal Seeker versus 52 percent for overall Deal Seekers).

The third level of passion involves the product category enthusiast. For these shoppers it's not about one brand—they are enthusiastic about the entire category. They immerse themselves in the category, spending a significant amount of their discretionary time keeping up on the latest product releases, industry news, and product development. I mentioned some of these enthusiasts already (i.e., tech-thusiasts, auto-enthusiasts), and there are more, including gamers, fashionistas, wine connoisseurs, or craft beer enthusiasts.

Their shopping behavior centres on enjoyment. The category enthusiast revels in the fact they get to buy a product within their area of passion. For category enthusiasts, the level of Journey shopping is elevated, which makes sense. This enthusiast is already investing significant discretionary time staying up on category news and events, so why wouldn't their shopper behaviors be consistent?

There are split results on whether the enthusiast shopper becomes more Price Blind or more of a Deal Seeker. For mobile phone shoppers, the tech-thusiasts score significantly higher than the norm in Deal Seeking (65 percent for category enthusiasts versus 52 percent overall). Why? Well, keep in mind the Deal Seeker shopper is trying to find the best deal on the product they want. As I discussed earlier in the book, switching phones is not just about the price of the phone—it is about the features of the phone and the monthly service. A shopper will define their deal based on the plan monthly payment, and whether the payment is more or less than what they expected to pay.

The highest passion level is personal passion. Personal passion is something in a person's life that is a part of their persona—it defines who they are. There are many personal passions, from family or pets to a leisure activity (e.g., golf, travel) to fitness activities (e.g. running, biking) to food.... I could go on, but you get the idea. Some of these passions impact a person's purchases. If someone is a foodie, pet-thusiast or golf enthusiast , there purchase behaviors will be altered by their passion.

Personal passion impacts shopping behaviors in ways very similar to what we see in category enthusiasts—they will more likely be a Journey shopper and socially active. The travel enthusiast's behaviors with regard to hotels are slightly different than the normal hotel shopper DNA; the travel-thusiast is more likely to be a Journey shopper, a Deal Seeker, and more socially active.

The foodie can be a passion enigma. Whenever I bring up foodies, there is a debate on what a foodie even is. Is it a person who is epicurean, taking chef classes, drinking fine wines, going to eclectic restaurants? Or is it a person who loves food whether they find it at Five Guys Burgers or Outback Steakhouse? The debate can be a subjective nightmare. The answer lies with the person filling out the survey. They may see being a foodie as fondness for fine dining or just a general love of food. They may see it as chef creating baked salmon with honey mustard and pecan panko crust, or someone just coming up with a new recipe for tacos. Both are right. If you ask a general question, then you leave the interpretation up to the person taking the survey.

Passion to me is about commitment and effort; therefore the questions should be about the effort invested in a person's passion and how much discretionary time is required. If you are testing for a foodie the following questions could gauge the level of passion:

1. Do you subscribe to a food magazine (e.g., *Food & Wine, Bon Appetit*)?
2. Have you made a new recipe in the past two weeks?
3. How much time did you spend online reading about food, recipes or cooking techniques in the past two weeks?
4. Have you taken a cooking class in the last six months?

If you compare the results of the foodie question you see a variance. The following table breaks out the foodie question along with two additional questions for both fast casual and family dining restaurants.

	Foodie	Subscribe to Food Publication	Tried New Recipe
Fast Casual	44%	23%	51%
Family Dining	49%	30%	58%

The takeaway from this example is that when you analyze how much effort someone puts into their passion, the numbers tend to be lower than when you simply ask about a person's perception of who they are. (In short, not everyone backs up the talk with the walk.) For instance, subscribing to a food publication is a measure of a person's interest based on the cost of the subscription and time needed to read the publication. (For subscriptions, the family dining numbers skew higher because the people who took the survey were older and more likely to subscribe to magazines.)

Interestingly, more people said they had tried a new recipe than said they were foodies; however, we don't know what the person was making. It is hard to discern if the person is a chef or a cook. If knowing the level of food fanaticism is important, then the question must probe what type of recipe was tried.

In summary, passion is critical in many product categories if one is to understand the nuances and shifts in shopper behavior. By triaging brand advocacy we get a deeper insight within a person's Brand Citizenship. Understanding a person's passion provides insight into the shopper's level of enjoyment and their social shopping behaviors.

The Passion Alter-Ego Principle
Passion alters a person's shopping behaviors specifically because passionate shoppers are more likely to be Journey shoppers and exhibit elevated social shopping behaviors.

NINETEEN
Impulse Buying

"I'm an impulsive buyer. I don't really go out with a list."
—Sophie Kinsella, bestselling author

A shopping receipt can reveal a lot about a shopper. If you decipher the list you can learn the shopper's brand affinity—when brand matters and when it does not. The receipt can reveal the price sensitivity of the shopper—when the shopper is price blind and when the shopper seeks out a deal. You can also learn much effort the person is willing to exert to get the deal, from taking advantage a deal in the store (easy effort) to creating their own deal through coupons or visits to multiple stores (extended effort). If you ask the right questions the receipt can also can tell you whether the shopper had a plan or just improvised their way through the store.

The shopping receipt was a crucial artifact in uncovering a shopper's actual DNA. I have spent a lot of time in this section discussing pre-meditated buying. An aspect of the receipt I haven't discussed yet is the insight into shopping improvisation or impulse buying that it provides. I mentioned in the first section how we asked participants to complete a diary in addition to filling out the survey to ensure we were getting an appropriate read on the shopper's DNA. In addition to the diary we had the shopper provide a shopping list (if they made one) and the receipt. On the receipt we had them highlight products they bought impulsively in the store.

As you can imagine, there was a significant variation among shoppers in how many products were planned versus impulse purchases. You could tell the Journey shoppers were more impulsive than the Mission shoppers (who tended to stick to their lists). Some of this had to do with the detail orientation of the shopper. If the shopper put a lot of forethought into their list, there were far fewer impulse items, while people with a short list of scribbled items tended to improvise in the store with most items chosen as they shopped up and down the aisles.

I want to point out something here: there is a difference between "improvising" and impulse buying. Improvising is buying necessities for the week without a script. For example, a shopper may do meal planning in the store, knowing they need to buy four dinners for the upcoming week. Their improvisation may lead to a haphazard shopping experience, but the shopper knew they needed four dinners—they just didn't plan ahead of time.

If the same shopper is in the store, ventures down the seasonal product aisle, finds a cute snowman to decorate the house, and purchases it—*that* is impulse buying. Impulse buying is an in-the-moment purchase where there was no prior intent. This is an important distinction.

To illustrate this point I want to draw on a convenience store study I fielded a few years ago. The purpose of the study was to assess the intent to purchase of the shopper going into the convenience store. Each shopper had specific items in mind entering the store (planned), and some also purchased items they did not intend to buy (impulse). Overall the top three items purchased in the study were cigarettes (33 percent), soda (32 percent) and snack food. If you look at planned versus impulse purchases, the top five items shoppers planned to buy were cigarettes, beer/wine, coffee, energy drinks, and newspapers. The top five impulse items purchased were candy, snack food, bottled water, lottery tickets, and juice/juice drinks. Worth noting in the study is that for every item, there were a certain amount of shoppers who planned to buy and a certain number who bought impulsively. Cigarettes showed the highest proportion of planned purchases, with 90 percent of the shoppers who bought them planning to do so, and only 10 percent buying impulsively. In fact there were only two items, candy and snack food, which more shoppers bought impulsively.

The study doesn't reveal too much. Sure, you can argue substance-addicted purchases (e.g. nicotine, caffeine, alcohol) are more planned out—not a big surprise. On a superficial level the study just tells us what shoppers did; it does not get into why they acted a certain way. For that we will have to lean more into the psychology of the buyer.

Considerable work has been carried out on impulsive buying. What interests me are the core motivations—why someone would buy on impulse. In an article in *Psychology Today*, Ian Zimmerman suggests four different motivations for impulse buyers:

First, impulse buyers are more social, status-conscious, and image-concerned. The impulse buyer may therefore buy as a way to look good in the eyes of others.

Second, impulse buyers tend to experience more anxiety and difficulty controlling their emotions, which may make it harder to resist emotional urges to impulsively spend money.

Third, impulse buyers tend to experience less happiness, and so may buy as a way to improve their mood.

Last, impulse buyers are less likely to consider the consequences of their spending; they just want to have it.

These underlying motivations make a person susceptible to impulse buying. The act of buying within the store is a spontaneous action based on a seeing the product and then buying it. The impulse action is triggered by different emotions. The first emotion is pleasure. In the convenience store survey, most of the products purchased on impulse were pleasure products (i.e., cigarettes, soda, snack food). The products fulfilled a craving and gave the customer plea-surable feeling upon consumption.

Pleasure can also relate to passion. A person may be passionate about fishing, food or fashion. They may indulge in an impulsive purchase to feed their passion. The shopper may have entered a Bass Pro Shop with the intent of buying fishing line. The fact the person left the store with a new Waterworks Lamson Arx Fly Reel is a sign of their passion. At $439 it was hardly a deal, but no matter—the customer is already dreaming of the next fishing trip to the Manistee River to catch the trophy trout.

A powerful emotion prompting impulse purchases is fear of loss. This can involve a number of different product categories, such as holiday shopping, seasonal products, or a limited time offer. The shopper sees a product in the store they decide they want. They fear that if they don't buy the product now, it will be gone the next time they are in the store. Fear of losing out on the product drives action.

The last emotion is the desire to save. This is particularly relevant for Deal Seekers. Whether stumbling across a deal on the aisle end-cap at a Target or perusing the clearance bin, the Deal Seeker finds a deal and feels compelled to act. They didn't anticipate purchasing the product, but they couldn't pass up the savings.

Based on all of this, which DNA strands lend themselves to impulsive pur-chases?

Journey shoppers are likely to exhibit impulsive tendencies for several reasons. The Journey shopper likes—or loves—to shop. This emotive under-pinning keeps the person in a shopping mindset longer, thus increasing the likelihood of purchasing items they did not originally intend to buy. After all, once they have purchased everything on their list, the shopper may still be in the shopping mindset, looking for other items to purchase.

Secondly, the Journey shopper is exploratory. They like to search for the find—find something new; find the deal; find a product worth talking about. Exploratory buying leaves this shopper open to the possibilities. And when they come across a product they want, they will often rationalize why they need it.

Trader Joe's is an example of a store built for impulsive purchases. Shop-ping at Trader Joe's can be an eclectic exploration into the unknown. Since the majority of products are private label, the shopper needs to get accustomed to the merchandise carried at the store. Even then, there are special buys available only for a limited time—products a shopper didn't anticipate buying, like aged manchego cheese and rosemary marcona almonds.

As I stated above, desire to save is an impulsive emotion. Deal seekers live for the "deal they can't turn down." Since the savvy deal seeker is price aware, they can spot a good deal when they see it (or just come across it). They are willing to buy it if they can project a future need. In grocery shopping a term frequently used is "stock-up price," meaning the price is so good it is worth purchasing the product even if there is no immediate need. Costco represents the epitome of stock-up deals for many shoppers. The combination of Costco's bulk sizes and warehouse pricing create many impulsive deal opportunities.

Stock-up pricing can be a "tweener" because it lives between a planned and unplanned purchase. Social media feature a persistent stream of stock-up price deals every day (to view this in action, search Twitter for "stock-up price"). Many times stock-up purchases are added to the list because the shopper found the deal while researching their shopping trip. Is this a planned purchase? The shopper had no intention of buying the product until they stumbled upon the deal; however, they did plan on purchasing the product when they entered the store. Planned? Unplanned? Actually, it doesn't really matter because shopping is a fluid journey.

If you combine the Journey and Deal Seeker (along with the Free Agent), you get the Bargainista. The Bargainista is in it for the find. They like to browse to find deals. Some stores are built for this typology. TJ Maxx is a store built for the Bargainista. The store increases the number of "finds" by cycling through inventory at a rapid pace. This has two effects: the first is that the shopper expects to find different items every time they shop in the store, and secondly, they are more likely to buy on the spot because the item may not be there on the next trip. The store also displays the original price and the TJ Maxx price on the tag. No reason for the shopper to remember the price—the store displays the deal for you.

Drug stores or pharmacies are designed for impulse buying. Many shoppers are on a mission when they go to a pharmacy—to get a prescription filled, purchase medicine for an ailing family member, or buy beauty products. The store's mantra is "just one more." The store's goal is to get the shopper to add one more item to their basket. These stores have displays up front designed to entice the shopper to impulsively buy more.

Another common tactic designed to encourage impulse purchases is putting end-caps at the end of every aisle. These high-traffic locations are designed to get a shopper to impulse buy. There are several tactics to maximizing the effect, including focusing on high-frequency promotional items or offering different types of solutions. A "solution" can be a meal solution at the grocery store, a pain management solution (e.g. cold and flu medicine) at the drugstore, or a fashion solution at a clothing store (with or without a mannequin).

In summary, impulse buying is a combination of shopper susceptibility and store design. Impulse buying is heightened when the shopper is motivated through pleasure or desire to save, and the tendency can be encouraged by stores that cycle through inventory quickly, increasing the shopper's fear of losing out on a product and therefore inspiring them to buy.

The Impulse Buying Principle

Impulse buying is driven by three core emotions: desire for pleasure, fear of loss, and desire to save.

TWENTY

Scenario Stress

"Some things are so unexpected that no one is prepared for them."
—Leo Rosten, American humorist

Your phone is like an extension of your person. It is a catalyst for life. Your schedule, your connection to others, your tether to on-demand information which helps you navigate throughout the day. What if you lost your phone? Or dropped it on cement and shattered the screen? How desperate would you be to replace it?

A study in the UK looked at how people would respond to such a scenario. Most people would suffer anxiety until the phone was returned or replaced. They referred to the heightened anxiety as *nomophobia* (from "no mobile phone"). Nomophobia represents the loss of order in one's life and it is more common than you may think. Of people who reported replacing their mobile phones in the mobile phone survey, about one-quarter of them did so because their phone was lost, broken or stolen.

Nomophobia also can cause tension with your Shopper DNA. If a person is a Bargainista (Free Agent Deal Seeker, Journey), they love to shop and take time to find the deal. They want to try different phone brands to see which is right for them and find the best deal. This enjoyment of shopping and discovery conflicts with nomophobia. The desire to replace the phone and get their life back in order trumps their natural desire to shop.

Counter this with a Loyalty Laser (Brand Citizen, Price Blind, Mission). This type of shopper would feel more comfortable shopping in a nomophobia scenario. Even in a normal situation, the Loyalty Laser prefers to just replace their brand—they don't care about price nor the shopping experience. Many iPhone owners who just upgrade their phone would be Loyalty Lasers (as I said earlier, try to get a deal on an iPhone!).

So our Bargainista shopper needs to act like a Loyalty Laser to replace their phone in order to get their life back in order. The shopper would have the anxiety of nomophobia combined with the stress of shopping outside their comfort zone. Imagine how a Bargainista would feel if they had to make a quick decision on a phone (probably their same brand) and pay full price. Their primal instinct would be to take a step back and think through the purchase. Find the best deal. And even if they can't enjoy the shopping experience, at least look at and try different phone options. As they pay for their phone, a wave of defeat would come over them even though their life is back in order—they conceded the necessity of the purchase and are now locked into a phone for the next several years. While their nomophobia subsides, their purchase regret increases.

Phones aren't the only category where this occurs. The automotive category is even more extreme. About 15 percent of people who buy a new vehicle do so because their previous vehicle was either totaled in an accident or repairs to their vehicle would be too costly. This is like nomophobia on steroids.

The car buying process can take weeks or months. Envision a person who realizes they have no car and must replace it as soon as possible. The problem is two-fold: they need short term transportation and they face uneasiness negotiating a deal on a new vehicle. The need for short-term transportation could involve sharing a vehicle within the family, but most likely will entail renting a vehicle until a new one is purchased. This short-term cost weighs on the shopper in addition to the impending cost of another vehicle.

The uneasiness over negotiating the purchase of a new car is an even bigger problem in the shopper's mind. If the shopper preference tends toward a negotiator profile like Deal Surgeon (Free Agent, Deal Seeker, Mission), they want the latitude to work the deal. They want to survey the local area for different deals and possibly pit one dealer against another to get the best deal. They want to have the luxury of walking away from a deal if they feel it is not to their benefit and then strike up another negotiation with a different dealer. The negotiating shopper revels in the deal and looks forward to going into battle to get the best deal. They love the adrenalin of the price dickering and they love winning the negotiations. This is fun and fine when the shopper has time, but they may feel differently if they walk away from a deal and get back into their rental car.

The stress caused by unexpected scenarios is not surprising. The gravity of impact or disruption to the shopper's life dictates the stress. A few years back I was reviewing research on drivers' attitudes toward servicing their vehicle. We split the results into two groups: people doing preventative maintenance on their vehicle versus someone dealing with an unexpected problem with the vehicle. The first finding was that customers dealing with unexpected problems scored their satisfaction with their service experience about 20 points lower than customers carrying out scheduled maintenance. More surprising is the fact satisfaction did not vary by brand. It did not matter if a person was driving a Lexus, Volvo, or Chevy, the scores between the expected and unexpected service visits were consistently twenty points apart.

Unexpected stress in a person's life automatically shifts them to a more negative state. This negative state is carried into the shopper journey. For a Mission shopper this is no big deal because they usually don't care to shop anyway (so they go from bitter to angry). But the Journey shopper, who generally enjoys shopping, now sees a negative cloud hanging over their impending purchase. There is no celebration—no enjoyment. The journey feels less like shopping and more like a basic transaction. Their internal preferences encourage them to try to shop as opposed to just buying.

A negative state for a Deal Seeker is being forced to pay full price. Imagine living in Minnesota and your furnace suffers a catastrophic failure. Sure, the Deal Seeker know it's 10 degrees outside, their furnace is broken, and if they wait any longer their pipes could freeze—but they crave a deal. Their natural preference is to call around to get that deal, maybe even negotiate a better price. But the temperature keeps dropping. Eventually, the Deal Seeker signs on the dotted line, the furnace is fixed, and they just want to put the situation behind them—that is, until the credit card bill arrives, haunting them with the reminder they paid full price.

Before I leave this subject, let's return to our nomophobia victim. I talked about the negative states experienced by the Journey shopper and the Deal Seeker in this scenario, but what about the Brand Citizen? The Brand Citizen buys brands they know and trust. Imagine the Brand Citizen traveling abroad when their phone breaks and nomophobia begins to set in. They go to a nearby store and the only phones available are a local brand they have never heard of. What does the Brand Citizen do? Transfer their line to the unknown phone or forgo getting a phone for several days until they can buy a phone they are willing to keep? While it is not life and death, it's a difficult scenario to fathom until you find yourself in it.

In conclusion, there are some typologies that react well to scenario stress, while others struggle with the purchase because they are working against their shopping preference. If a person is a Free Agent, Price Blind, and a Mission shopper (Shopping Minimalist), they will face far less stress than someone who is a Brand Citizen, Deal Seeker, and a Journey shopper (e.g., Brand Fanatic).

The Scenario Stress Principle

Life's unexpected scenarios can disrupt a shopper's natural preference, causing anxiety, stress and possibly buyer's remorse.

TWENTY-ONE
The Emotional Trump Card

"I continue to be fascinated by the fact that feelings are not just the shady side of reason but that they help us to reach decisions as well."
—Antonio Damasio, neuroscientist and author

Years ago I was working on team charged with rethinking how to sell new cars to shoppers based on different types of motivations—different mindsets. There was a wide array of mindsets we were contemplating, including adrenalin seekers, safety conscious, status seekers, and cost conscious. The cost conscious mindset was an outlier because many people on the team felt this person was making a rational purchase while the other mindsets were buying based on emotion.

There was considerable debate on this subject within the team. Finally, one person argued there is no such thing as a rational purchase. All car buyers are emotional. No one logically needs a new car, this person argued. If a person were looking at transportation logically, they would purchase a used vehicle or find some other form of transportation. Therefore emotion is always a significant part of buying a new car and it is our job as marketers to fuel this emotional decision.

This argument is accurate, but does not go far enough. All shopping decisions require emotion. If you look to the field of neuroscience you will find evidence to support this claim. Antonio Damasio, a Portuguese neuroscientist, studied people with damage to the part of their brain that generates emotion. These people seemed like normal, intelligent individuals except for one thing: they couldn't make a decision. Due to their brain damage they could not feel emotions and this affected their ability to decide. It wasn't because they didn't know how to decide. They could logically lay out the facts and outline the decision-making process; they just couldn't bring that process to a conclusion.

Shoppers are faced with decisions on every shopping trip. Do I buy the national brand or the store brand? I am leaning toward the national brand but is it worth $1.50 more? Wait, there is Brand C, another national brand, and it's on sale—only 50 cents more than the store brand. Hmm, I think I will go with Brand C because it seems like the better deal.

The internal debate bounces between facts and emotions. We try to be rational and make a decision based on facts, but do we really? Or are we rationalizing an emotional decision that has already been made? Emotions are guiding our decision process—the emotions tied to our shopper DNA. A Deal Seeker is motivated to get the best deal. They are emotionally charged to find the deal and buy it. If they get a deal, they are elated. If they don't get the best deal, they are dispirited. While emotions affect our decisions, feelings are the residual effect of success or failure.

Is there an emotionless purchase? Sure, if you consider a habitual purchase non-emotional. When a shopper buys on habit, they buy without thinking. No deciding between different brands. No deal searching. For the non-habitual purchases there is an emotive component that helps the shopper decide.

There is already emotion embedded within the shopper DNA. As discussed earlier, people become emotionally attached to their brands. The emotion can be subtle, like a feeling of comfort—of the known. The emotion can also be overt and more pronounced. For example, a brand can provide a feeling of achievement, becoming a status signature within a person's life.

There is emotional attachment to the deal—the adrenalin rush a shopper receives when they feel they got a great deal. This rush can be addictive and can fuel deal seeking behavior.

There is definitely emotion within the retail environment (love it or hate it). There are shoppers who love to shop and view it as a leisure activity. Conversely, there are the shoppers who loathe shopping. They find no pleasure in the experience and prefer to limit the time spent on it. Also, a shopper can switch between loving shopping and hating shopping based on the product category. They may love clothes shopping, but would rather have a root canal than grocery shop every week (perhaps that is a little extreme but you get the idea).

The emotions I want to discuss in this section go beyond shopper motivations. They are emotions rooted in the passage of time. This "chronological stimulus" affects our shopping behavior.

Sometimes the stimulus can be simple as the fact it's Monday. People handle Mondays differently. Some people detest Monday. Monday signifies the end of the weekend and the beginning of a long work week. Other people see Monday as a new beginning—like a mini-New Year's every week, complete with resolutions.

Regardless of a person's perspective, Mondays are emotionally charged for many people, but how does this affect shopping? Looking at online shopping you see an interesting trend. Somewhat surprisingly Monday is the second busiest online shopping day in the U.S. behind only Sunday, according to a study completed by Similar Web measuring the top 25 online shopping sites. Why is online shopping so popular on Monday? Is it a by-product of a person planning their week? Or is it an attempt to chase away the Monday blues?

Chasing the blues away is an idea worth exploring. Shopping addiction is linked to depression. The results can be as innocent as "retail therapy" where people shop to improve their mood. Compulsive Buying Disorder (CBD) is less innocent. CBD is an addictive loop in which the person shops to relieve their depression—for a while. The person will continue in this vicious loop until they are able to break the cycle. This kind of impulsive buying short-circuits shopper motivations. The primary motivation—for the person to get themselves in a better mood—trumps other shopper motivations.

People are willing to invest in themselves whether it is to improve their mood or achieve an aspirational goal. New Year's resolutions are the annual epitome of people aspiring to a better self. People are also willing to invest money to become healthier. They may invest in exercise equipment, a new diet program, a gym membership, or buy healthier (and more expensive) food.

The intention behind New Year's resolutions is perhaps sincere, but there is a reason January 17 is dubbed "Ditch Your New Year's Resolution Day" (assuming a person made it that far). A commitment to becoming a "better you" means changing habits—changing motivations. Spending money will not necessarily change habits (unless you invest in a personal trainer). This isn't news—it is something that happens every year for many people. Yet the idea of achieving an ideal state is the primary motivation and trumps a shopper's other motivations.

The weather is a regular stimulus altering our emotions and affecting our shopping preferences. Imagine extreme weather like an impending storm. A hurricane or snowstorm will create immediate demand for specific survival products like water, non-perishable goods, first aid supplies, and batteries. Now picture a Deal Seeker trying to find a deal on water or batteries during the mad scramble to stock-up for the coming storm.

Less extreme weather also affects our mood, sometimes unknowingly. A rise in temperature may lead to increased purchases of certain items. The demand for barbeque foods increases dramatically when the temperature is near 70 degrees. A study by Tesco, a British supermarket, found that when the temperature rose from 68 to 75 degrees the sales of hamburgers rose by 42 percent as people looked to barbeque. Sales of coleslaw also soared while purchases of green vegetables fell.

Conversely, when winter rolls in, our eating habits switch to comfort food. Google searches for pork chops, meatballs, lasagna and chocolate chip cookies soar during a cold snap. According to Google's Food Trends, the popularity of pork shoulder dishes is growing annually, albeit seasonally, with searches spiking in December. Pasta also is trending upward. Searches for rigatoni increased 26 percent year over year from January 2015 to January 2016. Food cycles are probably not much of a surprise. However, very few people think about their shifting food habits—they just happen naturally because of how we feel about the weather.

Sunny days make people more positive, and they buy more. According to three studies by *Psychology Today*, sunlight increases people's positivity and also their spending. The studies focused on tea-related products. In several other studies, including a review of six years' worth of retail sales, researchers found sunlight was associated with higher levels of spending.

Emotions influence our purchases. When we go shopping we are never devoid of emotion, meaning our shopping behaviors are grounded in an emotional foundation. Those emotions stem from our lives, our relationships, and our environment, whether it be the time of the year, day of the week, or weather conditions. And then there is the added factor of emotions associated with making a decision in the store itself.

One of the most emotionally packed times of the year for many people is the holiday season. Social engagements, holiday gift shopping, and caloric explosion all combine to put many people on edge. A major contributor to stress is the fact that the holiday season creates tension within our shopping preferences. In the next chapter I will deconstruct that tension.

The Emotional Trump Card Principle
Emotions are at the center of a shopper's decisions. A shopper's emotions can be intrinsic to the person or affected by different environmental stimuli.

TWENTY-TWO
Fight, Flight, or Buy

"Once again, we come to the Holiday Season, a deeply religious time that each of us observes, in his own way, by going to the mall of his choice."
—Dave Barry, humor columnist

In 2015 Amazon decided to create a new shopping holiday. They invented Amazon Day, which fell on July 15, their birthday (sort of—actually, Amazon was founded on July 5, 1994). The first-year promise of Amazon Day was lofty—they hoped to create a Black Friday (or more like a Cyber Monday) in the middle of the summer, and even promised "more deals than Black Friday." Deals people could not turn down—every hour on the hour. On July 15, 2015 Amazon Day took off and then it landed with a loud thud.

Why did the promise of deals not fulfill the dreams of shoppers?

First off, during the holiday season a person is buying for the "Them," not the "Me." There is a pent-up demand encouraging shopping by holiday gift-givers. Most holiday shoppers have a list of people ("Them") they need to buy for. As you are well aware the list could include family members, friends, co-workers, and appreciation gifts for people who assist us throughout the year (e.g., teachers, hairdressers, mail persons). To check off every person on the list takes effort, time and money.

In July, there is very little (if any) of this pent-up demand. Shoppers are more egocentric and are honestly shopping for the "Me." Sure, there may be some "Them" purchases for occasions like birthdays, weddings, anniversaries. However, even if you combined all the "Them" purchases, there isn't a significant pent-up demand. So while Amazon's hype to deliver the deal was well received, their promise was miscalculated. When retailers hold Black Friday sales throughout the year it is like a punch line to a bad joke for the Deal Seeker. The only true Black Friday is the day after Thanksgiving—the official kick-off of the holiday shopping season. To be sure, some people have already been shopping for months; however, whether that's the case or you are yet to begin, Black Friday is the recognized starting line, and retailers deliver with sales, door-buster deals, and promotions to lure the holiday Deal Seeker.

The day itself is the pinnacle of the shopping season for the true Deal Seeker. It is more than just shopping; it's a competition to see who can get the best deal. It is a badge of honor that they woke up in the middle of the night to wait in line to get the best deals—deals they can brag about.

Think of the holiday shopper as the primal shopper. Stress is a core factor in making shoppers go primal, with 84 percent of people stating they are stressed out about holiday gift giving. This time period amplifies a shopper's instincts, their preferences, sometimes to an extreme. Those instincts take over and we don't really think twice about it. In searching for the deal, the effort a shopper exerts will increase. A deal seeking shopper is willing to wake up early on Black Friday to get the best deal. They are also willing to wait in line—much longer than at any other time of the year. Also, the amount of research they're willing to do will increase, mostly because of the sheer number of gifts a person needs to purchase.

Shopping attitude will cause extremes, too. If a person enjoys shopping (think Journey shopper), and especially shopping for others, they will be exhilarated by the prospect of holiday shopping and motivated to find a cool gift or a great deal. The Mission shopper loathes the holiday shopping season (bah humbug). Their anxiety increases proportionately with the length of the list of gifts they need to buy. They will try limiting the time they spend shopping. This is why online shopping is a holiday blessing for the Mission shopper. They will try to do the majority of shopping online and probably through as few sites as possible. Evidence of holiday Mission shopping can be found by analyzing Amazon's impact. Amazon dominated online holiday sales in 2016 with a share of about 37 percent. The next highest share for online retailers was Best Buy at about 4 percent. In addition to online shopping, gift cards are another time saver for Mission shoppers.

Time is an obvious factor and the amount of time a person has to shop can either contribute to or mitigate stress. I am referring to whether the person is a planner or a procrastinator. Does someone begin their holiday shopping in August or are they hectically rushing from store to store on Christmas Eve? As a reference point, about 40 percent of people begin their holiday shopping before November with 15 percent waiting until the last two weeks before the holiday to begin their shopping.

Planning or procrastinating behavior is layered onto a shopper's underlying DNA. A Mission shopper is more adaptable regardless of whether they are a planner or procrastinator because they minimize the time spent shopping. A Journey shopper, on the other hand, will find life difficult if they are a procrastinator. This combination will induce stress because it is hard to enjoy shopping knowing there is very little time left to purchase gifts. Stress will then result from a Journey shopper forcing themselves to function like a Mission shopper. It is unnatural and therefore stressful.

Worth reviewing is the matter of how some typologies are amplified during the holiday shopping period. Following are several different holiday shopping archetypes that are based on the seasonal magnification of shopper preferences. The two DNA strands driving the archetypes are Wallet and Time. Brand could matter, especially in reference to a specific gift request, but it has less impact than the other two strands.

Black Friday Champ

The Black Friday Champ is an amplification of the Deal Surgeon and Mission Shopper. The deal is paramount for this shopper and they have a plan. Actually, they *need* a plan due to the tension between the desire to get a deal and a disdain for spending too much time shopping. They are willing to put in the effort to get the deal prior to going to the store. This shopper is a planner—they will put in the effort to scour sources of shopping information to locate the gifts they need and where they are on sale. These shoppers aren't browsers. Their preference is to get in and out of the store efficiently and then onto the next deal.

Holiday Celebrators

These shoppers are an amplification of the Deal Seeker and Journey Shopper. They revel in the holiday shopping season. They like shopping, and they will spend the time needed to find a gift. This shopper has no problem going to a mall and browsing store after store. They are in their holiday groove and will keep on shopping up until they finish their list or they run out of time. While this shopper enjoys spending time shopping, time may not be on their side. Since their approach often lacks a plan, their holiday anxiety increases, especially if they still have a list of items to buy when the end of the season draws near.

The Perfect Gifter

Some shoppers have no limits. They pride themselves in finding the perfect gift for people on their list. The Perfect Gifter's shopping preference combines Price Blind with Journey DNA. They normally don't have a specific gift in mind; rather, they prefer the hunt to find the gift that feels right. They revel in a person's surprise when opening their gift. Their ego is bolstered by compliments on finding something so unique—so perfect.

Their stress isn't about money. Money they will spend, even on credit. It is time that is their arch-enemy. If the Perfect Gifter has a large number of presents to purchase, they may easily feel overwhelmed, especially if they lack a plan. The amount of time needed to shop will feel too short, therefore increasing their stress. In the end they may have to concede to necessity, purchase a less-than-perfect gift, and forgo the compliments—at least for this year.

The Blitzen Shopper

Speed kills and these shoppers are all about getting their list done. They don't like holiday shopping and want it over as soon as possible. The Blitzen Shopper's preference combines Price Blind and Mission DNA. This archetype will find the path of least resistance to complete their shopping. They prefer the recipient provide the gift ideas—the more specific the better—so they can get their shopping done as quickly as possible. Buying online is a godsend to these shoppers, allowing them to minimize the time spent shopping. Most likely these shoppers are planners, not procrastinators, so they experience very little anxiety in completing their holiday shopping. Their only anxiety would be caused by would-be recipients who don't provide holiday gift ideas soon enough to allow them to complete their shopping as early as possible.

Worth noting is the fact that these archetypes aren't mutually exclusive. A shopper may be a Black Friday Champ for the majority of their gifts, but shift to a different archetype like the Perfect Gifter when shopping for that special someone on their list.

I mentioned that Brand DNA mattered less than the other two strands. There is one exception to consider—gift risk. Some shoppers may feel insecure about choosing gifts. They know very little about the brands and their quality. For example, they may be deciding between different brands of wireless headphones for someone on their list. Their original intent was to purchase Beats by Dr. Dre for a family member who requested them. When they get to Best Buy they notice the Beats are over $200, JBL headphones are about $150, and Jam headphones are under $50. They had planned to spend less than $100 and find themselves in a bind. Do they go with an unknown brand? Or do they spend more than they planned and get the Beats?

Each of our holiday archetypes would act a little differently in this scenario. The Perfect Gifter and Blitzen Shopper would probably just get the Beats. The Perfect Gifter is aiming for holiday gift hero status, and Blitzen just wants to get it done. If your preference is Price Blind, the decision is also pretty straightforward.

The Deal Seeking holiday archetypes will struggle. They didn't intend to spend over $200 and their first reaction will be to find a deal; however, there are very few deals on Beats headphones. They will look for online coupons, search sites like Overstock, and maybe check out their warehouse membership. The goal is to get the price down, probably to no avail. So, their final decision would be to be Price Blind and pay full price (the internal tension would be brutal) or buy a more inexpensive brand.

Lastly, holidays are a time for sharing, and social sharing about purchases increases significantly during the holiday shopping season. This makes sense as people are trying to find and buy gifts for people on their lists. But the frequency of sharing is somewhat startling. Some 72 percent of consumers share content at least once daily and 18-to-34-year-olds share content every couple of hours! If you look on public social media channels like Facebook and Twitter you will find some holiday chatter, but not much. The majority of the sharing is done on "dark" social channels (e.g., emails, IM, text messages).

The holiday shopping season brings out the primal shopper in all of us. A person can fight their natural tendencies, causing internal tension. Or a shopper can go with the flow, knowing it may lead them into a stressful situation (especially for Journey shoppers). In the end most shoppers end up somewhere in between—sometimes going with the flow, sometimes not—just to make it through the holiday shopping season.

Fight, Flight, or Buy Principle
Holiday stress level increases if a shopper is forced to shop against their natural tendencies.

TWENTY-THREE

The Decision Path

"There is no car-buying path to purchase. Car buying is chaos."
—Nameless marketing consultant

Decrypting the shopper journey is the Holy Grail for many marketers. They believe if they can identify the influential sources that affect a shopper's purchase, then they can hone their marketing tactics to increase the number of shoppers buying their products. This seems a realistic goal given the ever increasing ability to track a shopper throughout their journey.

In the late 2000s I was in charge of a project to uncover the shopper journey of a new vehicle buyer. The focus was online, where we hoped to find common purchase paths of shoppers as they meandered from site to site learning about what vehicle to buy. I turned to a web analytics company using ISP (Internet Service Provider) traffic to analyze online shopper behavior. The company's forte was the ability to identify shopper paths for different industries like financial services and technology.

Our initial meeting was not promising. The company analyzed millions of different shopper online journeys and was unable to find any consistency. Sure, there were common places that shoppers visited—manufacturer websites, third-party sites (e.g., Kelly Blue Book, Edmunds, Cars.com), and car forums. The company examined paths between hundreds of different sites, but no common path was discovered. The head consultant concluded, "Car buying is chaos." The sources used by consumers in the automotive buying process are consistent, but the path a shopper takes between them is not. There is not set order in which they visit sites. The journeys seem to be as unique as the shoppers themselves.

Great. I really couldn't go back to my client and say, "Hey, you know that shopper journey request? Can't do it. Turns out automotive shopping is chaos."

This conclusion is not unique to automotive. It is common for many high-consideration purchases. It is unrealistic to think all shoppers will buy the same way. I have spent this section discussing different shopper preferences and motivations. Add to this different buying situations and different purchase histories, and you quickly can extrapolate numerous journey permeations. So instead of designing *the* shopper's path, we need to think differently. We need to design an approach to intercept the shopper whatever their path may be and to influence their decision.

Identifying sources of influence in a shopper's purchase process is not a new idea. Many marketers survey recent buyers to determine which media influenced the purchase. The research encompasses a litany of media, from traditional (e.g. television, radio, newspapers) to digital (e.g. websites, banners, social sites) to in-store (e.g. signage, inserts), as well as the influence of friends, family or co-workers, thus allowing the marketer to identify which media drive a purchase (and which do not). The marketer can then optimize their media mix to increase their media ROI.

The problem with such research is it is not specific enough—*it does not tell us what shopper decisions the source influenced.* A shopper researching a purchase goes to a source to gain knowledge that will help them determine what is the right product for them. To get to the right product, the shopper needs to answer a series of question in order to narrow down the list of alternatives.

Think about an effective salesperson selling kitchen appliances. When the salesperson engages a new customer, they ask a series of questions and intently listen to the shopper's responses. The salesperson is determining the shopper's needs and wants. In no particular order, they will ask the shopper about key features, colors, brands, and price. What the sales person is doing is working through a series of decisions with the shopper that is necessary to reduce the list of viable products, ultimately helping the shopper decide on what product to purchase.

With this example in mind, consider that *in order to affect the journey you need to affect the shopper's decisions.* So, instead of identifying a journey, the key is to analyze the decision path. If you think about any high-consideration purchase, there are normally a series of decisions that a shopper will make on their way to the final purchase. For example, think of a mobile phone shopper and what decisions they need to make. The decision path may look like the diagram below.

Phone Decision Path

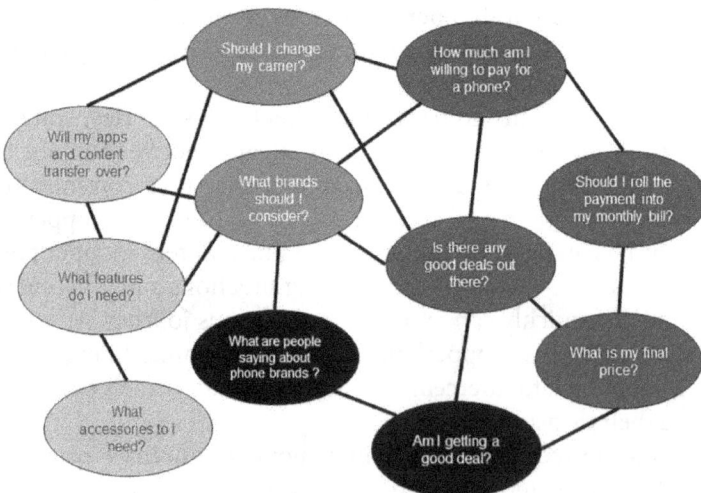

The decision path isn't necessarily linear. There normally is a logical order for such questions (i.e., *What are my needs?*, *What are my brands?*, *What is my price?*, *What do you think?*); however, the shopper may approach the questions in a completely random order. The shopper may also revisit certain questions as they progress through their shopping journey. For example, a shopper may have an idea of what their needs are when they start shopping, but may add to those needs as they research different brands.

To answer all these questions, the mobile phone shopper will use different sources of information. Some sources the shopper will seek out. Other sources will seek the shopper out. Interruptive sources like television, radio, and digital display ads will affect the shopper, because of their heightened awareness during their shopper journey. The shopper may spend a significant part of their journey seeking knowledge by researching product options through sources like consumer/brand web sites, word of mouth (friends/family), and salespeople. While using each source the shopper will try to answer one or more questions to help decide which phone they should purchase.

So, let's go back to the automotive research scenario. The goal switched from defining a journey to identifying the decisions that a new vehicle shopper makes. Using different methods, we were able to identify twenty-two different macro decisions made by a new vehicle shopper. As in the mobile phone example, the decisions fell into four categories:

- **My Needs:** What do I truly need in my new car?
- **My Car:** What car meets or exceeds my needs?
- **My Advice:** What do you think about my choices?
- **My Price:** What am I willing to pay for my car?

Make sense? Defining the decision path allows a marketer to focus their marketing so as to influence the final purchase and not only to influence the overall journey, but also to determine how influential a single source can be in moving a shopper closer to purchase.

Another example is to think about how a travel planner decides on the family vacation. Making vacation plans requires the person to answer a number of high-level questions that usually follow each other in a logical order. To answer these questions, the planner will use as sources of information various travel sites (e.g., Trip Advisor, Lonely Planet, etc.), online travel agents (e.g., Hotels.com, Expedia, Hotwire), and/or transportation sites (e.g., Delta, Enterprise Rent-a-Car).

As the planner gathers information from these sites and makes decisions, the number of options available to them in answering the remaining questions begins to narrow. Depending on the complexity of the vacation, it may be weeks before a final itinerary is decided. The extended length of time required to plan likely has to do with the fact that no one site or resource can provide all the information necessary to make every decision (unless they call a travel agent). Keep in mind this is a logical decision flow, one which is illustrated in the following chart.

Travel Decision Path

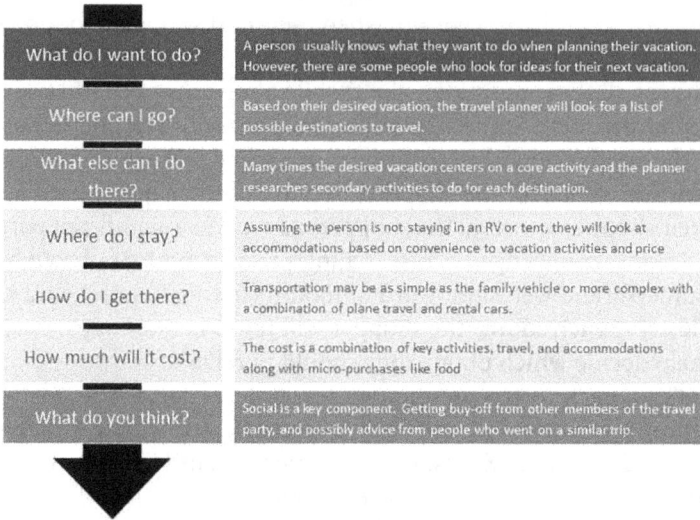

What do I want to do?	A person usually knows what they want to do when planning their vacation. However, there are some people who look for ideas for their next vacation.
Where can I go?	Based on their desired vacation, the travel planner will look for a list of possible destinations to travel.
What else can I do there?	Many times the desired vacation centers on a core activity and the planner researches secondary activities to do for each destination.
Where do I stay?	Assuming the person is not staying in an RV or tent, they will look at accommodations based on convenience to vacation activities and price
How do I get there?	Transportation may be as simple as the family vehicle or more complex with a combination of plane travel and rental cars.
How much will it cost?	The cost is a combination of key activities, travel, and accommodations along with micro-purchases like food
What do you think?	Social is a key component. Getting buy-off from other members of the travel party, and possibly advice from people who went on a similar trip.

Shopper preferences bring emotions into the decision-making process. A Deal Seeker may obsess over every cost, trying to get the best deals on hotels, rental cars, and airlines. A Brand Citizen may be conflicted between a convenient hotel they have never heard of and a known hotel that is out of the way. The Journey planner may seem as though they have fallen into planning paralysis, but they just may be enjoying the exploration of all the things they could do on their vacation.

In conclusion, the decision path is the shopper's road map to purchase, but this thought process is only half the equation. In the next section I will discuss how to assess the effectiveness of different sources in influencing a shopper's decisions.

The Decision Path Principle
The shopper journey is not a path from one channel to another; rather, it is a series of decisions leading to a purchase.

TWENTY-FOUR
The Shopper Principles

To conclude this section I feel it would be useful to summarize the principles in one place. While the discovery of the shopper DNA was fascinating, uncovering ther reasons why shoppers behave the way they do generates insights that drive solutions—in short, that drive better marketing.

Principle	Principle
It's a Matter of Brand	Brand influence is about emotional attachment. If brand does not matter, the shopper views the product category as a commodity.
The Brand Rotation	In some product categories shoppers prefer brand variety. Uncovering the reason for a shopper's desire for variety will also uncover the role of the brand in the shopper's decision process.
The Life Stage Eraser	Shoppers experience brand amnesia as they move through different life stages, causing them to disscover (or rediscover) brands.
The Brand Tattoo	Loyalty is a generalization best defined through a functional relationship (shopper motivations) or an emotional relationship (customer motivations).
The Deal Effort	The propensity for a shopper to be a Deal Seeker is directly correlated to the effort they exert in getting the "deal." Effort is measured in their willingness to use their discretionary time to seek out the deal.
Feel the Deal	Deal perception is a combination of brand value and getting a great price as defined by the shopper experience, shopping situation, and/or the shopper's social circle. The deal strength drives the likelihood of sharing it with others.
The Final Number	For contract purchases, the deal is not the price of the product; rather, the shopper's deal perception relates to the price they expect to pay each month.
The Ghosts of Purchases Past	There is a natural desire to reduce necessity payments; however, action only occurs at a point when the reward is worth the effort to switch.

For the Love of Brick and Mortar	The shopper's time motivations (e.g., those who love shopping versus those who hate shopping) will heavily influence the number of brick and mortar stores within a retail category.
Shopper Bragging Rights	Shopper bragging is a result of an egocentric connection point between people based on novelty, brand, passion, or expertise.
Beware of the Brand Governor	There are three primary shopper influencers: owners they know, experts they trust, and the Brand Governor, whose opinion may be as powerful (if not more powerful) than the other two influencers.
A Tale of the Lone Wolf	The Lone Wolf is socially inactive in their purchasing, most likely because they are a Shopping Minimalist and they don't shop—they buy.
The Passion Alter-Ego	Passion alters a person's shopping behaviors, especially if they are more likely to be Journey shoppers and exhibit a higher degree of social shopping behaviors.
Impulse Buying	Impulse buying is driven by three core emotions: desire for pleasure, fear of loss, and desire to save.
Scenario Stress	Life's unexpected scenarios can disrupt a shopper's natural preference, causing anxiety, stress and possibly buyer's remorse.
The Emotional Trump Card	Emotions are at the center of a shopper's decision. A shopper's emotions can be intrinsic to the person or affected by different environmental stimuli.
Fight, Flight or Buy	The holiday stress level increases if the shopper is forced to shop counter to their natural tendencies.
The Decision Path	The shopper journey is not a path from one channel to another; rather, it is a series of decisions leading to a purchase.

PART THREE
Don't Paddle Upstream!

"You don't paddle against the current, you paddle with it. And if you get good at it, you throw away the oars."
—Kris Kristofferson, singer and songwriter

If you are a marketer reading this book, the one thing you should take away from it is this:

Don't paddle upstream.

I get it. You like your brand—your product. You invested millions in product development, creating differentiation from your competition. You are proud of the company's product innovation (and you should be). You launched a new brand campaign and it is moving people's perception of your brand, your product, and/or your company. These are powerful assets in the market, but just remember:

Don't paddle upstream.

I spent the last section discussing different natural motivations within shoppers. I discussed in depth how brands are used by shoppers to guide their choices or, sometimes, how those brands may be insignificant in shoppers' decisions. How saving money can be a primary motivator and often trump brand. How a shopper's journey can be sheer enjoyment or a laborious chore. And, finally, I talked about the social aspects of shopping—about the advice people seek out and the experiences they share.

While I covered a lot of territory, I am pretty sure I did not talk about your specific brand.

Your brand is unique in the marketplace. Every product category (and brands within that category) can experience a different shopper flow. By understanding the different shopper flows, you can best deploy the appropriate marketing tactics to redirect the shopper's trajectory. The key word here is "redirect"—not to reverse that trajectory and ask the shopper to act in a way that is unnatural for them. Sure, you can market against the flow, but the odds are this will be as futile as paddling upstream into rapids.

This section is about different advertising practices and how they affect the flow—about tactics that work and others that are the equivalent of paddling upstream. And as you can imagine, different tactics will work for different combinations of shopper motivations.

TWENTY-FIVE
The Persuasion Continuum

"Ninety-nine percent of advertising doesn't sell much of anything."
—David Ogilvy, advertising icon

Television is king.

Yeah, it seems as though we're always hearing about new social apps. But make no mistake about it—TV is king. Every year there is a new music service on a new phone that makes your current phone seem like it's from the flip-phone era. Still, television is king. There always seems to be new voice-activated technology just around the corner that can adjust the temperature of your home, access the latest weather forecast, and keep track of your grocery or honey-do list. And, oh yeah, despite all this, television is still king.

Even after three digital decades television is still the glamour medium for many marketers. Advertisers spend billions of dollars on TV advertising to interrupt your day and (hopefully) change your mind about their brand—to buy their product. Creating a commercial can be pricey too. With production costs sometimes running into the hundreds of thousands of dollars, a marketer is limited in the number of television commercials they can make. Even with the proliferation of advertising outlets available to marketers today, most continue down the same road they've been following since the 1960s. The simple reason for this is because (one more time!) television is king.

What if I were to tell you that television is one of the least effective ways of converting shoppers?

Shoppers are skeptical of advertising, especially advertising that interrupts their lives and imposes a belief system that may differ from theirs. The problem may be relevance, or timing, or maybe it's just that the ad is on the wrong channel. The conventional wisdom is that if a marketer can reach the shopper in the right place at the right time with the right message, they can convert them. While true, this is extremely difficult to do when using mass media, because by definition a mass message is being communicated. If the majority of shoppers share a mass belief or perspective, then television (or any other mass medium) can be effective, but how many universal beliefs can you think of?

Try to think of the last time a commercial aired that had mass impact. The Super Bowl is as much about the ads as it is about the game. The game is full of commercials that viewers see for the first time. Some are memorable, most are forgettable. The memorable commercials usually strike an emotional chord with the majority of people viewing. Some consistent themes emerge over the years in the best ads. There may be horses playing football, cute kids building a time machine to get snack food, monkeys working in an office. A talking baby orders stocks from his crib. Elderly women in a fast food restaurant ask "Where's the beef?" Horses hold a reunion. An elderly woman eats a candy bar because she is not herself. More monkeys doing something else. More babies talking, dancing … you get the idea.

The commercials that create an emotional connection make an impact. However, how many commercials accomplish this? And for how many people? This is not an efficiency play. In fact, for the majority of products being advertised, their target audience is in the minority. For example, only four to six percent of the population is in the market for a new car at any given time. Now consider how many car and truck ads there are on television! Just as a point of reference, each car ad targets only a subset of this four to six percent. In actuality, one car model may be only appealing to less than one-half of one percent of potential new vehicle buyers.

I said that persuasion involves the right message in the right place at the right time. Let's think about this for a second. The right time is, for the most part, up to the shopper. The right time is when the shopper is thinking about shopping for a new product. Now combine this with the right place. The right place is a channel that has captured the shopper's attention—the channels the shopper seeks out to inform their purchase decision. Finally, the right message is about influencing that shopper, and, as I have discussed throughout this book, different shoppers are influenced differently. This makes creating one message that appeals to everybody shopping for a specific product extremely difficult.

In fact, the right place can't be limited to one channel. The marketer needs to be pervasive throughout the shopper's decision path. This is why I devised the *persuasion continuum.*

Persuasion Continuum

| Interrupt Media | Intercept Channels | Trusted Advisor | Product Trial | Product Ownership |

Less Persuasive   More Persuasive

The persuasion continuum looks at different sources and their potential influence on the shopper. The continuum moves from least persuasive to most persuasive. However, there are trade-offs within the continuum. As the continuum becomes more persuasive, it also moves from most efficient to least efficient in terms of both cost and time to execute. Logistically, this means it is easier to create a traditional campaign than to overhaul your entire customer service approach.

First let me introduce the continuum's five levels: interrupt media, intercept channels, trusted advisor, product trial, and product ownership. And before people freak out, let me say that *all* sources can be influential; however, from a shopper perspective, some sources are more influential than others. As we move across the continuum, each source is more progressively influential than the previous. For instance, while interrupt sources can be influential, intercept sources are more persuasive, and trusted advisor trumps intercept, and … you get the idea.

Interrupt sources, like television, seek the shopper out and interrupt their life. Sources like television, radio, and online advertising interrupt content to get the shopper's attention. These media can be compelling, but it is hit or miss on whether interrupt can be influential. It's a hit if the message finds the right shopper at the right time. It's a miss if the message reaches a non-shopper or a shopper at the wrong time.

Interrupt media is bought on the marketer's time with the marketer's dime—meaning the marketer spends a significant amount of money to get the necessary reach and frequency to change a shopper's perception and (hopefully) move the shopper behaviorally. This reach and frequency is necessary because the shopper may not always be in the mood to accept the message. They are not always in a shopping mindset, and when they aren't, the message will be less influential than when they are.

Interrupt media can work well to move a person attitudinally. Rarely is a commercial compelling enough to drive action immediately after viewing—this is not realistic. Over time a good commercial can shift a person's perception of a brand, though it still may not lead to a purchase, because the viewer may not be in the market for the product.

Interrupt sources seek out the shopper, while shoppers seek out *intercept sources*. Intercept sources are sources a shopper researches when making a purchase decision. These are more influential because in this case the shopper finds the information on their terms and at the right time for them. The only question mark is whether the marketing is providing the right content to answer the questions the shopper has as part of their decision process and move them closer to purchase. Providing the necessary content is critical when someone is buying a product that requires a certain degree of knowledge to make an informed purchase. Think about health insurance. As in many industries, the category's language is not shopper friendly. You need a decoder ring to decipher information provided by insurers in order to choose a plan which is right for you. If the information fails to persuade the shopper, then the source fails to influence the final decision.

And here is the rub: in intercept mode, there is no shortage of information. If you Google "health insurance" you will find no shortage of sites with information meant to assist the shopper. There are sites that explain the different options that are available, brokerage sites offering not only explanations but providing a platform where you can compare the prices of different policies from different brands, and brand sites touting why they are better than their competitors. A shopper will sift through the options and try to find the content that's right for them—the content that will answer their questions.

Content influence is predicated on the ability of the content to answer the shopper's decisions and connect emotionally with them. Content needs to be constructed in such a way that it assists the shopper in gaining the knowledge they want and need. It seems simple enough except that many marketers prefer to write about how their product is better than the competition. Marketers use a shorthand phrase—"Why Buys"—for such descriptions of why a product is superior to its competition. But instead of actually assisting a shopper in their decision, the content reads like a brand resume and fails to make an emotional connection.

If the shopper is a DIY'er, they will lean on intercept sources to answer their questions. To this end you can bucket shoppers into two categories: DIY (Do It Yourself) and DIFM (Do It for Me). The former will typically stick to their own efforts and not rely on others. This is no different from asking for help in a store on where to find something or how to use a product. While DIY'ers have been characterized as primarily male, it is more of a mindset of independence (or insecurity).

The DIFM'er, on the other hand, will reach out to others. This gets me to the next source: *trusted advisor*. The trusted advisor is a person or source the DIFM'er will use to help make their decision. This source is more impactful than interrupt or intercept for two reasons. First, the person or source will most likely have experience with the product and therefore firsthand knowledge. Secondly, if the information is relayed through a conversation, the source can answer specific questions rather than just providing generic information.

Advice is a critical word here. Often marketers think testimonials are what shoppers are looking for. Actually, this is not true. Shoppers are looking for advice in order to confidently make purchase decisions. When a travel planner goes onto a forum like TripAdvisor, they are looking for information specifically for *their* trip, not just general comments and ratings about another person's trip. *They are looking for someone like them.* Someone who has been in a similar travel situation so the information is relevant to their decision process. If someone is planning a trip to Disney, they will find no shortage of information on how to do Disney. The challenge for the travel planner is to sift through all the information and find the traveler like them—the traveler who has two children ages 3 and 5 and is traveling with grandparents and will be at Disney for 3 days …

Disney created a unique solution to assist travelers: the Disney Parks Mom's Panel. The mom's panel offers advice to travel planners on how to get the most out of their Disney vacation. The thirty-plus panelists are passionate about Disney. Disney gives them specialized training to help them become more knowledgeable about the parks and their operation. The panel is an effective approach because these moms have been there—they have planned vacations to Disney. They can empathize with the planner.

As I discussed in the chapter "Beware of the Brand Governor," people have three options for trusted advisor: people who bought the product or a similar one; experts within the category; and the brand governor, i.e., people with no product experience but who have an opinion on what brand to buy (or not to buy). If the shopper trusts the individual or source (e.g., *Consumer Reports*), the advice given will be highly influential in their final decision.

You can easily see why trusted advisor trumps interrupt and intercept. Referencing trusted sources in interrupt or intercept content can increase the degree of influence. Adding an endorsement like "Good Housekeeping Seal of Approval" or "Recommended by *Consumer Reports*" can add unbiased influence.

Be careful though, because not all sources are recognizable. The source must be recognized as a trusted source by the shopper. On the face of it, a "5-star crash rating" seems like a superior endorsement. A few years back I was working with a group that was researching how to improve the safety perception of cars. We were surprised that not only did the focus group find the "5-star crash test rating" meaningless, but some people in the group thought the manufacturer made up the ratings because they were unaware of what the National Highway Traffic Safety Administration (NHTSA) actually was and therefore skeptical of the source.

Another example of using experts to influence purchasing behavior involves awards in the wine industry. There is no shortage of such awards, from international events down to local competitions. They give out so many awards you would swear there is one just for participating. Well, one wine taking advantage of this vast array of awards is Barefoot. Next time you are in the store look at the bottles and see which awards they won. You will find a double gold award winner at the 2014 Monterey International Wine Competition; a gold award for the Pacific Rim wine competition; and gold at the 2012 Riverbank wine competition.

Is this influential? Most shoppers probably have no clue how credible the Pacific Rim or Riverbank competitions are; however, this is an interesting tactic that will work due to the sheer volume of expert evidence. While a shopper may not know anything about a specific competition, the number of awards influences the shopper simply because "this many experts can't be wrong".

The next source is the most impactful one short of *ownership*: *product trial*. The multi-sensory firsthand experience will trump all others because, well, it's the shopper themselves using the product. Whether it is sampling a product in the grocery store or test-driving a car, trial will influence a shopper more than any other source or experience.

Red Bull built a brand through such experiences, and by focusing on the extreme. Red Bull is found integrated into extreme sports, extreme stunts like the supersonic free-fall from the edge of space, and their own extreme events like Flugtag, in which competitors make homemade flying machines and launch them off a twenty-foot deck in hopes of soaring to victory (hey, do you have wings?). Integrated into many of these events was the Red Bull Sampling Team. You couldn't miss them; they were usually driving a VW Bug painted with the Red Bull logo and sporting a 12-foot can on top of the vehicle. Sure, Red Bull could have just sampled its products in stores, but the context of sampling at these extreme events built the brand and reached the right target (in this case reaching the right target at the right place and the right time with the right experience).

According to an old adage, is it is easier to retain existing customers than attract new ones. By and large I believe this to be true. Many marketers are more interested in finding new customers than investing in their existing ones. Most likely a marketer needs to do both.

Investing in customers begins from the first time they purchase the product. It's all about exceeding customers' expectations. The shopper has an expectation about how the product will benefit them. Things can go two ways. If the product functions as expected or exceeds expectations, a customer is more likely to purchase it again. If the product falls short of expectations, another purchase is much less likely.

A secondary aspect of the first purchase is novelty. The first time a customer uses a product or brand the experience is a novel one. The result of the usage can drive different outcomes when it comes to word of mouth. If the product considerably exceeds the customer's expectations there is a good chance they will share their experience. The brand just acquired an advocate who may share their experience like a trusted advisor. Conversely, if the product experience severely disappoints, the brand possibly created an adversary.

Sometimes a customer is forgiving of a brand even though it does not meet their expectations. This forgiveness often is a result of how the brand deals with a problem. Customer service can either mitigate some of the ill will or exacerbate it. Some of the best brand stories that customers share are occasions when a customer was treated with empathy and their problem was resolved quickly.

Getting the first purchase is only the beginning of the challenge for many retailers—they need to turn the visit into a habit. A general rule of thumb is that it takes three visits to create familiarity with the store environment and build habit. However, getting someone back three times is easier said than done. For high-frequency retailing environments (like grocery shopping) it is easier to build frequency within a short period of time. Creating initial frequency is a challenge; however, displacing an existing grocery store within the shopper's rotation is an even bigger challenge. The majority of grocery shoppers shop in more than a single grocery store, and they build familiarity over time. A shopper gets comfortable with the store layouts and where to find the products they frequently buy. Walking into a new store (even the same brand) requires a shopper to orient themselves to the new store.

The power of the persuasion continuum is leveraging each source based on the marketing situation. It is not necessary to make use of all five types of sources, but I would argue that a marketer who is using only one or two of the sources is missing influential opportunities.

Timing is a factor to consider, too. If immediacy is paramount, then interrupt is necessary to get the message out. Interrupt media are a quick release. Their power is to get the target's attention *now* and persuade them to take action. Other methods are a slower burn. Intercept works, but requires the shopper to be inquisitive and searching for content themselves. And there is no guarantee a shopper will actively look for additional information, especially in a low consideration purchase. Using a word-of-mouth campaign can be more effective but requires patience on the marketer's part. Trial (assuming it is viable for the product in question) has its logistical challenges.

I began this chapter by saying that TV is king. In a shopper-centric world *context* is king. The industry knows this. We talk about the right message at the right place at the right time. If you boil these three factors down, you get context. The power of persuasion is a function of understanding shopper motivations and then influencing them through different methods—the more influential the better.

TWENTY-SIX

Mindset over Millennial

"I think I do speak to all ages, but the emphasis is, unlike everybody else
who is chasing the Millennials, I'm not chasing the Millennials."
—Oprah Winfrey

Millennials are the marketing rage for a while (Gen Z will soon become the bright shiny object). Every marketer who does not have Millennials as a significant part of their customer base seems to be trying to find a way to capture them. The logic is simple for many marketers: if we can establish a brand relationship with twenty-somethings, they could carry it through their entire lives. Seems logical. However, if you are over the age of 40, think about how many brands you began using in your twenties that you still use today. Over 50 percent? Under 10 percent? Most likely your answer is closer to the latter figure.

While I am all for refuting conventional wisdom, let's get back to the Millennials. Over the years I have discussed the idea of targeting Millennials with numerous clients. One exercise I do is a twenty-something projection. I begin by prompting people to share what it was like to be in their twenties. It doesn't matter if you were twenty-something in the '70s, '80s or '90s; just focus on what it was like to be that age.

Many characteristics emerge. In their twenties most people were more egocentric and felt the world revolved around them (at least to a certain degree). In your twenties possibilities are boundless and it is only up to you to decide your future. You are early in life—early in your career and eager to get to the next level. Patience is a virtue you have not yet mastered.

You are more carefree. It is one of the few times in your adulthood you have time on your side (until you become an empty nester later in life). You spend time with friends and others and engaging in lifestyle passions, whatever they may be. Your life tends to be based on experiences. A simple but important factor for many twenty-somethings is that they are early in their earning years and money is limited. Buying things will come later; right now it is about enjoying life's experiences.

Of course not all twenty-somethings are the same. Many may be single while others are progressing through life stages like marriage, the purchase of their first home, and having children. These life stages impact freedom through the demands of time and money (or lack thereof). Inevitably twenty-somethings wake up one morning (as we all do) and realize they're now middle-aged and the new rage is the next twenty-something group (enter Gen Z).

Twenty-somethings share many similar characteristics regardless of when they grew up, but there are differences, too. One of the most pronounced differences between Millenials and prior generations is how they are digitally tethered. The connectivity of this generation opens up communication channels like never before.

As a teen in the late '70s I can tell you the most-desired purchases were clothing, your own phone line, and a car. Fast forward 40 years and you would find clothing still tops the list. However, the (mobile) phone has overtaken the car in order of preference. Over 75 percent of teens have a cell phone today; by contrast, in 1980 about 50 percent of 16-year-olds had a driver's license, while 30 years later only 28 percent of teens had one. Big difference, or is it? What the generations share is the desire for connectivity—the desire to stay in touch with friends. In the '70's this meant having a car so you could meet up with them whenever, wherever. Today, a person is never out of touch. They can reach their friends anytime, anyplace—they are only a text away.

It may seem hard to believe, but if you look at the fundamentals of how we act, you will find more consistencies than inconsistencies among different generations. People tend to confuse the evolution of behavior with the evolution of motivation. With any smartphone we carry a store in our hand. We can get a deal at a moment's notice. Shopping is evolving at a rapid pace; however, shopper motivations are more glacial in their movements.

Let's discuss Deal Seekers for a moment. Do they really change by generation? Hypothetically it seems that when you're younger you have less money and are more likely to spend time to save money. So you would expect the proportion of Deal Seekers to be higher among younger people. The chart below displays deal-seeking propensity by generation for four different product categories.

Deal Seeker Propensity by Generation

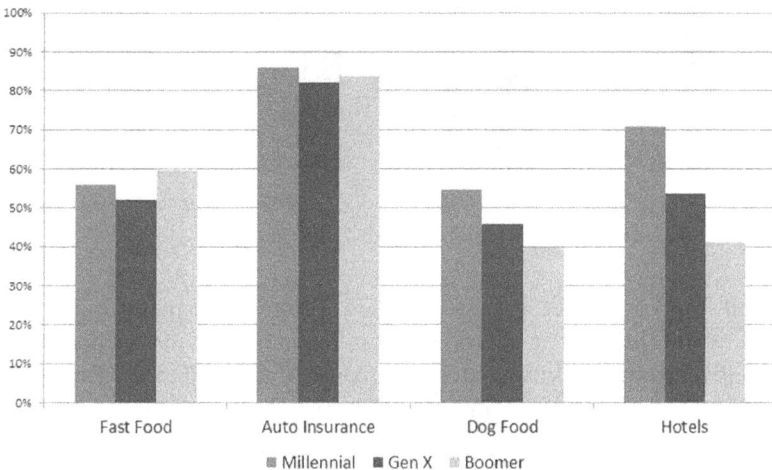

Millennial ■ Gen X ▨ Boomer

As you would expect, Millennials score the highest in three of the four categories. The variance is sometimes subtle, as in auto insurance where everyone is looking for a deal. Compare this to hotels, where Millennial travel planners are much more likely to be Deal Seekers. If you look more closely at the data, this variance relates not only to age, but also to the income of the respondent. An important point here is that while there is a variance by generation, there is a significant proportion of people with a Deal Seeker mindset within each generation.

If a marketer decides to target a generation (and not the mindset), they are missing out on a significant opportunity. In fast food, over 50 percent of Millennials are Deal Seekers. Sounds like a big target, right? However, if a marketer decided to target Millennials only, they would be reaching only about 20 percent of all Deal Seekers. If they targeted the deal mindset regardless of age, they would increase their opportunity fivefold.

What about Brand Citizenship? The conventional wisdom is that a shopper's brand affinity will increase as they age. The following chart displays the propensity toward Brand Citizenship for each generation.

Brand Citizen Propensity by Generation

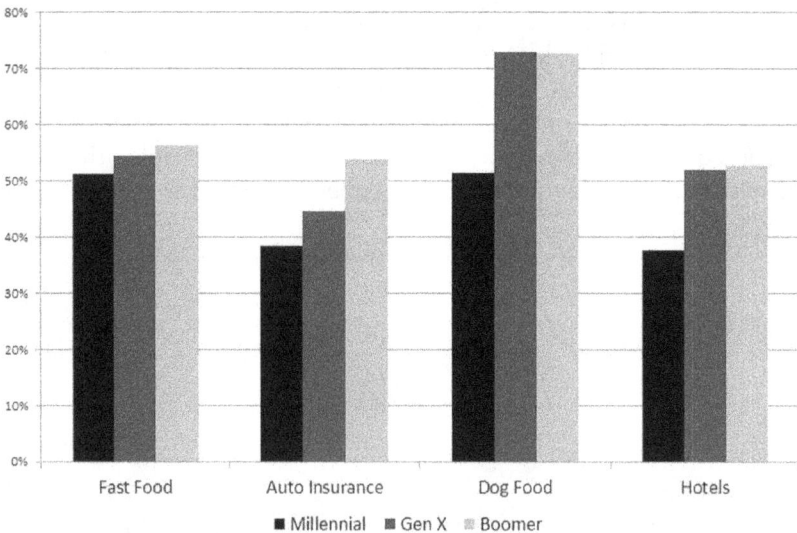

In all four categories, yes, as expected, Brand Citizenship increases with age. But while this is true there is a significant proportion of people with a Brand Citizen mindset within each age group. Marketing to the Brand Citizen mindset is about building an affinity, a loyalty. While a marketer should focus on increasing the loyalty of Millennial customers, why limit those efforts just to Millennials?

Hotels provide a good example of this thought process. If you look at both Deal Seeker and Brand Citizen mindsets, you will see that they run opposite to each other (that is, when Brand Citizen is low, Deal Seeking is high). This is because the target mindset views hotels as a commodity. The marketers' responsibility is to increase the value of the brand through marketing and customer service with the goal of moving the target from "all about the deal" to a brand-centric mindset. Sure, the marketer could focus on just Millennials with a Deal Seeker mindset; however, this only represents about 30 percent of all Deal Seekers.

What about the social factor? Conventional wisdom holds that younger targets are more socially active. While this is most likely true of social *media*, is it also true for sharing a shopping experience generally? The following chart shows the Social Shopper propensity for each category. Keep in mind a Social Shopper is someone who seeks out advice prior the purchase and also talks about their purchase experience post-purchase.

Social Shopping Propensity by Generation

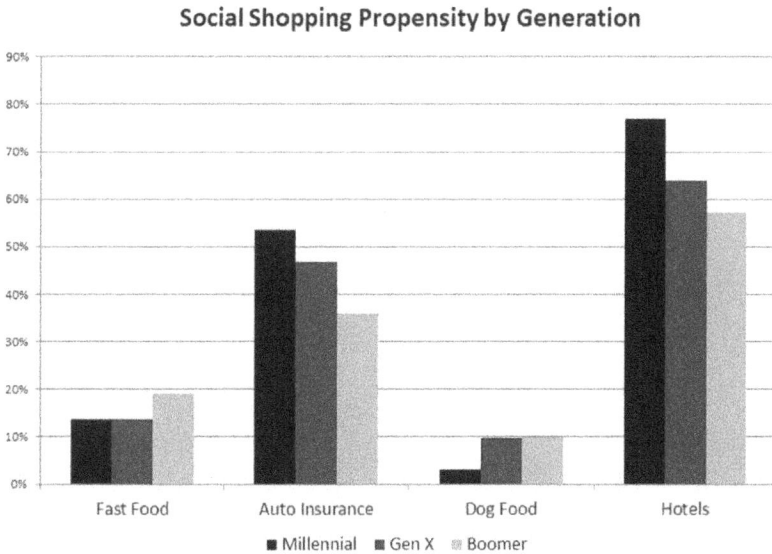

Millennials are more likely to be socially active shoppers in two of the categories, but not so much in the other two. Part of the reason lies in Millennials' Deal-Seeking mindset. In general, Deal Seekers tend to be more socially active because they are asking others (both online and offline) where to get a deal, and they also share more information after the purchase.

The other two categories (fast food and dog food) show low propensities toward social behavior for different reasons. To find a deal in fast food you just need to turn on the television set or go into the restaurant—there is something always being promoted. Add to the current promotions the ever-present "value menu," and you can see why there is no need to deal seek. Dog food, on the other hand, has a high proportion of Brand Citizens; people tend to buy the same product over and over (about 75 percent of respondents stated they buy on habit).

The take-away from this chapter? *Focus on the opportunity mindset that will drive the most sales.* Avoid the conventional tendency to focus on generational targets or just demographics. There will always be statistical differences between generations, but the goal is to focus on the motivational differences across the entire population and then market to the mindset. After all, marketing is about moving a shopper both attitudinally and behaviorally. Later in the book I dedicate a chapter to marketing to the mindset.

TWENTY-SEVEN

The Left Turn

"Marketing is a contest for people's attention."
—*Seth Godin, American marketer and author*

The average online banner click-thru rate is 0.1 percent. That is a 99.9 percent failure rate. I have been in many a client meeting where people were high-fiving when they got a 0.2 percent click-thru rate (after all, that is double the norm!). All I have to say is that someone is a genius. Somewhere along the way a digital media person had a stroke of genius and decided to invert the normal way of reporting a success rate, and it caught on. While I consider myself a glass-half-full type of person, this glass that's 0.1 percent full seems a bit of a stretch.

My point of bringing up this nuance of measuring digital success is to focus on why the click-thru rate is so low. The answer is simple (and one word): life. When a person is online they are living life. The person is checking their email and catching up on the daily news, sports, or entertainment. Social media is a big part of our online life, accounting for two hours a day. Gaming is a time-filler for many—a way to pass the time between life moments.

The reality is that online advertising accounts for roughly 15 percent of total online activity. It lives on the perimeter of the screen. A person's focus is on the center of the screen or page—on the content they desire. They move from page to page, blind to the banners—blind to the advertising. Rarely in life does someone seek out advertising; rather, they live life and shop when they want to or have to.

In fact, for many of our day-to-day purchases, we operate on autopilot. Whether it's getting the coffee at Starbucks on the way to work, fueling your car at Citgo around the corner from your house, buying your usual brands at the grocery store—the brands you've bought hundreds of times before. Most shoppers have a comfort level with brands and stores they purchase (or purchase from) on a regular basis. They are not looking for alternatives—not looking to change. There are just looking to live life.

To get a person's attention we need to interrupt their life. We need to get them to take a left turn in their day.

I don't care if we are talking online, a commercial on television, or an outdoor billboard along the highway. Success lies in the ability to interrupt a person's life and shock their system. We need to engage the shopper part of their mind and make them think. The ability to interrupt and get noticed (in a persuasive manner) defines whether a marketer is successful or not.

There is one time a year that people tune into advertising and that is (as I mentioned earlier) the Super Bowl. For some people the ads are bigger than the game. The ads are designed to generate buzz—to create conversations. The commercials are big, bold and memorable (and typically expensive), and make an emotive connection with the audience.

And then there is the rest of the year. The rest of the year, I often feel, marketers just phone it in. Sure, marketers produce quality advertising, but is it bold? Is it disruptive? Does it challenge a person's brand perception? Does it interrupt a person's life and get them to think? Why isn't every ad a Super Bowl ad?

There are several reasons for that. But let's start with what works. With Super Bowl ads, marketers entertain—they make an emotional connection. They design communication which makes its way right into the shopper's life. It is funny, heartfelt, and provocative. Following are the top 10 Super Bowl commercials of all time as selected by *Advertising Age*.

The Super Bowl Top 10

Rank	Brand	Commercial	*Ad Age* Take
1	Apple	1984	"Was there ever any doubt?" *Ad Age* asked. In one interpretation of the commercial, the nameless heroine represents humanity's hopes of escaping corporate "conformity."
2	Monster	When I Grow Up	Children voicing stunted aspirations ("I want to claw my way up to middle management") evoked a response "for adults in dead-end jobs," said the magazine, "and resulted in the perfect message for a job site."
3	Budweiser	Respect	A "simple but spectacular" tribute to America by the famous Budweiser Clydesdales in the wake of 9/11.
4	Coca-Cola	Hilltop	The magazine singles out the 1971 ad's "epic cinematography, infectious music and lyrics and … unmistakably Coke-esque flavor."
5	EDS	Cat Herders	"Dry humor and a dead-on product message cleverly converge in this 2000 spot … that turns grizzled cowhands into herders of cats who ford streams, climb trees and risk bodily harm from claws."

6	Coca-Cola	Early Showers (Mean Joe Greene)	"The interplay between the young boy and Pittsburgh Steeler, and its end line, 'Hey kid, catch' is a part of advertising history," said *Ad Age*.
7	Nike	Hare Jordan	Basketball legend Michael Jordan teamed up with Warner Brothers animation icon Bugs Bunny to vanquish bullies.
8	Volkswagen	The Force	A miniature Darth Vader learns he has undiscovered powers and in the process captured Super Bowl viewers' hearts.
9	Ram Trucks	Farmer	Excerpts from ABC newsman Paul Harvey's "So God Made a Farmer" speech, voiced over striking photographs of American farms and farmers.
10	Budweiser	Whassup!?	The magazine's Bob Garfield said the spot "hit upon not merely the latest beer-ad buzzword, not merely an inside-black-culture joke, not merely a universal expression of eloquent inarticulateness, but the ultimate depiction of male bonding."

Some of the top ten commercials were feel good spots that built brand equity. Most generated water cooler buzz the next day at work. Still other commercials not only moved the mind, but also drove behavior. Monster.com was tracking about 1.5 million visitors per month prior to airing their Super Bowl commercial. Post commercial they averaged 2.5 million visitors per month for the rest of 1999 and the number of searches on Super Bowl Sunday increased three-hundred-fold.

It seems as though during the balance of the year most marketers shift from creating an emotive connection with the shopper to what I call a "Brand Resume" commercial. The Brand Resume ad is a litany of reasons why someone should buy a product. These ads tend to lean toward the logical rather than the emotional. The better ads focus on a core benefit for the product. The less effective ads list a series of features that differentiates the product from the competition. I talked about these "Why Buys" before—while differentiating the product, are they creating an emotional bond with the shopper?

If the goal is to interrupt the shopper to get them to rethink their current brand choice(s), then the commercials must be disruptive. They need to disrupt the shopper's current beliefs and grab their attention. In other words, the brand must move the mind before the shopper changes their behavior. There are different methods to carry out such disruption as to get the shopper to take a left turn. Let's consider five of them.

Startling Price Promise

Price is a primary motivator for the Deal Seeker. Extreme pricing conditions can shock Deal Seekers into action. Geico provides one example. Geico made insurance all about price and not about the relationship with the agent. Their classic line, "Spend 15 minutes and save at least 15 percent," brought the deal to the forefront of the insurance category (I discuss this at length in the chapter titled "The Geico Effect").

General Motors Employee Pricing is an example of redefining a deal within the automotive category. In 2005, GM launched a campaign to "Get America Rolling Again." At the center of the campaign was the employee pricing offer. Employee pricing was synonymous with the "insider deal" and the approach soon was adopted by other automakers. It didn't stop there. Other retail categories such as electronics and home furnishings picked up the language. As employee pricing offers became ubiquitous, the effectiveness of the term "employee pricing" became less impactful.

Innovative Product Benefit

Innovation can drive people to rethink their current product choice. One of the best examples involves the introduction of the iPhone, which redefined the mobile category. While the advent of the iPhone appealed to the public at large, it also fueled advocacy of Apple—it was the must-have device for Apple fans. iPhone ads didn't need to do much, since word-of-mouth was as interruptive as any ad could be.

Every so often a marketer exploits their competitive product benefit by making things simple for the shopper. An example of a simple ad that became a cultural riff is the "Where's the Beef?" spot for Wendy's. This basic ad, which featured several elderly ladies poking fun at the competition, became an overnight sensation. The campaign impacted sales too, generating record-breaking revenues in 1985.

Profound Brand Shift

Sometimes a campaign can propel a brand to a new level of relevance. A successful brand shift works against a person's view of the brand—the shift forces people to take notice and reassess their current perception of the brand. To accomplish this, the shift must be dramatic and compelling. A dramatic expression of the brand can send ripples through the category, resulting in a social riff.

In 2011, Chrysler was still reeling from negative customer sentiment from taking the government bailout. They needed to shock the public to get them to rethink their brand. So Chrysler did just that. Chrysler launched the "Imported from Detroit" campaign during the Super Bowl with a two-minute commercial. It had an immediate impact on many viewers. The commercial directly attacked the negative tension toward the Detroit automakers. It also caught people's attention. The Chrysler 200 (the vehicle in the ad) saw a 1619 percent increase in site traffic on Edmunds.com. Over the weeks after the game traffic to Chrysler.com was 87 percent higher than in the weeks prior to the Super Bowl.

Domino's Pizza was a brand in distress in the 2000s. The pizza was so bad it placed dead last in the chain's own customer survey. Something had to change. In 2009, Domino's launched a new campaign aimed at overhauling the business, culture and brand. The campaign challenged the conventional perspective of Domino's by relentlessly trying to do the unthinkable—to act differently. The campaign put humanity into the brand. Results soon followed. Domino's experienced five straight years of same store sales increases and their stock price increased by 1,200 percent.

Breakthrough Brand Action

Actions speak louder than words. A brand action can redefine the brand and do more than a litany of ads could ever accomplish. Brand actions tend to be counter category, shocking both shoppers and the competition.

In 2014, CVS decided to stop selling tobacco products because it was inconsistent with its health care mission. None of CVS's key competitors followed. The action had an impact on its customers and its bottom line. In an analysis published by *American Journal of Public Health*, it was reported that CVS customers were 38 percent more likely to stop buying cigarettes. As far as revenue is concerned, CVS lost about $2 billion in annual sales by dropping tobacco products, but still increased sales overall thanks to new business from the Affordable Care Act and by growing its medical services businesses.

Tom's Shoes is classic example of a brand action that is also their brand promise. Tom's "One for One" promise gives a needy person a pair of shoes for every pair of shoes sold. To date Tom's has donated over 70 million pairs of shoes. Tom's has expanded its philanthropic actions to include additional donations like eyewear, safe water, and the training of school staff and crisis counselors to help prevent and respond to instances of bullying.

Redefining Shopping

Redefining how people shop a category can be result in competitors following suit or in some cases can disrupt the category so much that it's never the same. There are many instances in the digital age of categories being created and then disappearing. The digitization of content, specifically music and books, has redefined how people shop for (and consume) both. In the wake of digitization, many long-established retail establishments disappeared, like the vast majority of bookstores and music/record stores.

At time of writing, Amazon had opened its first brick-and-mortar store, called Amazon Go, to the public, with plans for additional locations. The store is unique because it doesn't have a check-out or cashier. A shopper scans their Amazon Go app when they enter the store and Amazon takes care of the rest. Amazon Go uses sensors and cameras to determine the items a shopper picks up, and charges them for the items when they exit the store. If the concept catches on, it might redefine the retail experience and make it easier to get in and out of a store and on with your life (something that would be very attractive to Mission shoppers).

In summary, getting a shopper to take a left turn is not an easy task. The examples I've discussed represent the extreme, and the extreme isn't always necessary to change behaviors. With that said, subtlety does not disrupt. If a marketer wants to get a shopper to rethink their brand choices they need to disrupt the shopper's thought processes.

TWENTY-EIGHT

A Quest for Knowledge

"Getting information off the Internet is like
taking a drink from a fire hydrant."
—Mitchell Kapor,
software entrepreneur and founder of Lotus Software

We live in the age of information. Access to information is one browser search away. Timely information such as weather reports, news, stock market figures, or the latest celebrity gossip keeps us informed in our daily lives. Shopping information is pervasive on the internet. No matter the product, someone has probably posted information about it. That information may be in the form of a brand website, product demonstrations, specifications and comparisons, and, of course, reviews.

Sources for shopping information usually fall into three genres: the brand, the expert, and the customer. Each source plays its role in the marketplace. The brand provides a positive perspective on the product. Sure, such information probably is biased, but what brand is going to come out and say, "Yeah, our product is okay. There is a very good chance it will meet your needs. Well, maybe. Just trust us." Shoppers know marketers are taking a positive perspective; therefore they weigh the information accordingly.

Expert information comes from the perspective of a recognized expert in the category. The source could be a publication (e.g., *Consumer Reports*, *Travel & Leisure*, *Car & Driver*), a renowned blogger, or a celebrity (e.g. Oprah, Ellen). The expert information balances cheerleading brand information. It provides an "unbiased" perspective. However, from a shopper's perspective, it does not provide a complete answer.

Past customers are an influential source of information for the shopper because they have firsthand experience with the product. Their input can convince a shopper to purchase or scare them away from a product. In a hotel study, 67 percent of respondents included a brand because of a positive review (either online or word-of-mouth) while 55 percent rejected a brand because of a negative review. Yelp! is a source many people use in choosing a restaurant and information and ratings posted there impact prospective customers' decision on where to dine. On average a one-star increase equates to a 5 percent to 9 percent increase in revenue. Conversely, one negative review can cost a restaurant up to 30 customers.

As you can see, reviews provide powerful input that can sway shoppers. Whether a product review on Amazon, a hotel review on Trip Advisor, or a review of a particular brand of TV on the Best Buy site, such reviews influence the psyche of the shopper. On the surface, reviews seem to provide very little information relative to other sources. Their most important component is a rating of the customer experience. Without context the shopper would not know the reason for the rating—did the product fail or it was an issue with shipping or customer service?

Also, customers may think they are objective, but in reality each shopper subjectively rates their purchase based on their motivations—their preferences. One customer may give a product a negative review based on the smallest defects or lapses in customer service. Another customer may give a product a 5-star rating because the product met or exceeded their expectations, even if there were deficiencies in the overall experience.

You can Google information, but you cannot Google knowledge.

The irony today is that, despite all the information online, there is a lack of knowledge. Each source provides a different perspective, yet they have one thing in common: each source is just information. But the shopper is not looking for information; they are seeking *knowledge* to make the right buying decision. The overarching question shoppers are trying to answer is "What product should I buy?" Beneath that are a series of micro-decisions, each requiring the shopper to seek out information from various sources to analyze, decide, and then continue on their path to purchase.

Knowledge is critical as to whether a source is influential or just informational. In this context "knowledge" can be thought of as the shopper's relevant acceptance of information because it relates to a shopper's situation—their needs and motivations. Let me explain. In the information spectrum, content ranges from product information to solution scenarios. Take as an example a vacuum cleaner. A brand website can list all the product features—amperage, cord length, suction power, so on and so forth—but it is up to the shopper to interpret the product specs to determine if this vacuum is the solution for them. Now think about a solution scenario. Shoppers' "vacuum scenarios" can range from an older couple without pets in need of a vacuum cleaner to do weekly spot cleaning to a mother of three young children and owner of a golden retriever in need of a powerful daily-use machine that can suck the mess out of their life. There could be many different variations for vacuum scenarios, such as a person's mess threshold, where they live, and the time of year.

Solution content is critical in providing knowledge and convincing the shopper that the product is right for them. A repeated theme of this section will be what I call the *brand resume* approach. In a brand resume, a marketer focuses on the competitive differences between their product and the competition. A vacuum marketer may talk about how their cord is five feet longer than the competition's or how their machine has 100 AW (air watts) more than the competition (for the vacuum-uninitiated, "air watts" is one measure of suction power).

Solution content is about reality. A solution shopper searching for a new vacuum cleaner thinks in terms of life scenarios as opposed to product attributes. The shopper with the golden retriever is probably going to Google "best vacuum cleaner for golden retrievers" or "best vacuum cleaners for pet hair." It is doubtful if they are searching for vacuum cleaners with the most air watts.

Solution-based content can be difficult to execute for a marketer. There are several reasons for this. First, there may be too many scenarios for which to create content. Think of this as the difference between a 30-second commercial and a 30-minute infomercial. The brevity of the 30-second ad forces a marketer to either focus on one scenario (or feature/benefit) or a list of reasons why their product is better than the competition (i.e., the brand resume). A 30-minute infomercial allows the marketer to show a multitude of persuasive usage scenarios. This approach can be optimal for many direct response products, but also can be expensive because of the cost of purchasing media time for the ad.

Solution-based content also applies to information provided by expert sources. Many experts already provide such content. They will compare products based on real-life scenarios. For example, there are thousands of online sites comparing the features of new high-definition televisions (HDTV). However, what if the shopper's primary scenario is finding the best television for gaming? Sources like Game Radar+, Tech Radar, and CNET compare televisions based on gaming scenarios. Some of the sources go beyond generic gaming and even offer television recommendations based on specific gaming systems (e.g., Xbox, PS4).

As I stated earlier, customer reviews can also be persuasive in influencing a shopper's final decision. But there are inherent problems with many reviews. The shopper wants advice that will help them make their own buying decision. They could care less about another person's good or bad experiences. Most reviews, however, focus on overall impressions as opposed to breaking out the customer experience. For example, Yelp! allows patrons to rate a restaurant and provide general feedback. But the assessment is not broken down according to different aspects of the restaurant experience, such as service, food quality, ambiance, and value for money. This fact does not make Yelp! a bad source by any means; my point is simply that the general nature of the review limits its helpfulness to prospective customers.

A second flaw that's characteristic of reviews is their frequent failure to correlate the motivations and preferences of reviewers and shoppers. For example, let's revisit our television gamer scenario. What if a gamer shopper was able to filter reviewers on Amazon based on whether they bought the television for gaming? By finding "reviewers like me" the shopper is able to filter through advice and get to customer reviews/advice that will be more meaningful in their purchase decision.

In conclusion, influence is based on solution relevance. It seems like a simple, obvious concept, yet many marketers continue to create brand resume ads.

To affect a shopper's decision path the marketer must focus on getting into the shopper's mind and world. They need to go beyond what they have to say and integrate experts and customers in an influential chorus. This leads me to the next chapter, where I discuss the power of using these three sources together.

TWENTY-NINE
We Say, They Say, You Say

"Word of mouth is the best medium of all."
—William Bernbach, advertising creative director and co-founder of
Doyle Dane Bernbach

Marketers are believable. They can be persuasive. But they are not transparent, because they tend to be one-sided—their side. Every marketer puts their best foot forward, and they should. Why spend money on an ad and just claim that your product is okay? Or that you have good prices, so if a customer is too lazy to travel to a warehouse club, we can save you some pennies. Could you imagine a car manufacturer saying that all mid-size sedans are pretty much the same, so you might as well buy ours or not—your call.

In an industry where transparency and authenticity are often discussed, very few marketers actually manage to be either of those things. Sure, a lot of marketers punk people by switching a high-quality product with their own (e.g., Walmart steaks served at a high-end steak restaurant), but at what point is deceiving people genuine? And in these situations everyone seems to love their product anyway (no surprise!). By the way, that "everyone" is the problem. As a society there are very few things we all agree on, so when a marketer uses real people and they all agree on something, many people are skeptical because the outcome seems so predictable, and no different from a marketer saying their products are "fresh" or "high quality" (whose aren't?).

Believability comes through trust. In the chapter on the persuasion continuum, I discussed how the trusted advisor is sought out in the course of a considered purchase to assist in the decision. A shopper doesn't seek out just anyone; they seek out a person or source they trust. Whether it is a friend or family member, or a publication like *Consumer Reports*, the source is trusted and therefore believable. Oh yeah, and marketers are *not* believable unless you trust them—and how many marketers do *you* trust?

Believability comes through transparency, and transparency is built in layers. The three layers I like to refer to are *We Say, They Say, You Say*. These phrases come from the Ford Fusion launch. It was 2009 and social campaigns were in vogue. The concept was simple: we would combine the marketers' message (We Say) with recognized experts (They Say) with testimonials from customers who bought a Ford Fusion (You Say). This approach, while not perfect, does increase the believability of brand claims, because third-party validation from experts and customers increases the trust of the marketer. The power comes from using all three layers, with the second two layers (They Say, You Say) balancing the one-sided nature of the marketer's layer (We Say).

The We Say message is, as I mentioned earlier, predictable. It can get worse if you listen to the category in aggregate. What you will hear are what I call tired words. Tired words are overused "easy" words that are persistently used by all competitors. They don't differentiate and become white noise the shopper ignores.

Let's look at one such word: *quality*. This term is used to describe products in many categories, including restaurants, automotive, appliances, and consumer package goods. Quality is expected. Quality is unoriginal. Quality is white noise. There are other words and phrases which are more illustrative, more compelling and less predictable (e.g., artisanal, locally sourced, hand-crafted, trail-tested). Better yet, tell a product story illustrating how the product embodies the concept of quality.

The We Say approach must be transparent to be successful. If the results are all good, then believability decreases. If a product on Amazon had only five-star reviews you would probably be suspicious, especially if there several hundred reviews of the product.

An important point about transparency involves the believability of the environment containing the customer reviews. Over the years I have worked with different marketers who wanted to place customer reviews on their brand site. I always recommended against it for several reasons. The first reason centers on the shopper—how believable is a review on a brand site? Not very. A shopper will be concerned the marketer cleansed the negative reviews to give their products a more positive spin (and in several cases the shopper would be right!).

Allowing a customer to vent on a brand site tests the marketer's vigilance, which gets me to my second point. Whenever this topic came up, I would ask the client one simple question—"How thick is your skin?"—because they were very likely to get one or more negative reviews. Reviews they would want to remove….

Transparency is not limited to websites. Many marketers create commercials with "real people" reacting to their product. And guess what? Those reactions are always positive! There are no naysayers, skeptics or critics. An example of this was a Microsoft campaign called "Laptop Hunters." The campaign premise was that a shopper was challenged to find a Mac or PC laptop for under $1,000 that met their needs. If they could find it they would get it for free. The shopper visited an Apple store and was unable to find a laptop under a grand that met their needs. The next visit was to a retail store selling PCs where the shopper easily found such a laptop. As you can imagine, no one ever bought a Mac (at least there was no commercial showing a Mac purchase).

Transparency is depicting the real world, where some people buy one product and others buy another (e.g., remember four out of five dentists—not five out of five—recommend Colgate). Transparency is a spectrum of product reviews, ranging from five stars to one star. Transparency is recognizing the positives and negatives of a specific product.

Transparency is believable. But in my opinion, I don't think it is realistic for a marketer to be totally transparent in their advertising. Why should they? They are spending a lot of money—potentially millions of dollars—to advertise their product. A marketer should put their best foot forward in their advertising in order to persuade people to purchase their product. But they shouldn't be faux transparent.

Believability comes from a chorus of people talking about a product. In addition to the marketer, there are two other active participants: experts (They Say) and customers (You Say).

Experts are recognized by a large number of people to be authorities within a particular lifestyle genre or product category. Experts range from writers for a publication to celebrities to paid bloggers. Experts may be viewed as more believable than the marketer because they usually put the product in a "real world" context and assess its pros and cons. More often than not, these experts have reviewed other products, something which increases the credibility of their product review.

An important aspect of believability involves the expert's following. Within the context of their social following the expert is believable and persuasive. If the expert's review is taken out of that context, its persuasiveness and believability will decline. "Mommy bloggers" are used by many marketers to spread the word about their products. There are roughly four million mommy bloggers, each with their own following. And while they can impart knowledge to their following, their take is less persuasive and possibly meaningless in other social groups. The same goes for a tech journalist on CNET. A CNET writer may have credibility and following on CNET, but this would diminish if the writer's review was used outside of CNET (especially if there was no reference to CNET).

You Say is what the customer has to say about their product experience. This takes on different forms. The purest is when it is brought up in a conversation within their social group. The customer is persuasive because they can describe their pleasant (or unpleasant) product experience and put it in context for the person they are talking to. A marketer may say that a vacuum has the best suction power within its category, while a customer may tell their neighbor how the vacuum easily sucks up the hair of their golden retriever without clogging and would no doubt do the same for hair from the neighbor's three cats.

Word of mouth marketing works best when it is about personal context— when the customer describes the pros and cons relative to their own personal experience (similar to the expert). Their experience will be relatable to some and not others. However, the review will be powerful for those who can relate.

They Say and You Say can be used as either interrupt or intercept. From a shopper perspective these two sources are an intercept within a shopper journey. The following word cloud depicts influential sources when purchasing a new phone.

Mobile Phone Influential Source

Television Online Video Online Search
Expert Blog In-Store Signage
Direct Mail Brand Website Retailer Email Outdoor Board
Social Media Post *In-Person Conversation*
Carrier Website News Story
Radio Online Banners Retailer Website
Consumer Review Website Salesperson
Magazine Ad In-Store Materials

The influence of the marketing content in the decision path is balanced with They Say (consumer review website, expert blog) and You Say (in-person conversation, social media post). The They Say and You Say are highlighted in darker type within the word cloud. Interrupt media can influence the shopper if the ad exposure comes at the right time. However, for the mobile survey, interrupt media were much less influential than intercept channels. The shopper will seek out different sources as the need to make decisions arises. Intercept brand content that may be influential ranges from website content to in-store materials and interactions with sales personnel.

Integrating the three is less about putting all three on the same website or in the same commercial as it is about layering, which is the most natural form of integration. The We Say is the overarching mass communication disrupting the shopper's perceptions and making an emotional connection. It may be persuasive enough or it may require validation from experts and customers, which brings us to the layering.

A marketer layering on experts (They Say) needs to engage enough experts to be effective. The expert can be a direct link to the shopper (think about mommy bloggers) or to influencers like foodies, tech-thusiasts or auto enthusiasts. These influencers are the social beachhead a marketer is trying to reach and persuade—that is, influencers within a person's social network. These influencers are the people who have a passion for a product category and stay on top of product trends and news (e.g., the auto-enthusiast you know, the epicurious friend who is into food trends). In this scenario the expert is a gateway to the influencers and secondarily to the influencer's social network.

The customers' layer (You Say) fuels the one-to-one conversation and/or prompts the customer to share their thoughts on the product. Fueling the conversation may be the novelty of the product or the fact it exceeds the customer's expectations. Since word-of-mouth involves the natural desire to share, it is difficult for the marketer to control. However, a marketer can monitor conversations about their product and leverage those conversations.

The native channel in which a person shares their perspective on a product is the most believable and most transparent expression of that perspective. To leverage the native channel, a marketer should do a transparency redirect and invite people to check out what others are saying. Transparency redirects can be as simple as linking to an external site or to a blog containing the review. For customers this may mean sending them to a social source like Twitter or Instagram by using a hashtag (e.g., #KrogerFan, #AppleFan).

A transparency redirect is a sign of brand confidence. Sending a shopper to an uncontrolled environment is a sign the brand believes the majority of conversations out there are positive. It's like saying, "Well, if you don't believe us, just search Twitter for #BrandFan and see what others are saying about our new product."

The bottom line? A marketer should never say their brand is "cool." By definition a person or brand who says they are cool is not. Others need to say it on their behalf. Experts and customers define whether a brand is cool or not.

THIRTY

The Geico Effect

"Good advertising does not just circulate information. It penetrates the public mind with desires and belief."
—Leo Burnett, advertising icon

Can a category make it all about price?

Can marketers condition shoppers to focus on price over brand?

Auto insurance companies spend billions of dollars every year to get people to switch—to change their policies from one provider to another. From commercial pod to commercial pod people are reminded that they can get a better deal, or better coverage, or more forgiving coverage. Maybe cash back, good driver privileges, or if you suck at driving we won't penalize you like the other guy. Bottom line: there is a better deal out there; all you need to do is spend 15 minutes and you can save.… Well, you know.

But does this constant barrage of teasing people to switch really work? Sort of. Annually, about 39 percent of people shop for auto insurance; however, only about 11 percent switch. The persistent teasing of the deal has created a Deal Seeker mentality within the category. A phenomenal 84 percent of auto insurance shoppers are Deal Seekers. Think about that: 84 percent!

There are several reasons why this is so but the most interesting one is the influence of television. Thirty–one percent of shoppers stated that television influenced them in their shopping experience. This is interesting because most of the time Interrupt media (e.g., TV, radio) are underplayed by shoppers taking a survey, who do not want to admit that marketing affects them. They believe they are in control of their own choices, and therefore sources they seek out are rated higher than sources that seek them out. But not in auto insurance.

Another interesting aspect of the industry is how different brands attract different typologies. Take Geico and State Farm for example. Forty-two percent of Geico shoppers are Deal Surgeons. Deal Surgeons (Free Agent, Deal Seeker, Mission) are looking to get a deal and then get on with life. Further, they don't believe that brand matters. (By the way, that 42 percent is over three times the norm of 12.5 percent in the category.) Twenty-three percent of State Farm shoppers are a Brand Tracker (Brand Citizen, Deal Seeker, Mission). This typology is similar to Deal Surgeon in that they want to get a deal and then get on with their life. The difference is that for a Brand Citizen, brand matters.

The difference is reflected in their advertising. Geico ads are popular because of the use of amusing characters and situations all driving to the same point: spend 15 minutes and you can save up to 15 percent. State Farm, on the other hand, focuses on their agents, who magically appear at the beckoning of the policy holder—always telling them they are covered.

Ironically the advertising reflects the customer experience. When you buy insurance from Geico, you buy it from a faceless entity. If you need to process a claim, you call a person, but that person is there to process your claim, not strike up a relationship. State Farm policies are bought through agents and if you need to process a claim or manage your account it's all done through the agent. I believe this human connection is the reason brand does matter for State Farm shoppers but not for Geico customers. Interestingly, some shoppers/customers prefer a human relationship and that need builds a relationship with the brand.

The "deal first" approach is unique to auto insurance—or is it? Another category fixated on deal-vertising is travel. There are numerous Online Travel Agent (OTA) sites like Hotels.com, Expedia, and Priceline all trying to impress upon travel planners that they should never pay full price when they travel.

The situation in the hotel category is not as dramatic as for auto insurance, as you can see from the diagram below, which illustrates differences between new and repeat hotel guests and the influence of various sources of information.

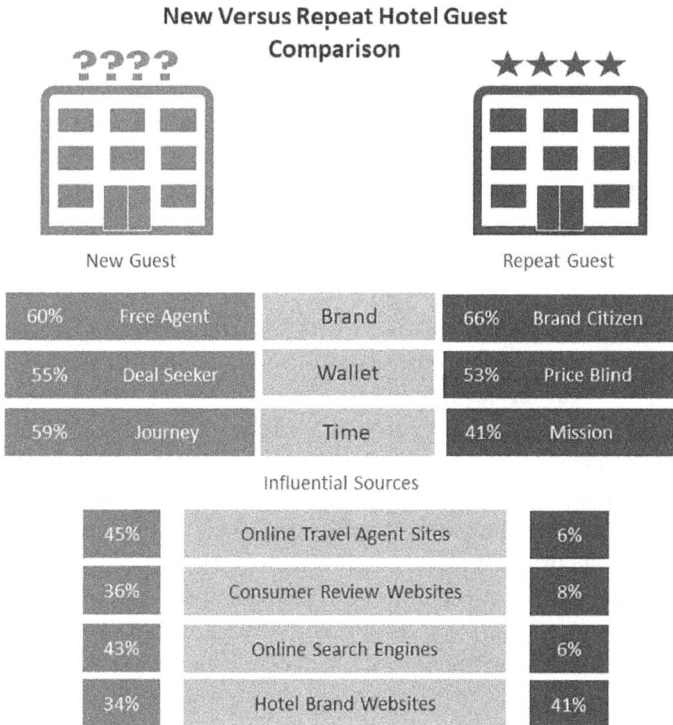

New Versus Repeat Hotel Guest Comparison

New Guest				Repeat Guest	
60%	Free Agent	**Brand**	66%	Brand Citizen
55%	Deal Seeker	**Wallet**	53%	Price Blind
59%	Journey	**Time**	41%	Mission

Influential Sources

New Guest		Repeat Guest
45%	Online Travel Agent Sites	6%
36%	Consumer Review Websites	8%
43%	Online Search Engines	6%
34%	Hotel Brand Websites	41%

First off, note the percentage of Deal Seekers in the hotel category, 52 percent, compared to the 84 percent found in auto insurance. This stark difference may be a function of who is actually advertising. In the auto insurance category the brands themselves are promising savings. Within the hotel category it is not the brands promising savings but, rather, the "brokers" or OTAs. This is reflected in the influence of television advertising: only 1 percent of hotel shoppers stated they were influenced by television in their most recent booking. This doesn't mean TV advertising for OTAs was not effective. Sure, only 1 percent of respondents stated television was influential; however, overall 27 percent of hotel planners in the hotel study were influenced by an OTA site.

So at the category level the deal appears to have less impact. Looking deeper into the category, you see a dichotomy between new guests versus repeat guests. The first-time guest is more likely to be a Bargainista (Free Agent, Deal Seeker, Journey) based on higher Deal Seeker and Free Agent preferences. They also are more exploratory about what is available and where they prefer to stay. They are active users of online sources to find their hotel, and those online sources are influential in their decisions. Much of this is due to the fact that they do not have past experience with the hotel to use as a reference.

Compare this to the repeat guest. The repeat guest has experience with the hotel brand. The core typology for repeat guests is the Loyalty Laser (Brand Citizen, Price Blind, Mission), focusing on a brand affinity and having less sensitivity to the best deal. They are also on a mission to just book the room, and tend to focus on brand-centric sources for their hotel.

Many retail categories use the latest and greatest deals to try to get shoppers in the door every week. Home furnishings, home improvement, electronics and grocery play up the deal to generate foot traffic and sales. Of these categories, grocery involves the most frequent purchases with many shoppers making a weekly trip to the store.

Grocery marketing is a weekly deal war with each marketer trying to win the week. Deal noise dominates the category, from BOGOs to 10 for 10s to Fuel Perks. The promise from the majority of brands within the category is that you should never pay full price. This is very appealing to two typologies: Bargainistas and Deal Surgeons. Both typologies are Free Agents and Deal Seekers. The only difference is that one enjoys shopping (Bargainsta) and the other sees it as a chore (Deal Seekers).

Brands set their own expectations for the "deal." Some brands promote the weekly deal, while others promote it subtly or not at all. Brands like Walmart, Winn Dixie, and Kroger are all about the deal—about saving the shopper money every week. By contrast, brands like Trader Joe's, Whole Foods, and Sprouts Farmers Market focus on their products. While they may have a "deal," it is not a part of their brand promise, nor do they compete directly with the deal brands.

The weekly circular is the bible for the grocery shopper. Many shoppers actively use the circular to determine which store(s) to go to and what products to buy. It doesn't matter if it is the physical copy that comes in the newspaper or if it's accessed online, the circular is the deal trigger when it comes to planning their trip. Like television in auto insurance, circulars are the dominant medium in the category. According to research by Market Force, nearly half of consumers review printed circulars at least once a week, with 63 percent of those consumers comparing prices between competing supermarkets.

I want to touch on a final category: restaurants. Restaurants range in quality, deals offered, and time. Fast food restaurants are about the quick deal. Fast casual focuses on time and quality in lieu of the deal you would get in fast food. Casual dining is sit-down and table-service so time considerations are not paramount, but quality and deals do factor into the decision.

Based on their brand promises restaurants in different categories attract different shopper typologies. In general, fast casual is dominated by three Price Blind typologies: Comfort Zoners (Brand Citizen, Price Blind, Journey) at 35 percent, Loyalty Lasers (Brand Citizen, Price Blind Mission) at 21 percent, and Solution Shoppers (Free Agent, Price Blind, Journey) at 16 percent. The three typologies represent 72 percent of the shoppers in the category. This is not a surprise; fast casual restaurants are rarely on the airwaves, and when they are they are advertising the quality of their food. The brands within the category are all primarily Price Blind, too. Boston Market is the highest Deal Seeker brand, but even so only one of four of its customers are seeking a deal.

Compare fast casual to family dining restaurants. Like fast casual, the family dining category is dominated by two Price Blind typologies: Comfort Zoners (Brand Citizen, Price Blind, Journey) at 35 percent, and Solution Shoppers (Free Agent, Price Blind, Journey) at 19 percent. The two typologies together represent 54 percent of shoppers in the category. While many of the brands in the category are primarily Price Blind, there are some outliers. One is Denny's with about 40 percent of their patrons being Deal Seekers. Denny's is about the deal. Part of their menu is deal-based, offering offering items for $2, $4, $6, and $8. This approach is less like other family dining restaurants and more like a fast food restaurant approach.

A parting thought: Can a brand break out of category-driven deal inertia? If a category shopper is looking for a deal, the challenge is to create an emotive connection to counter the deal-driven DNA. In fast food, brands are attempting to fight deal-vertising. A primary tactic is product innovation. Taco Bell is constantly reinventing their products from the chalupa to the gordita to anything on the menu plus Doritos. They are even broadening their meal offerings, from breakfast to happy hour beverages, and they also invented the "fourth meal" for those with late night cravings. Constant food invention is disruptive and increases the brand's profile. Is Taco Bell still a deal brand? Sure, but they are not considered a commodity within the category. This prevents their brand being lumped in with the burger brands or the sub brands or fried food.

THIRTY-ONE

Deal Now or Deal Later

"If you are depressed, you are living in the past. If you are anxious, you are living in the future. If you are at peace, you are living in the present."
—Lao Tzu, Chinese philosopher

"Live in the moment" is many people's mantra—especially many Deal Seekers. I am going to return to the deal seeking savant, Monica, I wrote about earlier in the book. There is an aspect of Monica's shopping preferences I would like to examine—needs versus wants. Monica incessantly focuses on her product needs and her family's needs, and on saving as much as possible on those needs.

She felt loyalty programs conflicted with that goal, because loyalty program incentives prompt her to buy products other than those she needs. For example, if she earns $10 in Kohl's cash, she feels pressure to use the "free cash." The incentive haunts her—it's like free money she would hate to see go to waste. The problem is she doesn't need anything else from Kohl's, and she especially doesn't want to spend more than $10 on something she doesn't need. So what she will do is browse the store looking for an item as close to $10 as possible that she or another family member needs.

Monica's perspective on loyalty programs highlights an intriguing question—are deal seekers more motivated to get a deal now or build up to a better deal later?

From a marketer's viewpoint, loyalty programs are pretty straightforward. The goal is to increase over time the frequency and amount that the shopper uses the product or service. By and large these are highly Pavlovian tactics which when removed can result in the person reverting to the previous behavior.

From a Deal Seeker's perspective, loyalty programs are less straightforward. Using a loyalty program requires effort and often decreases brand choice. Let's start with effort. Effort is normally not a problem for a Deal Seeker, because they expect to exert effort to get a deal. It would be one thing if there was only one rewards program—it would be easy for a shopper to remember to use it. However, the average household belongs to 29 loyalty programs and is actively using 12.

Why is there a gap between subscribing and usage? There are several reasons. Start with human nature. There is a limit to the number of things we can keep top of mind at any one time. Do a quick test: Write on a piece of paper the number of loyalty programs you subscribe to. How many did you recall? Did you end up with more than 12? Another question: How many have you used recently, say in the last month?

Each person's results may vary, but several consistent themes emerge with regard to usage. Ease is critical to usage. Ease is not necessarily access. Just because I belong to a program does not mean I will remember to use it. Ease is about linking the deal to the reward. Many times a shopper must be prompted by the cashier to use the program. This prompting may or may not result in a habit; however, if the deal is linked to usage the shopper will be more likely to use it unprompted.

So there needs to be a synergy between ease of use and the loyalty reward. The easiest method is to integrate the reward into the existing shopper behavior. This is often done with credit cards. Many cards offer some form of cash back based on purchases, while others help the customer earn airline miles or hotel loyalty points. The card recipient doesn't need to think about the rewards. They're automatically accrued every time they use the card.

But if they have multiple credit cards, well, that's another story. Credit card rewards provide an example of two different ways of incentivizing a person: (1) give me an immediate reward (cash back), or (2) let me work toward a long-term goal (earning frequent flyer miles). For the shopper there is tension between the deal today and getting a reward in the future. The deal today provides immediate gratification. You make the purchase and the cashier informs you of your savings based on the loyalty program. The "deal later" scenario needs to establish an emotive connection with the Deal Seeker to shift away from the "deal today." Are frequent flyer miles enough to prompt change? For some people, sure they are. They are dreaming of that next trip—they are striving for the dream. An emotive dream relevant to the shopper is a strong stimulus to change their preference from the deal today to the dream later.

Getting a deal today versus delaying the deal may be a function of the product category and shopper expectations. Take two different restaurant categories: fast casual and fast food. The percentage of Deal Seekers in the fast food category is about 48 percent while for fast casual it is only 16 percent.

Fast food is about the deal today. For many people it is a utilitarian activity—getting food for as little money as possible in order to survive to the next meal. If Maslow were to classify the usage of fast food, it would probably be on the bottom rung of his famous hierarchy of needs. While some fast food restaurants may dispute this perspective, they still act the same way: wooing customers with the latest deals, from $1 menu items to "5 for $5." The category creates deal-vertising to constantly entice the shopper with the latest deal.

This immediate reward focus makes it very difficult to create a delayed deal scenario. It doesn't mean certain brands are not implementing rewards programs. McDonald's has been dabbling with different rewards programs over the years. Probably the most successful of their "deal later" programs is the Monopoly program, which began in 1987. The promotion sells the dream: a $1 million prize (additional cash prizes range from $25 to $50,000). The program has proven an annual success with same store sales increasing anywhere from 1 percent to 6 percent over the three decades of the promotion. The Monopoly promotion is not a classic rewards program, however; its annual success sells a dream (probably better than many rewards programs out there), and gets people to return throughout the month to McDonald's to participate.

So does fast casual do any better? Not really. They are a step up from fast food from a quality perspective, and you see this in the low Deal Seeker percentage. The category also refrains from heavy deal-vertising. Rather the goal for a fast casual restaurant is to (1) get into the diner's rotation and (2) increase the frequency once in the rotation. I discussed this fact in the Brand Rotation chapter, where I noted the desire for variety among fast casual diners. Panera has only 32 percent exclusivity, with the remainder of diners going to at least one other Fast Casual restaurant.

So are fast casual restaurants using the deal later strategy? Part of diners' loyalty to Panera can be explained by their rewards program, MyPanera. Over 22 million customers enrolled in the program through the end of 2015. The impact on sales is impressive. Panera states that 50 percent of the transactions at their bakery-cafe were attached to the loyalty program. MyPanera rewards range from complimentary bakery-cafe items to exclusive previews and tastings and cooking and baking tips.

Is MyPanera usage a function of the patron remembering to use the card or the cashier prompting the patron? Probably a little bit of both, but in my experience the cashiers at Panera always prompt me if I belong to the loyalty program (very much like Kroger). I don't believe the rewards offered by Panera are strong enough to elevate Panera above the competition; rather, the loyalty is more likely based on brand preference or habit.

Deal Now

Deal Now is meant to be an accelerant to get the shopper to act now. Most retailers attempt to get the shopper in today; however, some brands layer in the deals to increase the adrenalin—increase the desire to act now. Take retailers like Kroger and Target, who stress getting the deal in a shopper's current trip.

Shopping at Kroger is like walking into a hyper deal environment. The aisle is marked with "New Low Prices," "10 for $10," and "Buy 5, save $5" signs, as well as the "Wahoo" deals, which I am assuming would make a shopper yell "Wahoo." However, I have yet to actually hear that exclamation in the store.

A second feature of Kroger loyalty is impressive: over 90 percent of shoppers use the Kroger card. This is almost double any other store chain. At first this may seem astounding, but think about it: a Deal Seeker at Kroger wants to *save today*, and Kroger makes it easy by just joining their rewards program.

Target's Cartwheel is a Deal Now program allowing shoppers to save anywhere from 5 percent to 50 percent on specific items. A shopper can also stack additional manufacturer coupons (if available) and use the Target RedCard (5 percent off purchases) for an even deeper discount. As of January 2017, 27 million Target customers were using the card.

Deal Later

The Kroger example represents the present reward but what about the future reward? Normally, these are points-based systems where a shopper will be rewarded based on the amount they purchase. The higher the amount spent, the more rewards points they receive. The rewards vary from complimentary items to monetary rewards.

The goal of the rewards program is to build the shopper's brand loyalty and encourage as many trips as possible. Many times all a reward program does is give a customer free items after so many visits—visits the shopper was going to take anyway. Is this a bad thing? No, not really. The complimentary items acknowledge the shopper for their patronage. This type of reward is more of a good will gesture than an incentive to get a shopper to come back.

If you break down Deal Now and Deal Later, you are speaking to different typologies. The Deal Now is obviously speaking to the Deal Seeker and most likely the Free Agent. These two core typologies are Bargainista (Free Agent, Deal Seeker, Journey) and Deal Surgeon (Free Agent, Deal Seeker, Mission). Deal Later still speaks to the Deal Seeker, but most likely the Brand Citizen. These core typologies are Fanatical Finders (Brand Citizen, Deal Seeker, Journey) and Brand Trackers (Brand Citizen, Deal Seeker, Mission). The difference between the two lies in the expected commitment of the shopper to buy the brand long-term to get the loyalty reward.

This dichotomy between Free Agent and Brand Citizen is evident in the hotel category, especially when it comes to using an Online Travel Agent (OTA) in booking the hotel. If you split Deal Seekers into Free Agents and Brand Citizens you see a significant difference in OTA bookings. In the hotel study, 40 percent of Free Agent Deal Seekers booked their room through an OTA, while only 22 percent of Brand Citizen Deal Seekers booked through an OTA.

There are multiple reasons for the difference in booking rates, but start with the fact that the Brand Citizen does see a difference between hotel brands. Sure, they want a deal, but are not willing to go with the cheapest price. The strength of the OTA is to provide the best price over a vast range of hotel options. If the shopper is only considering a short list of brands, then the utility of using an OTA declines—the shopper can just as easily go to the hotel-brand site and book.

Is there another reason for the difference in booking rates other than brand preference? Yes, and it is the hotel's loyalty program. Seventy-two percent of Brand Citizen/Deal Seekers were more likely to be influenced by loyalty programs either always or often (compare this to 33 percent for the overall hotel study).

The hotel statistics demonstrate how a Deal Seeker shopper can build brand preference in the long term. The Deal Seeker DNA doesn't subside; rather, it redirects from a short-term deal to possibly a long-term reward. For some Deal Seekers their immediate deal remains a priority, even though their brand preference is increasing. This preference shift will alter their shopping path. Instead of focusing primarily on price, the shopper will begin their search with their brand(s) either in an OTA site or by perusing brand sites. If they feel like they are getting a deal they will book. If not, they will most likely broaden their brand set, reverting back to a Free Agent.

Ideally, if a brand wants to attract the Deal Seeker, they will not Deal Now *or* Deal Later; the brand will try to do both. The reality is Deal Now and Deal Later provide two different types of behavioral reinforcement. Deal Now is an accelerant to get the shopper into the store today. Deal Later is an amplifier to get the shopper to come back again (and again).

Kohl's department store does both well. Their Deal Now accelerant is a direct mail piece with a peel-off sticker offering shoppers 10 percent, 20 percent or 30 percent off their next purchase. At the checkout, the shopper is rewarded with $10 in Kohl's Cash for every $50 they spend. The Kohl's Cash, like the discount coupon, can only be used for a limited time in order to get the shopper back into the store in the near future.

Kohl's approach is more of a "plus-one" strategy, i.e., get one more visit from the shopper. Plus-one builds brand preference in the short term. Once the two-visit cycle is complete, the Deal Seeker has very little reason to go back to Kohl's as opposed to another store. However, one cycle may be enough. Most people do not buy clothes on a weekly basis. The tendency is to buy in the spring (for summer) and fall (for winter). If the Kohl's deal cycles are aligned with the high-traffic purchase periods, then this may be enough to attract loyalty.

Worth noting is that Kohl's also has a Yes2You Rewards program, which earns subscribers an additional $5 for every $100 they spend, plus ancillary incentives throughout the year. This may be an amplifier for some shoppers, but does not have the same deal energy as the Kohl's Cash cycle.

There are many different methods to consider when developing a rewards program. Some are effective, others not so much. In the next chapter, I will discuss how to integrate incentives into shopper behavior in order to shift that behavior.

THIRTY-TWO
Can You Change a Shopper's Stripes?

"Motivation is what gets you started. Habit is what keeps you going."
—Jim Ryun, Olympic medalist in track and field

For the past 25 years, a friend of mine, Mike, has taken several snowmobile trips a year with his buddies in Michigan's Upper Peninsula. Normally they take three or four trips a year. Some are weekend trips while others extend over three or more days.

In the beginning, the group's perspective on hotels was a bed for the night. They wanted to maximize their time on the trails, sometimes spending as much as 12 hours a day snowmobiling. Given their utilitarian views on hotels, they were very deal driven, trying to spend the least amount possible on rooms. For years they chose the cheapest hotels.

But as they grew older, 12 hours on the trails was more difficult to recover from, and the hotel grew in importance, becoming a bigger part of the trip, not "just a bed." Hotel amenities and nearby activities became integral to the trip. The group was (and is) still price sensitive; however, they began to pay more to get a better experience.

Recently, they began to stay at the Kewadin Casino in Sault Ste. Marie, Michigan. They paid double the price they normally did, but were able to have dinner, do some gambling and enjoy a nicer room (which was very welcoming at the end of the trip). They also switched their hotel in Munising from one outside the town to one near the water. The price wasn't that much more, but allowed the group to walk to the South Bay on Lake Superior and do some ice fishing. Over the past few years they developed a relationship with the hotel owner, Larry, and are even friends with him on Facebook. Ironically, this social connection makes it difficult to switch to a different hotel in Munising without Larry finding out (unless they choose not to post on their trip).

So why am I telling you about an annual snowmobile trip with a bunch of guys? Well, worth noting about these guys is they are on the frugal side, especially when it comes to lodging. Why spend any more than you have to on a bed for the night, especially if the next morning you're back on your sled again, headed to the next waypoint? But while Mike and his buddies are frugal, they changed their stripes over time as they found places that became more integral to the trip.

This was the crux of a presentation I gave at a hotel convention. Can you—or how do you—change a person who is a Deal Seeker into one who is Price Blind?

This shift works against the shopper's nature and so seems unlikely, but it is not impossible. Let me explain.

Many shoppers booking travel in the industry go through an Online Travel Agent (OTA) like Expedia, Hotels.com or Hotwire. These sites show the shopper available rooms in different hotels at their destination. The shopper can quickly survey the results and choose the best "deal." The benefit from the hotel's perspective is that they fill a room, the downside is that they pay a fee to the OTA for the booking—a fee that cuts into their margin.

Moving a person against their innate shopping preferences requires a progression. First off, it is very difficult to do if the person is a one-time or infrequent traveler to the destination. However, if the traveler does return on a regular basis, there is an opportunity to shift them toward being more brand loyal. The following diagram displays this shift and the effect on the likelihood of using OTAs of each stage in the shift.

Shifting a Shopper's DNA

	FD	BD	BP
	Move from Free Range to Brand Citizen		
	FD Free Agent Deal Seeker	**BD** Brand Citizen Deal Seeker	**BP** Brand Citizen Price Blind
Online Travel Agent Influence	44%	31%	10%
Booking	40%	22%	7%

The first shift is from Free Agent/Deal Seeker to Brand Citizen/Deal Seeker. This shift is built on the repeat nature of the travel, combined with the traveler's familiarity with the hotel. Just like the example of Mike's snowmobile trip, if there is a regular trip the hotel has an opportunity to shift the shopper's DNA.

The key to doing so will be to anticipate the traveler in their planning process, and to get them to book directly with the hotel as opposed to going through an OTA. Fundamentally, if a hotel has a good customer profile, they can track the reason and frequency of the trip and then intercept the traveler next year through direct marketing activities. So if the person is on an annual "buddy trip" or a couple are taking an anniversary getaway, the hotel can entice them back based on the timing. Critical to this communication is the deal. The planner may be familiar with the hotel; however, they still are a Deal Seeker. The hotel needs to feed the Deal Seeker motivations and offer something enticing to close the deal. This could be a reduced room rate, but it doesn't need to be. It could be free amenities that will make the booking more appealing.

Another option is to shift the temporal nature of the deal. Shifting the deal lens from transaction (Deal Now) to relationship (Deal Later) will feed the traveler's desire to a Deal Seeker. The only issue with this tactic is frequency. If the person does not frequent the location (or chain) enough, the Deal Later scenario will lack the energy to feed the Deal Seeker's needs.

The second shift is moving someone from Brand Citizen/Deal Seeker to Brand Citizen/Price Blind. This is a bigger shift because the hotel is asking the Deal Seeker to forgo the deal. This requires changing the value equation. If the hotel is offering just a bed and the traveler perceives it that way, accommodation is just a commodity and therefore it is easy to shop around to get the best "bed." Sure, throwing in amenities like free breakfast and WiFi may help, but that tactic may lack differentiation and can be easily matched by the competition. Changing the value equation means becoming a larger part of the person's vacation. Let me give you two examples.

There is a travel target I like to use called the "Romantic Escape Artist." This person is typically a guy planning a romantic getaway for his significant other. His desire is simple: he wants to be the hero. The problem: he may have some idea of what is romantic, but honestly needs help to become that hero. The solution is for the hotel to act as a romantic concierge—to assist the Romantic Escape Artist prepare an itinerary from check-in to check-out. This itinerary is not limited to the hotel, but takes advantage of the surrounding area's restaurants, entertainment, and experiences to create a memorable getaway.

Another travel target to consider is the "Vacation Mediator." The vacation mediator tries to build consensus within the travel party. The mediator will attempt to fulfill some or all of the needs and wants of each member. Not the simplest thing to do, especially for a family. The hotel can assist the vacation mediator by highlighting core family activities nearby, as well as evening activities to keep the kids busy (and ultimately tire them out). By providing suggested secondary activities, the hotel moves from a place to crash after hitting Busch Gardens to the "Family Fun Hub." Becoming a part of the experience increases the value and therefore moves the planner from a pure Deal Seeker to leaning toward being Price Blind.

A cautionary note: the experiences need to be different than those offered by the competition. If nearby hotels all offer complimentary family breakfasts, outdoor pools, and gaming rooms, the hotel goes from Family Fun Hub to one of several hotels with family-friendly amenities—and the Vacation Mediator continues to look for the best deal.

Feed the Deal Seeker

If the Deal Seeker found the product based on a deal (or incentive), it is likely that behavior will be repeated to find the next deal. Therefore the marketer needs to feed the Deal Seeker to maintain loyalty. Let's assume a person switched their insurance to get a better deal, saving 20 percent annually. The person will wonder in a year if they can get a still better deal (as they are haunted by the monthly price combined with the reminder they can save to 15 percent or more at every commercial break). The insurance company must find a method to satisfy the person or possibly wave goodbye. Allstate, for example, offers its customers Good Driver Checks twice a year. Will this change a person's stripes? Probably not; they likely won't become Price Blind. But the question is really if the semi-annual checks are enough to quell the Deal Seeker's desire to look around.

The auto insurance example highlights the tension between getting customers in the door with a deal and then keeping their Deal Seeker DNA satisfied so they don't bolt to another brand. If the external marketing for the brand is deal-vertising and the inner view of customers is monthly payment with no loyalty incentive, then the brand is misaligned from a Deal Seeker's perspective. The brand is screaming "Hey, if you switch to me, look at this great deal I'll give you," while existing customers are treated to a mundane monthly payment—a monthly payment lacking deal energy when compared to the brand advertising.

The cable companies spiff people to jump from brand to brand based on great deals. After a period of time the deal usually expires, and normal rates are charged. The Deal Seeker subscriber then begins to look for a better deal with another brand. The deterrent from jumping from brand to brand is the effort required to uninstall one system and install another. This is hardly a case of being Price Blind; it is more an issue of convenience. But eventually the Deal Seeker DNA is strong enough to compel the subscriber to action.

At this time no cable company is offering a reduction in price for loyalty (on the contrary, many subscribers' bills creep up a little every month). Could a cable company offer loyalty incentives? Possibly. However, I am sure the financial models show the company that it is easier to take the risk of customers switching to a competitor.

An interesting recent trend is the proliferation of different options for "cutting the cord." Companies like Hulu, Sling TV and Netflix offer programming at a fraction of the price of cable. Every major provider is assessing an option to just sell on-demand programming, where a person can select and pay for only the channels they want.

Deal Seeker Blindness

Frequent deal seeking can cause a shopper to go from active deal seeking to the passive belief they are getting a deal, particularly if they often find the best deals at the same retail location. Take fueling a car as an example. A shopper may deal seek by observing prices along their route and stop at the cheapest station to fuel. This behavior continues for weeks, months, and possibly years. Heuristically the person begins to gravitate to the same station because they learned over time the best deal was at that station. Their deal seeking went from active search to regular routine to unthinking habit.

In habit mode they may believe they are getting the best price, but may actually be overpaying relative to nearby stations. This is the case in a fuel study where I asked Deal Seekers if price was the primary motivator in choosing the station. In this survey the respondents were also asked for the nearest major crossroads so I could assess whether they truly got the best price relative to nearby stations. The results showed one-third overpaid versus a station close by, sometimes by more than ten cents per gallon. The remaining two-thirds either got a comparable price or truly paid less than nearby stations. Of those who overpaid, over 50 percent habitually went to the same station (habit is defined as going to the same station four or five times in the past five fill-ups).

Can a Deal Seeker change their stripes? Sure. Affinity for a brand may steer them toward being Price Blind. While Deal Seeker DNA still exists within the shopper, the specific shopping scenario behaviorally reinforces an atypical action. The customers in the fuel example evolved from deal seeking to loyalty, all the while still believing they were getting the lowest price compared to nearby stations.

The key question in this chapter is whether brand marketing can change a shopper's stripes. A brand would prefer a shopper who is a Loyalty Laser (Brand Citizen, Price Blind, Mission). In the hotel example I discussed how the goal of the hotel is to counter OTA advertising and change the shopper's behavior. It is easier for a hotel brand to do this because in the beginning it wasn't the hotel itself that was luring the shopper with a deal—the shopper was reacting to information provided by the OTA.

If a brand itself is trying to attract customers based on a deal, then it is difficult to change the customers' stripes. With the brand's advertising rooted in the deal, they would need a second stream of marketing to shift the shopper from Deal Seeker to Price Blind. In short, they would need to change the value equation and de-emphasize the deal (and the Deal Seeker would have to be willing to go along with that). Not an easy task when the interrupt media constantly trumpet the deal!

THIRTY-THREE
Owning the Deal Ecosystem

"Happiness is paying $0.29/gallon for gas ... that's $7.25 to fill up my
#ChevyTahoe #fuelperks"
—Sally L on Twitter

Back in 2009 I worked on an initial Fuel Perks concept for Shell and Kroger. From Shell's perspective the idea was pretty simple: How do you take a deal-seeking target and get them to buy premium fuel, which is often 10 cents or more higher in price than the nearby competition? The solution was to hijack an existing loyalty program in another category and redirect shoppers to Shell by offering a 10-cent discount on a gallon of gas if they bought groceries at Kroger. The idea was to redirect the Deal Seeker from one retail brand to another.

Well, Kroger liked the idea too. They liked it so much they began opening their own fueling stations adjacent to their stores. And instead of 10 cents a gallon, Kroger allowed customers to keep accumulating Fuel Perks throughout the month and then cash them in—up to a whole dollar per gallon. While a Kroger customer can still get 10 cents off a gallon of gas at Shell, they can get ten times as much at the Kroger station.

What's fascinating about the example is that Fuel Perks is a critical part of increasing the share of grocery shopping a Deal Seeker makes in a given month. In fact, rewards that help consumers save on the cost of gasoline ranked #1 in 2016 as the most popular loyalty program.

There were three elements to Kroger's attempt to own their customers' deal ecosystem: the planning, the first trip, and other trips within a month's time.

Kroger's approach is comprehensive because it parallels the grocery Deal Seeker's journey. Think of a Deal Seeker's journey as falling into three parts (see the visual on the next page). It feeds the Deal Seeker as they search for their best deals prior to their shopping trip. It provides the deal energy within the store from aisle to aisle and at check-out. And it provides an overarching incentive to save on fuel if you continue to shop at Kroger throughout the month.

The Deal Seeker spends time to make money. They survey the competition, clip coupons, and are not afraid to go to multiple stores to get the most for their money. What Kroger does within the planning process is incorporate manufacturer coupons into their site so a shopper can simply load them onto their card. This convenient shortcut fulfills the couponer's need to save more through manufacturer coupons and combines it with the convenience of a closed system. Obviously Kroger will take physical coupons too, but the convenience of

Kroger Deal Ecosystem

| Before:
Personalized Deals | During:
Impulse Deals | Over Time:
Fuel Perks |

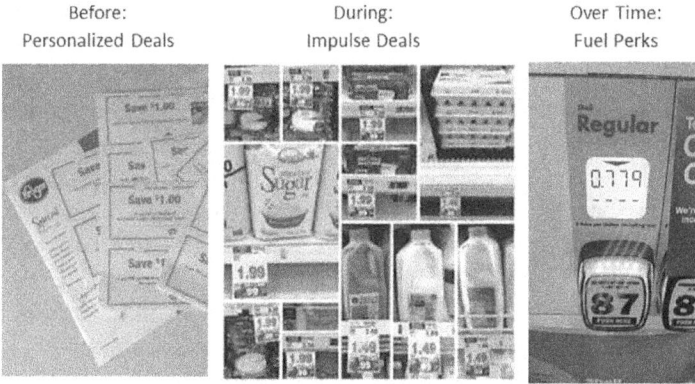

offering coupons within their own system allows them to direct the attention of the shopper and just as importantly develop a routine to shop Kroger first.

In addition to the mass offerings, Kroger also gathers information about the shopper through use of the Kroger card and sends private offers to a shopper tailored to their buying patterns. This relevant couponing increases the likelihood of coupon redemption and therefore a trip to the store.

The second element is that trip to the store and Kroger's use of in-store deals. If you look up and down the aisles you will see a myriad of price promotions feeding the Deal Seeker. On any given week the shopper will find shelftalkers promoting BOGOs, 10 for $10, buy 6 items and save $3, and new lower prices. These promotions are definitively not unique to Kroger; however, there is an expectation from many grocery shoppers that they deserve a deal. So while not unique, the in-store deal energy is critical within the overall deal ecosystem.

Finally, during the trip the shopper receives catalinas they can use on their next trip. (A catalina is a coupon that is printed out by the cashier.) These coupons are triggered by what the shopper purchased that day. During the summer Kroger also offers a coupon for twice the Fuel Points for weekend purchases. Again, smart deal energy considering the greater mobility of people during the summer and the increased use of fuel.

Sometimes deal energy is increased by the little things like the cashier reading to the shopper the amount they saved in this trip or the amount of fuel points they have accumulated month to date.

This gets me back to where I started this conversation: Fuel Perks. Fuel Perks is the thread that runs through the month. It is the stimulus to get people to come back to Kroger throughout the month in order to build their Fuel Points and cash them in for savings. Fuel incentives may not work for everyone, especially considering not every Kroger has pumps, but it provides an additional stimulus to get deal seeking shoppers back throughout the month.

Kroger is an example of a retailer expanding its reach upstream within the shopper's journey and extending it to multiple trips to convert the Deal Seeker into a Deal Loyalty. Other retailers take a different tactic and double down on the deal. One example is Speedway gas stations, with over 2,000 locations primarily in the eastern states. Speedway is a brand that not only offers a deal on the roadside marquee (normally the lowest priced fuel nearby) but which also complements it with savings in the attached convenience store through a loyalty program called Speedy Rewards. The loyalty program rewards both the customers' fuel behaviors and on-the-go purchases. The duality of the program is important since the majority of people visit a convenience store/fuel station several times a week or more. Like Kroger's loyalty program, Speedy Rewards also offers customers a monthly reward to redeem their accrued points.

Many marketers use transaction-based rewards like Kroger. The challenge for some brands is that infrequent purchases make it difficult to create deal momentum in the same way a grocery store or fuel station can. Brands like Kohl's, Ace Hardware, and Walgreens offer loyalty programs based on how much shoppers spend. Kohl's even tries to get a shopper to return through Kohl's Cash, which the person earns based on how much they purchase. The Kohl's cash is good on their next transaction; however, there is an expiration date, so the customer needs to return soon.

Another method is to increase the number of places where one can get a deal. The goal of Plenti is to offer rewards over a group of brands, including Macy's, ExxonMobil, Rite Aid, AT&T, and Chili's. The idea is to increase the frequency of rewards by combining brands from different product categories. While the concept is sound, the question is: Will a shopper switch their current retail brand(s) to those included in the Plenti program? If the person truly is a Deal Seeker, they also lean toward being a Free Agent, and Free Agents are willing to swap brands for a better deal. So, is Plenti successfully converting Free Agents to Brand Citizens? In 2016, Plenti had 36 million active users accumulating over 40 billion in points. This translates to $400 million in revenue. From a partner perspective ExxonMobil can attribute one percent of its sales to Plenti. The numbers are impressive, but it would be interesting to see how many Plenti brands are actually being used on a regular basis, or are shoppers just getting points on brands they were already using?

An interesting outlier is Costco. Their niche is simple: own destination stock-up shopping that is carried out on an infrequent basis. Membership warehouses grant shoppers access to great deals—deals the general public cannot access unless they buy a membership. Costco removed the gimmicks, minimized store aesthetics, and offer a bare-bones shopping experience focused on the deal. While the Costco experience does not feed into the deal journey like Kroger, Costco lets shoppers enter their self-contained deal ecosystem by paying for the privilege of saving money.

Costco and other warehouse clubs can offer the best deals because of their merchandising approach. Their goal is to minimally mark up prices on products, passing the savings onto their customers. Their inventory strategy is to offer differentiated, high-quality merchandise. Costco's merchandising approach fits neatly into the definition of a deal: *high-quality product at an unbelievable price.*

However, not every product is a deal at Costco. If a person is a Deal Surgeon they will benefit the most from Costco, because they are on a mission to get the best deals and will do their homework ahead of time. If they effectively use Costco in their store rotation they will maximize their savings. Conversely, if the shopper is a Bargainista, they tend to fall for the find—the impulse buy. A Bargainista could probably discern if a frequently purchased item is a deal; however, it would be more difficult to determine if an infrequently purchased item was also a deal (however, they could always showroom while at Costco).

The goal of the deal ecosystem is deal loyalty. So, what does that look like? A brand needs to understand the deal journey in their category and incorporate deal triggers into their brand deal ecosystem. A shopper will slowly gravitate from being a retail Free Agent to a retail Brand Citizen based on persistent proof of deals in a specific store. Behaviorally, they will increase use of the store within their retail rotation until the store is either exclusively used or getting a larger portion of their buying dollars.

THIRTY-FOUR

The Private Public Deal

"If you post info about a secret sale on your website,
it is no longer a secret."
—David C. on Twitter

Over the past several decades I have spent a considerable amount of time working in digital marketing. I rode the wave of the dot.com rage and experienced the doldrums when the bubble burst. There was a lot of experimentation back in the early years as marketers tried to figure out what worked and what did not. Marketers went through a "Field of Dreams" phase where the belief was that if you built a website the customers would come. Then there was the "viral video" phase, where the belief was that anyone could create a branded video that would go viral. This was closely followed by the rise of Facebook and the "everyone is a friend of my brand (especially if I bribe them to Like my brand)" phase.

Anyway, one of the more interesting conundrums in my career occurred in the automotive space. Auto websites attract millions of unique visitors every month, and the desire was to convert these active shoppers to a sale. One way to convert is to give the user a deal to act today. The challenge as a marketer was that you just don't want to throw a bundle of cash (say $500) at every purchaser—it cuts into your margins. Be that as it may, this is what we initially did. As you can imagine, this was successful, but for a different reason than we originally thought. Once the first shopper went into the dealership with the coupon, the salesperson would ask where they got it. The salesperson would then encourage all their clients to go to the website and get the coupon as a way of closing the deal. Inevitably, the "private" deal was offered to every shopper coming through the door making it, in essence, a public deal. To counter the salespersons' behaviors, we would do "burst" incentives, meaning we would turn the incentive on for 24 hours and then turn it off. Most likely by the time the salesperson found out about the incentive it was already turned off. Still this was not good enough.

The incentive was designed to convert the fence sitters—shoppers deciding between the company's own vehicles and those of competitors. By sweetening the deal, the hope is to push them to buy the vehicle. There were different targeting methods we used, including studying online media behaviors and using algorithms to determine the likelihood the shopper was a fence sitter. As you examined the shoppers' behaviors you could discern several things. The first was whether they were a Deal Seeker. The simplest way to determine this involved a combination of how they interacted with pricing information and with finance information on the site. As I discussed earlier, there are three elements in the deal triangle, and if the person was exhibiting these behaviors we could trip a coupon.

However, there was one caveat—don't be desperate. The concept of patience was difficult for many clients. If they felt they had a hot lead they wanted to close the deal right then and there. What we needed to do was figure out *when* to trigger the deal. A shopper typically would come back to the brand website multiple times. Usually a shopper close to buying would review pricing, vehicle information, and incentives. These behaviors could trip the incentive. As you can imagine, using a behavioral algorithm also solved the other problem: the behavior of the salespeople. When the shopper went to the dealership, the shark smelled blood and looked to the coupon to close many deals. However, it was virtually impossible for the salesperson to trip the coupon unless he or she followed the specific behavioral sequence.

The success rate with these coupons was pretty good, because we matched the deal with the Deal Seeker. This is where the marketer has options—they can broadcast a public deal to convert the deal seeker. If the incentive is good enough, they will convert. There is a risk—they are also creating a deal seeking behavior in which someone may only purchase the product if they get a deal.

It's been over a decade since this experience, and if anything the public private incentive has become ubiquitous. What I am talking about are deal hacks or the ability of someone to easily hack the price of a product based on a deal. Normally a deal hack is only one Google search away. For example if I Google a retailer like Lowe's or Bed, Bath and Beyond along with the words "deals" or "coupons," a series of sites will come up listing active deals for the retailer. This is not new. This is not a secret. In fact most savvy deal seekers are fully aware of this fact and are conditioned to search for a retail deal prior to making any purchase.

Some marketers combine public and private to extend the deal cycle and get the shopper to buy more. Kohl's department store uses different incentive modes to entice people to shop. They use a combination of in-store sales, direct mail coupons offering up to 30 percent off (for credit card holders), a loyalty program, and Kohl's Cash, which is loyalty cash earned based on transaction dollar amount. This Pavlovian approach works to bring in Deal Seekers. The upside of this approach is that it generates deal energy, which drives traffic and transactions. The use of different channels allows Kohl's to be selective with promotion incentives. The downside is the creation of a behavioral reinforcement to shop only during the promoted periods (i.e., when a coupon is offered). Shoppers may feel compelled to shop elsewhere if there is no incentive.

Kohl's uses a combination of public offers and private offers. They will use channels to interrupt a shopper (for example, direct mail to nearby households), as well as private communications to customers via email and their app.

The use of different channels allows a marketer to marry the right deal with the right customer. It allows for personalization and also the varying of incentives to limit the amount of discount offered.

Earlier I discussed hotels and how to move a Deal Seeker from being a Brand Citizen to a Free Agent. A further nuance to this approach is the use of different channels to intercept the Deal Seeker who is looking for a hotel. The channels range from Online Travel Agents (OTAs) to brand websites to brand emails to previous customers. Interestingly, these channels align with converting certain typologies. The diagram below displays two levels of influence. The bubbles indicate the top sources of influence for a hotel shopper. The call-outs denote the most influential source for a specific typology.

Hotel Influential Sources

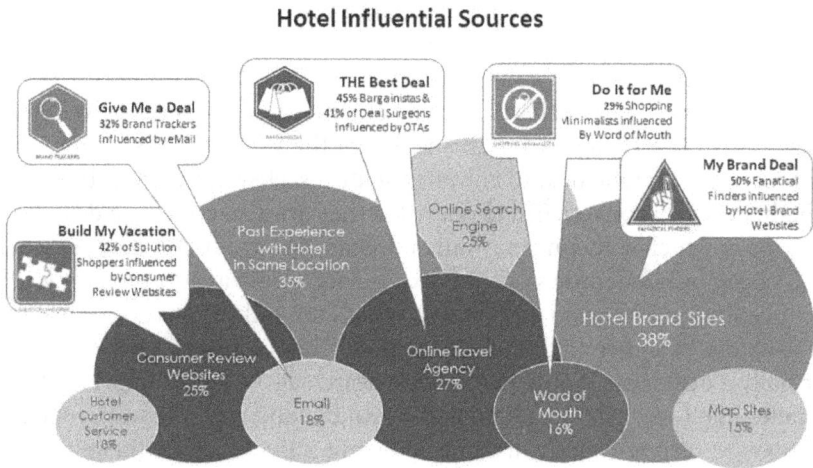

As you can see from the diagram, specific typologies are more likely to be influenced by certain sources. For example, the Solution Shopper (Free Agent, Price Blind, Journey) is simply interested in getting their hotel choice right. Brands and deals have little impact on this type of shopper. Not surprisingly, consumer review websites like TripAdvisor are more influential for them. The Shopping Minimalist (Free Agent, Price Blind, Mission) simply wants an answer and leans on others to give them one. Word-of-mouth input is a perfect match for a shopper who is looking for others to do it for them.

The deal spectrum ranges from mass offers to personalized offers. You can see this in mass typologies like Bargainista (Free Agent, Deal Seeker, Journey) and Deal Surgeon (Free Agent, Deal Seeker, Mission) and personal typologies like Brand Tracker (Brand Citizen, Deal Seeker, Mission) and Fanatical Finders (Brand Citizen, Deal Seeker, Journey). The mass typologies are more influenced by the OTAs due to their need to find the best deal regardless of brand. The personal typologies are more influenced by brand communication.

The hotel brand goal is to migrate repeat guests from OTAs to brand communications through personalized offers. The personalized offer can be more effective and also reduce the expense of re-acquiring the customer. There are several reasons for this. The customer is already familiar with the brand and therefore more likely to rebook (unless they had a bad customer experience and then all bets are off). Also, a shopper can naturally shifts from a Free Agent to Brand Citizen if the brand can create an emotive connection; however they still want a deal. The private deal operates as a proxy to make the customer feel good about the price/value of their booking (and hopefully prevent them from shopping for a deal on the OTAs).

I want to digress briefly to talk about the store versus the product deal. The store deal is designed for everyone because it offers a percentage off any merchandise in the store. A classic example is Bed, Bath & Beyond's ubiquitous 20 percent coupon. A customer with the coupon can save on any item they want. No restrictions.

Compare this to a product deal. The product deal is based on a specific item, like saving $30 on a Genie garage door opener at Home Depot. The product deal will be a great find for someone; however, its appeal is limited by the incidence level of how many shoppers buy a given product in a given year and the frequency of the purchase cycle. In the case of a garage door opener, less than five percent of people purchase a new one each year and the average duration between purchases is about 15 years.

As you can imagine the optimal approach is to blend both tactics. A public deal (store side) is designed to get the shopper in the door to buy and create familiarity. Then the product offer takes over, based on the purchase history of the shopper. Kroger applies this tactic, especially the product offer. The storewide offer is set out in their weekly insert, which offers a plethora of deals. If you look at each product individually you could categorize them as product deals; however, in aggregate there is something for everyone in the insert. Then Kroger balances this with a regular mailing of coupons to loyalty card members based on their purchase histories. The coupons offer an added incentive for the Deal Seeker to choose Kroger on their next stock-up trip. These coupons are more surgical in their approach. I am not privy to their algorithm so I don't know if they are targeting fence sitters to buy new products or rewarding shoppers for buying something they would anyway (free money).

I started this chapter talking about fence sitters and moving them to purchase. This is the role of the private deal. The marketer can use private deals surgically to move the fence sitter and thus increase sales. The alternative would be a public deal, which would increase sales but also reduce potential profit because you're basically throwing an incentive at a sale you would have gotten anyway.

THIRTY-FIVE
The Shopper Whisperer

"Social media can be a powerful tool to listen to, engage with and gain access to customers that you would otherwise not be able to connect with."
—Carol Roth, radio host and best-selling author

Social media is forever evolving. The latest and greatest fades and something else takes its place. Today very few people remember Friendster, Xanga, or MySpace. And five to ten years from now you wonder where Facebook, Twitter and Snapchat will be. They may be thriving, on life support, or in the social media graveyard in the plot next to Friendster. The reality is it doesn't matter what social media platform is hot or not, it is all about the conversation—word of mouth, something which has been around before the internet ever started. Shoppers' social behavior is an untapped resource that marketers often forget. Instead of worrying about being on the latest and greatest social media, they need to listen—listen closely to the conversation to learn about their shoppers, what makes them tick and what ticks them off.

There are many forms of shopper research. Most are biased one way or another because they artificially insert the marketer into the shopper's psyche. As I have stressed throughout this book, most shoppers act naturally. They go with the flow. In research there is an artificial occurrence. And at the point the shopper is aware of the marketer's presence they act differently, they answer differently, and the information received from the research is tainted.

This is where social media can be one of the purest forms of research. Shoppers are posting, talking and asking for advice. The conversation is a natural emanation from them and their shopping process. They are not paid and not prompted (normally) to share. If a marketer just listens they will learn much about their brand and their category.

A while back I did an analysis for Mackinac Island, a tourist destination island nestled between Lower and Upper Michigan. The primary way on and off the island is by ferry. The historic island itself is a throwback in time. There are iconic tourist attractions like the Grand Hotel, Fort Mackinac, and rides in horse-drawn carriages. Transportation on the island is limited to bicycles and horse carriages, since gas-powered vehicles are banned.

The island had a dilemma: too many tourists were coming for the day and not staying overnight. My role was to delve into the reasons why this was occurring, and (if necessary) change the island's marketing to emotively connect with the traveler to spend a night or two instead of just jumping on the ferry in the evening to get back to the mainland.

Through social analysis we looked at two different types of travelers: day and stay. They were starkly different. The day traveler was all about the activities. They talked about the iconic attractions like the Grand Hotel, biking around the island, the fort, and oh yeah, the island's world-famous fudge. On the negative side the day traveler complained about the cost for everything, and the hectic schedule to fit in all the activities. It seemed like each schedule ended with "and we just made the 5:35 ferry to get back to our hotel."

The stay traveler was part of a completely different conversation. They talked about the ambiance of the island shared with their friend and/or significant other. They described their experience more than the attractions. They may have gone to the Grand Hotel, but it did not seem like a prerequisite for their travel itinerary. The essence of the conversation ended with how refreshed they were and they couldn't wait until they returned next year.

If you compare the conversations, something stands out: the day traveler's emphasis on activities compared with the stay traveler's use of emotive words. We summed up the day traveler as Ferries, Fort and Fudge—very much a bucket list approach—while the stay traveler was Food, Photos, and Footpaths: an unplugging of the mind.

Comparing the two viewpoints on the island helped explain why the day traveler didn't stay. They saw the island as a list of activities, and once they checked the box on the activities the saw no reason to stay (and if they hurried they could complete all the activities in one day). On the other hand, the stay traveler saw the island as an experience—a romantic weekend, family getaway, destination wedding. They relished the seclusion of the island and were less likely to partake in many of the day traveler activities. The result of this listening exercise was to focus marketing more on the island as an experience and not just a list of activities.

I did the same exercise for Colonial Williamsburg. There were a lot of similarities between the two conversations. Colonial Williamsburg is very unique in that it is a working town from the time of the American Revolution. For a visitor there is plenty to do: over a hundred different activities. At the same time the place was a bit of an enigma. Unlike other attractions, you can just walk onto the streets of Colonial Williamsburg without paying. The cost comes when you enter the buildings and participate in the activities.

This fact caused confusion, with guests often not understanding why they should have to pay about $40 for a day ticket providing access to activities. One particular conversation on a travel site was revealing. The thread was about whether a person should pay for a day ticket. One person responded that they wouldn't pay for the day ticket, they would just wander the streets and check out the historic area. However, they went on, there was a cool ghost tour at night that was worth the price. In other words, walk around for free during the day and just pay for the ghost tour at night. This insight highlighted a bigger problem: the lack of premium language used to describe the experiences offered by the activities. The necessary shift was to sell premium experiences instead of focusing on the volume of activities.

At this point I would like to shift gears to completely different category, grocery shopping. If you listen closely to the online conversations in this category you will hear the voice of the Deal Seeker loud and clear. The Deal Seeker likes to share what they have found in their quest for savings. They like to brag about how much they bought for a certain dollar amount. They want to be seen as an expert. This is done in different ways; however, normally there is grounding point of relevance that others can relate to.

The Deal Seeker expresses their expertise through different themes. The most basic theme involves the product deal. An analysis of over 50,000 social media grocery posts found that about one in three mentioned a product deal. These posts basically amplified the deal promoted by the grocery store (hardly bragging, more an altruistic impulse to pass the deal on to others).

A more intriguing theme in my opinion is the "grocery haul." If you were to go to Google and search for images based on the phrase "grocery haul" plus a dollar amount, you would get a result similar to the image below.

Online Social: Grocery Haul $50

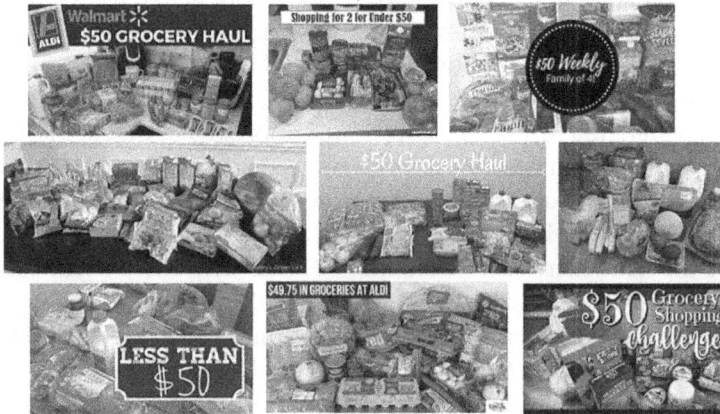

The grocery haul plus a budget is real world. Many Deal Seekers shop with the goal of getting the most for their grocery budget. A visual for a grocery haul shows product volume relative to the budgeted amount. Many of these images are part of a blog detailing the shopping trip that led to the deal haul. For what it's worth, I typed in $50, but other budgetary amounts work (e.g., $100, $150) work just as well.

I discussed the unboxing of tech products in a prior chapter. Well, if you search videos on YouTube for "grocery haul" you will get the equivalent of an unboxing video for groceries (it's more like "unbagging"). The grocery shopper details in the video how she/he saved so much money in their latest grocery haul. Many times the shopper is hitting multiple stores to get the most for their money in these videos. This is an important point—while the grocery store is shouting deal, the shopper is thinking "haul." They need to get the most for their money and it usually requires visiting multiple stores.

The product versus the cart is a conundrum for grocery brands. The grocer is shouting product deal. Some shoppers are listening and even passing the deal along to their social network. However, the shopper is thinking haul. They are not limiting their shopping to what the grocer may be promoting within their circular. No, they are trying to get the greatest possible amount of what they need. And when they are victorious they like to brag about it.

I would like to touch on one more example in this chapter and that is automotive. Automotive social media is dominated by enthusiasts and is found mainly on forums and blogs. They debate, share, and learn within the social environment. There are some vehicles with considerable conversation, while others are hardly a blip on the social media radar (unless the vehicle has a problem or recall). Normally you can gauge the amount of social media interest based on the number of owners combined with the sexiness of the design or desire for performance. This is why it is not a surprise to find conversations around Corvettes, Mustangs, or BMWs. Trucks like the Chevy Silverado, Ford F-150, and Ram have their own social stream debating the merits of different engine types, configurations, and aluminum use within the vehicle body.

One of the more surprising conversations I uncovered involved the Ford Flex about a year after it launched. For those unfamiliar with Flex, it is a boxy vehicle launched in 2008. Some people bluntly described it as a toaster on wheels. No matter how you looked at the vehicle it definitely stood out and was polarizing.

In researching vehicles through social media, our approach was to look at mentions per 1,000 owners. A typical vehicle had three to ten mentions per thousand owners. For example, the Mustang had about seven mentions per thousand and the Ford Edge about three per thousand. But when I looked at the Flex it had about six times the frequency of mentions as the Mustang. At first I was concerned the data was in error, but looking into the social data (which was indeed accurate) I discovered a significant portion of the conversation involved people who rented the vehicles. They were highly complimentary of the interior of the vehicle—it was spacious, luxurious, and the vehicle rode well. So, while the vehicle may have been described as looking like a toaster on wheels on the outside, people described the interior as a rolling living room of comfort.

What if no one is talking about a product? Yep, sometimes no one is talking. You probably already noticed the products I listed in this chapter were mostly high-consideration or deal-focused. This is the one downside to the Shopper Whisperer: you can only listen if someone is *naturally* talking. A marketer could force a conversation by bribing a shopper/customer to share; however, this is similar to research. The artificial stimulus will bias the conversation, resulting in a forced discussion. You will lose the natural insight into your customers.

THIRTY-SIX

The Channel Trap

"Technology changes all the time; human nature, hardly ever."
—Evgeny Morozov

Be careful of the channel trap.

The channel trap normally starts with a stat and a demographic. For example, over 90 percent of Millennial parents have a smartphone. The stat is impressive—that damn near includes the entire target population. And Millennials are the sexy target every marketer wants to capture in order to build brand loyalty over the shopper's entire lifetime. The stat and reasoning become a fixation: *How can we reach Millennial parents through mobile?* And the trap is sprung.

The channel trap then becomes a rabbit hole. In a short period of time, the mobile fixation results in an uncovering of every mobile stat. A deep dive into what Millennial parents do on their smartphones. Uncovering novel or cutting-edge technology to track and intercept the target. All this driving to the goal of pinging the target with a message in hopes of converting them to purchase. By the time a solution is crafted the marketer is so far down the rabbit hole, they have lost sight of the why their target would actually engage with their brand—their message.

The channel trap is alluring, especially when the channel is new. The novelty of doing something cutting-edge feeds many marketers' and channel experts' egos. They believe they are doing something press-worthy—making a name for themselves. In the digital space this is a common occurrence. Working in the space since the mid-1990s, I have seen the channel trap sprung many times. Often I was a part of the solution development. I built solutions that were far out on the digital fringe. For instance, I once was part of a team whose claim to fame was putting the first automotive video on a mobile phone—for the benefit of the 0.05 percent of mobile users who at that time had the capability to see it. However, the reality is that the majority of people live in the digital center—they use the tech device to live their life. They do not live for the tech device.

Now let's flip the Millennial parent opportunity into a scenario. Assume the person is grocery shopping. Sure, they have their smartphone with them, but now the question is: How are they using their mobile phone to make the most out of their shopping trip? What is the current benefit of the phone and possible future benefit?

The first thing to think about is the list. About 60 percent of Millennials (42 percent of shoppers overall) use a digital list, meaning the majority of shoppers overall are still using a paper list or no list at all. The purpose of the list for the shopper is simple: get the items necessary to live their life over the next week. Looking into list making, there are four primary sources for entries on the list: pantry, family, recipes, and menu planning.

Recipes are one of the primary reasons for use of a mobile phone in the store. About 66 percent of Millennials (47 percent of shoppers overall) occasionally or frequently look up recipes on a mobile phone while at the store. The recipe search may be for different reasons, but one major reason highlights the difference between planners and procrastinators. The planner will more likely create the list at home, looking at physical (e.g., cookbooks, food magazines) and digital sources (e.g., recipe sites, Pinterest) for recipe ideas and ingredients to build their list.

The procrastinator is a different story. They may have prepared a list, or, more likely, they are meal planning on the fly as they go through the store. As they mentally build their meal plan for the week, they rely on prepared solutions (e.g., frozen lasagna, frozen pizza), boxed solutions (e.g., taco kit, chili packet), or their mobile phone (I can imagine a Mission shopper reading this and getting anxious). While the mobile phone may be a meal assistant for the procrastinator, you can imagine how cumbersome it would be to combine multiple recipes and get all the ingredients in a store.

The deal journey is a critical part of grocery shopping. First off, in general Millennials are more price sensitive than other demographic groups, with twice as many Millennials checking prices than Boomers. About 67 percent of Millennial mothers look for digital coupons as a part of the grocery journey. Also, 55 percent look for weekly specials at their grocery store on their mobile phones. Finally, in a survey of the most popular apps used by Millennials, local grocery stores are second only to the Amazon app and ahead of Starbucks, Target, and Groupon.

My goal with the Millennial shopper journey scenario is not to overwhelm you with stats. The stats are used to make sure the mindset is significant enough to actually build a solution around, so the marketer stays away from the digital fringe. In general, I also prefer to focus on the mindset and not the demographic, since a mindset transcends demographics as I discussed earlier.

In building a solution for the grocery shopper, start with the scenario inherent in the shopper's journey. As with the case of the deal ecosystem, determine how you can extend the brand experience to integrate it into their journey. Let's say you want to increase the level of influence over the shopper's list making. Well, you need to look at the sources used (i.e., pantry, family, recipes, meal planning). Two stand out: recipes and meal planning. Both are viable options around which to create a brand experience.

So what about the device?

The reality is the device activates the shopper motivations. It is important to understand how a shopper is motivated first, then examine their behaviors second. A common example is showrooming. A shopper who is showrooming uses their phone in a store to search for a better deal online or at another store. Many times the goal of the retail visit is to see or use a product before purchase. Showrooming amplifies the Deal Seeker's motivation to ensure they are getting the best deal, either in the current store or elsewhere.

Searching for a deal predates the internet by decades (if not centuries). Shoppers have always been willing to exert the effort to get the deal. If this meant driving across town to save a few bucks, well, get in the car and let's go. If it meant clipping coupons, it was worth the effort. Better yet, save the coupons for double coupon days at the grocery store to maximize the deal. The difference between today and the time before the internet lies in the fact that devices provide omni-access to the ability to search for deals—any place, any time.

The digital age is not limited to just deal searching. Different typology motivations result in using sources differently even through the journey may be perceived as the same. Some sources are digital—some are not.

One shopper tendency I touched on earlier involved their approach to planning: *Are they a planner or a procrastinator?* Planners are more likely to be Mission shoppers. They like structure in their shopping experience; therefore they normally have a plan. The plan normally takes shape through a list. Generating a list is made easy through internet enabled planning tools and list generating apps. If the shopper is grocery shopping, they can use meal planning websites, Pinterest, or recipe sites like All Recipes or Food Network. Many sites support the creation of a shopping list; however, the shopper could also use list apps like GroceryIQ, or a grocery store's app. Digital devices provide the Mission shopper the means to structure their shopping experience so they spend the least amount of time in the store. This is where ecommerce inroads are being made with Amazon's Prime Pantry and many grocery stores' order and pick-up services (e.g. Kroger's ClickList, Walmart and Jet). These services combine the minimalistic approach to shopping with a planner's mindset.

Procrastinators are sketchy list makers and prefer to see what options are out there. Given this motivation, they have no problem making decisions while in the aisle of the store. Their device of choice is the mobile device because it assists them with their decision making. So what are they accessing? Well, they are accessing on-demand solutions. Those solutions vary by type of store. If they are meal planning in the grocery store, they may be accessing Pinterest to find a killer gumbo recipe or different ideas on how to cook the chicken breasts that are on sale for $1.99 per pound. The shopper may be in a hardware store trying to find the parts to fix a plumbing problem. They probably could ask the sales associate for help, or they may access YouTube to watch a video on how to fix their problem. Finally the shopper could be showrooming at an electronics store to ensure they are buying the right television at the best price.

Digital provides two divergent scenarios based on planning tendency. The procrastinator feels empowered because they can have a successful outcome with little or no planning. The planner feels empowered because their success is a combination of structure and an expeditious shopping experience.

The travel industry has had sweeping changes since the advent of the internet. No longer does someone need to use a travel agent. Travel has become self-serve with a myriad of sites to assist the shopper in planning their vacation or finding the best deals on hotels or flights. Once at the vacation destination, the traveler may make in-the-moment decisions like where to find an nice Italian dinner or what activities they can do indoors because of an unexpected rain storm on the second day. There are many apps to help travelers make these decisions.

Keep in mind: these are information sources, not motivations.

Travel planners are motivated differently. The desire to save money is paramount with the Deal Seeker and they are willing to sacrifice amenities at a hotel, accept low-budget meal options, and/or willing to take a layover (or two) to save hundreds of dollars on airfare. Their deal scenario is facilitated by the many websites and apps now available. An extreme Deal Seeker may have a commodity view of hotels and airlines. It is all about price.

Counter this frugal scenario with the travel planner who is not interested in the best deal but, rather, wants the most out of their vacation experience. They are into building their itinerary. They are looking for *advice* on the best destinations, hotels, and restaurants *based on their preferences*. Let me stress this point: *This travel planner is looking for advice from other travelers like them.* Many sites offer general ratings for hotels, restaurants, and entertainment options. This aggregated approach blends everyone together. This poses a problem for the advice seeker. Let's assume the planner is looking for advice on how to make the getaway to Chicago as romantic as possible. Most general sites don't offer that type of advice. Some come close by offering a filter based on the word "romantic." However, the results are often just generic ratings of the patron's hotel stay or restaurant experience. Instead of trying to find advice, the travel planner will most likely search the web for advice from a travel expert or blogger.

The point of all this is that there is no shortage of travel sites or information accessible to the travel planner. The problem for some travel planners is the lack of *relevant* advice based on the planner's motivation. This is because many digital experiences are created from the data "out," instead of developing an experience based on the travel planner's own scenario, which is rooted in finding the right solution for their travel party.

This is the channel trap in a nutshell. There is too much emphasis on a device, a channel, or a site, and people lose sight of *why* someone is accessing the internet. They are looking for advice to make a decision, and the device used just happens to be the most convenient device at that moment.

THIRTY-SEVEN

The Behavioral Funnel

"The Traditional Funnel is Kaput."
—*Adweek*, March 10, 2014

In marketing the funnel is a tired metaphor. Over the years I have read articles about inverting the funnel and flattening the funnel, and in one memorable instance the funnel looked like a three-dimensional cone with shoppers spiraling down it as if they were inside a toilet bowl. The most common phrase I have heard throughout my career is "Let's fill the funnel." The logic is sound: if we get more shoppers into the funnel, theoretically more should come out the bottom.

For the uninitiated, the funnel is a logical flow of stages a shopper will go through, from awareness through purchase. Typical steps for a high-consideration purchase may include the following:

Classic Marketing Funnel

Awareness

Opinion

Consideration

Preference

Purchase

There is a secret, a nuance, which lies in the depth of the funnel—a nuance that perplexes marketers. Normally, the top of the funnel (Awareness through

Consideration) has a healthy slope, slowly dropping as you would expect. But then something in the funnel breaks, falling off severely somewhere after Consideration. Most clients are perplexed. How can shoppers like their product, consider it, and then just drop out of their funnel? In short, they were trying to figure out why they had a *Consideration cliff.*

A typical marketer reaction is to scour data to determine the primary reasons why a shopper didn't buy the product. Why did they choose the competition? Why was there a severe drop-off after Consideration?

Normally the data is an introspective look at product attributes relative to the prospective shopper. This product-centric orientation will focus on key attributes of the product. The general strategy of many marketers is to find out why the product was not purchased and then adjust the messaging within ads so as to fix the funnel. Problem solved!

Not so fast.

The problem is that the client is most likely looking in the wrong place. There is a shift mid-funnel. If the shopper in the funnel could talk, they would probably say something like, "Dude, it's not you, it's me." Yep, the ultimate break-up line. The reason is simple—and it comes into play when a person moves from *thinking* to *doing*. This point occurs typically at or right after Consideration. The diagram below illustrates the point.

The Two Shopper Mindsets
Vacuum Cleaner Example

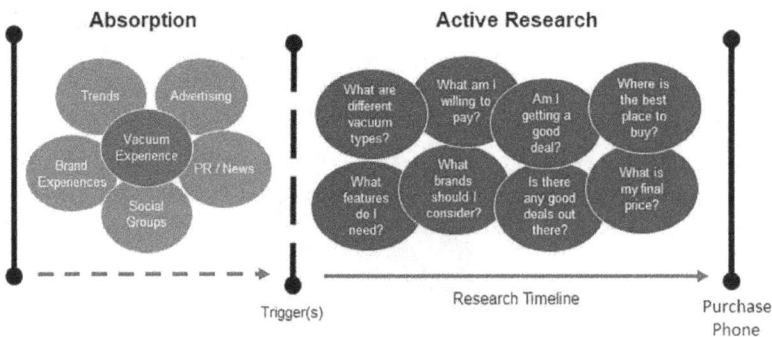

The shopper's journey can be split into two distinct phases for considered purchases: Absorption and Active Research. In Absorption, the shopper is thinking about the next purchase. The purchase may be weeks away, or even years. Since the shopper has not identified themselves behaviorally, the marketer needs to sprinkle the infield by reaching prospects through their media consumption. The goal is pretty simple: get on the Consideration list. Once the person begins researching, there still may be a chance to get on the Consideration list; however, it is an uphill battle trying to displace brands that are already there.

There is a trigger that moves a person to the active research stage. Depending on the product, the trigger will vary. Sometimes the previous product breaks, the shopper may get a windfall from (say) a tax refund, or they may feel they're finally ready to buy a new product. Whatever the trigger, the shopper moves from thinking to acting and begins actively researching the product.

In active research the shopper will move through their decision path, which will culminate in the purchase of the product. To make these decisions, the shopper will use different sources. This is where Brand, Wallet and Time influence the decision.

Let's say a shopper is buying a vacuum cleaner. They haven't bought one for years; however, they are persistently hearing about how good a Dyson is. During the Absorption phase they have Dyson in their *consideration set*. The consideration set is a non-binding set of brands that are not rooted in a shopper's reality, because they didn't apply their DNA to these brands. In the case of Dyson, the shopper quickly dismisses the product because they are unwilling to spend $400 on a vacuum cleaner. Their price tolerance is in the $100 to $200 range. Oh yeah, the shopper is a Deal Seeker and they want a deal (and Dyson does not typically offer deals).

It is easier for a marketer to address what they can control. Many times upper-funnel communication methods (like traditional media) are within the marketer's control, while the retail environment is not as easy to control. The belief is that if the value of the brand is increased through advertising then funnel throughput will increase, generating more sales.

Many marketers fail to assess the funnel behaviorally. The behavioral funnel is inverted. It begins from the purchase and works backwards. Why, you may ask? Well, true shopper motivations are revealed at Purchase. There is no hiding preferences then: all is revealed.

At purchase you can behaviorally assess the journey that shoppers took. In a study of mobile phone purchases, I analyzed the difference between shoppers buying from a cellular provider versus a big box retailer like Best Buy. The difference is stark, but makes sense, as the diagram on the next page shows.

It is no surprise the deck is stacked against Best Buy for different reasons. First and foremost is the relationship a shopper likely has with their cellular provider. When it comes to purchasing a new phone, the shopper will think AT&T or Verizon first—Best Buy may not even be considered. This is not for lack of effort on Best Buy's part. They have been advertising their brand as a mobile solutions store for years.

If the shopper does do research online, Best Buy may have an opportunity to get on the list; however, they need to intercept the shopper based on the

Mobile Phone: Behavioral Funnel

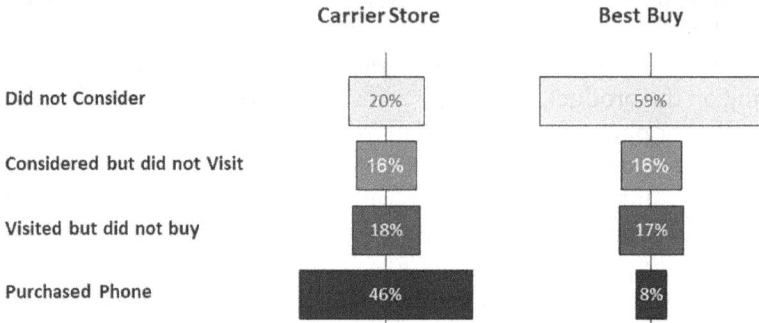

	Carrier Store	Best Buy
Did not Consider	20%	59%
Considered but did not Visit	16%	16%
Visited but did not buy	18%	17%
Purchased Phone	46%	8%

shopper's motivations (e.g., a deal, expert assistance, exclusive brands) to redirect them to purchase at Best Buy. Not an easy task.

To mine opportunities with the behavioral funnel you need to look at the *path of least resistance*. The idea is to work backward from purchase. (This is *not* a matter of flipping the funnel—another phrase as tired as the funnel metaphor itself.)

Looking at the purchase is very insightful because it tells a marketer who bought and, more importantly, *why* they bought. This provides a view of both the product and shopper in tandem. What typologies dominated the purchase? Were shoppers more likely to be Bargainistas, Solution Shoppers or another typology? This will help the marketer understand how marketing is resonating with shoppers, and therefore may be used to attract other shoppers with the same motivations.

Along with shopper motivations, the product needs to be scrutinized relative to the competition. What attributes of the product resonated with customer? Did they consider any other product? If so, was it a product-differentiated factor driving the purchase? Or did shopper motivations play the bigger part?

Consider a person buying a new truck. They may be looking at two trucks, say a Ford F-150 and Chevrolet Silverado. They view both products as good and are driven to who can give them the lowest monthly payment. Sometimes this decision can come down to nothing more than a ten-dollar difference on that monthly payment. Given pride in their brand and products, many companies don't want to believe the decision came down to (a relatively few) dollars and cents; however, the reality is that it does sometimes.

Moving backward from Purchase, consider those who bought the competition. Just as with those who bought your product, the idea is to triage the reasons why the shopper rejected your product. Again: was it a product attribute, shopper motivation, or a combination of both?

Or maybe the answer involves a dominant typology. This is a consistent problem with clients who turn deals on and off. Let's say a competitive buyer had the Deal Surgeon typology. This person is driven by the deal they know of or can find, prior to going in the retail environment. Their behavior is driven by coupons or sales. If so, the marketer would need to incentivize the competitive shopper to choose them in the future (or decide the margin on the shopper is not worth the effort).

If the product is a high-consideration purchase, the decision path provides insight into the core decisions the shopper made in choosing the final product. Instead of stepping through the funnel, a marketer could apply the decision path to individual sources to determine how shoppers used the source and how effective the source was in moving the shopper closer to purchase. (I will discuss how to execute this in an upcoming chapter.)

Moving up the behavioral funnel, the next stage is Consideration. This is normally the tipping point between thinking and acting. If shopping were a race, this is the starting line. The question at this point is: Was the product/brand in a leadership position? Or did they lag behind the competition? Or was the product possibly not even in the consideration set?

This was the case for Chamberlain garage door openers. The dominant brand is Genie and most people start with Genie on the list (sometimes it's the only brand on the list). If a person bought a garage door opener in three days or less, 61 percent of shoppers did not consider Chamberlain, with two-thirds stating they were unaware of the brand. However, for those who took longer than three days the likelihood of buying a Chamberlain garage door opener increased dramatically.

Garage door opener shoppers are a tough breed. They most likely are shopping under duress, with an immediate desire to replace their broken garage door opener. So, it is not a surprise to find that about one in three are Shopping Minimalists (Free Agent, Price Blind, Mission). They just want it done. Their perspective on brands is also minimalist, with about two-thirds of shoppers agreeing with the statement, *They didn't buy a brand, they bought a garage door opener.* This mindset does not bode well for any brand, let alone a brand like Chamberlain which has lower awareness levels.

So why were shoppers who spend more time more likely to choose Chamberlain? The reason was positive conversation about Chamberlain online. If a person did their own research, there was a tendency to gravitate toward and buy Chamberlain. Now, if you're the client, you have two choices: Ask people to do their due diligence (not happening!), or try to increase your brand's top-of-mind awareness. Increasing top-of-mind awareness for garage door openers is a daunting goal, especially when the product is bought only every 15 years or so. To increase top-of-mind awareness, Chamberlain needs to disrupt the belief that Genie is the only brand. This won't be easy, since under normal circumstances (i.e., when they are working properly) garage door openers are probably the last thing on people's minds. So, subtlety will not work.

One last thing to consider is the *trigger*. The trigger in a shopper journey is the tipping point that moves a shopper from "thinking about a purchase" to "actively shopping for the product." The trigger is important because it will provide insight into the timeliness of the decision process. Was there a life-stage transition prompting the person to act? Maybe the person came into some extra money from a tax refund or a bonus from work? Maybe the previous product broke or was stolen.

The behavioral funnel brings together shopper motivations and their decision path to triage the reasons why some shoppers buy a certain brand while others choose a different one. The reasons can be competitive, environmental, or scenario-based. The behavioral funnel (together with shopper motivations and decision paths) create an objective way to analyze what is really happening in the marketplace.

PART FOUR

Activating the Primal Shopper

"It's always about mindshare, not market share."
—Ron Johnson, Canadian politician

The marketplace is full.

Imagine a large rectangular box drawn on a white board. The box represents the entire market for a specific industry. What industry we're talking about really doesn't matter but for the sake of discussion let's choose grocery stores. The grocery marketplace box is split into puzzle pieces representing the market share for each grocery brand. Each brand wants to increase share—they want to make their puzzle piece bigger. There are only two ways this will happen: take share from someone else or get more people to grocery shop. Odds are there isn't going to be a surge of new grocery shoppers, so the box isn't getting any bigger. This means the brand needs to steal share from a competitor. They need to give the competitor's shoppers a compelling reason to switch.

The reality is there are plenty of grocery options for most people, and many of them already have a "go-to" grocery store or a rotation they use for stock-up, product and meat. As well, most people are probably content with their options. It is doubtful anyone is sitting at home saying, "Geez, I wish there was another grocery store I could go to." So, to get share a grocery brand needs to get the shopper to rethink their habit—their rotation. The marketing needs to be disruptive enough that the shopper takes notice and evaluates the new store relative to their current choices.

Disruption is a bit of a tired word but it is important to understand what I mean. Disruption in the holistic sense would change the marketplace. A brand would create a new offering or product that would redefine the category. The brand market shares in our grocery box would be repartitioned based on a new paradigm. In the grocery category this could be the growing use of ecommerce. Whether it is Amazon Prime or Kroger's ClickList (where the store packs the groceries and loads your car), the proliferation of ecommerce alternatives may redimensionalize the share chart (especially for Mission shoppers, who view grocery shopping as a chore).

This is not the disruption I am referring to.

The disruption I am focused on is disruption of a person's habit or beliefs. This kind of disruption is necessary to move the shopper attitudinally—to get them to consider a new product. Normally, disruption occurs through interrupt channels like television, online video, direct marketing, or word of mouth. Video has the sensory capacity to engage a viewer, but the message needs provocation to get the person to rethink their choice.

Word of mouth as an interrupt mechanism is even more powerful, yet harder to do. If someone lauds their brand purchase or experience, there is no better form of marketing. Believability and relevance are why it's so powerful. Usually, the person doing the advocating is known to the recipient and therefore believable, especially if they are someone the recipient trusts. Secondly, the communication can be more relevant since the participants know each other. Remember my mother's ALDI experience. ALDI's marketing did not persuade her. What persuaded her was a conversation with a group of women who advocated for two brands, ALDI and Costco, as the stores with the best deals.

Moving the shopper attitudinally is only half the equation. A marketer must also move them behaviorally. To do so, the marketer must speak to the shopper DNA. It's a combination of getting the shopper to try the product the first time and then reinforcing the behavior in the future. In the previous chapter, I talked about the Consideration cliff, the point at which marketers are able to move a target attitudinally but fail to convince the shopper to buy their product.

Intercept channels are critical in moving the shopper behaviorally. Such channels are the primary sources a shopper uses to make decisions. The sources could be online, traditional (e.g. inserts, direct mail), or within the retail store itself. The channels will change by product because of differences in the decision path to the final choice.

This section tells you how to activate the principles and practices outlined in this book. The first two chapters focus on the nuances moving a target attitudinally. The next two chapters outline how to create powerful experiences to influence the shopper's decision. The final chapter is an introspective look at ad agencies and how to deliver an integrated channel experience to move the shopper.

THIRTY-EIGHT

Marketing to the Mindset

A friend told me a story about focus groups he had attended to get a better understanding of pick-up truck buyers. The goal of the focus groups was to get insight on how owners related to their trucks. There was a divergence between owners. One set of owners used their trucks for work. Their trucks were like a tool in their toolbox—a critical tool. Without it, they could not get their work done.

The other set of owners viewed their trucks as a just-in-case functional part of their lives. Unlike the first group, they did not use the truck every day. They used it occasionally to haul a boat or camper, do yard work, or help someone move. They liked the idea they had this on-demand functionality in their lives, even if the truck was used this way only about 10 percent of the time.

Obviously two different mindsets. The key insight from the focus group is that each owner group aligned to a different brand. So what to do next? Does the brand market to the mindset or to the competition's customers? If you are targeting the 10 percent-usage group do you show real work or leisure activity?

This scenario highlights a conundrum in marketing: who do you target? There are different options. A marketer can target a demographic segment like Millennials or women 35–54 with children. Or they could target the industry (i.e., anyone who is a primary grocery shopper). Similarly, a marketer can target specific competitors to grow their share. Targeting the competition makes logical sense to many marketers because to increase their own share, a competitor's share must go down.

Fundamentally, however, these approaches are flawed because marketing just isn't about exposure—it's about persuasion. It's about convincing someone to try something they haven't tried up till now. It's about convincing an existing customer to keep buying a product. The first step in conquering the competition is getting the target to rethink their choices. It is about moving them attitudinally. The most effective method to move the target is to market to their mindset.

To illustrate the nuances of this approach let's look at a simple example. Let's say your company is selling a fresh salsa to grocery stores. The salsa market is relatively crowded, with national (e.g., Chi-Chis, Pace, Tostitos), regional and store brands.

Shoppers have different perceptions of canned and fresh salsa. There are several reasons for this. The canned salsa is stocked with the rest of the Mexican products, conveniently located where a shopper decides on their Mexican dinner or snack. Fresh salsa is not in the decision aisle. It is located somewhere else in the store where it can be refrigerated. The other nuance is price. Fresh salsa normally carries a premium price compared to canned brands.

In analyzing the salsa shopper there are different motivations to consider, but the first thing we need to discard is habit. If the shopper purchased the same brand the last five times they bought salsa, then we remove them from the analysis. Why? It would take an inordinate amount of marketing to get them to switch. Even then, they are probably operating on auto pilot and salsa marketing is like white noise to them.

From a shopper perspective the two primary DNA strands driving the decision are Brand and Wallet. If you break the DNA into a quadrant (see below) there are areas of opportunities and some territory that may be not worth the investment.

Salsa Shopper Matrix

Brand Citizen – Price Blind *Willing to pay the price for their brands.*	**Free Agent – Price Blind** *Looking more for food appeal based on their current situation.*
Brand Citizen – Deal Seeker *Typically buys the same brand(s) and is looking for ways to reduce the cost (e.g. sale, coupon).*	**Free Agent – Deal Seeker** *Most likely views salsa as a commodity and is looking to get the best price.*

For the sake of argument let's assume the salsa in question is a premium brand made of fresh organic ingredients with a limited shelf life. One quadrant would not be worth the effort: Free Agent – Deal Seeker. Price is paramount for these shoppers and unless you are going to deeply discount you would not be appealing to this target.

The Brand Citizen typologies (Price Blind and Deal Seeker) are viable targets but they will require some investment to interrupt the shopper. We would need to get the shopper to rethink their current brand(s) and/or add our salsa to their brand rotation. A key tactic to employ would be some type of trial. This could be through a coupon or sampling within the store.

The remaining target (Free Agent – Price Blind) is also a viable target. As with the Brand Citizen targets, we would look to deploy interrupt and trial techniques, but with a difference in messaging. The interrupt would be focused more on the originality of the salsa combined with promoting different flavors (e.g., peach salsa, black bean salsa, pineapple salsa).

Getting on the list is only half the battle. There is a secondary habit we would need to market against: their current shopping path. Given this is fresh salsa it would need to be located in a refrigerated area, apart from where the other salsas are sold. If the salsa decision is made in the Mexican food section, then our brand will neither be considered nor purchased. The location poses a challenge in attracting buyers, especially the Free Agent – Price Blind target.

We would need to be on the shopper's list or have some type of retail promotion directing the shopper to the right location in the store.

Salsa is a relatively simple example. As you can imagine, a high-consideration purchase is much more complex. There are two mindsets to consider: customer and shopper. The customer mindset can be defined as how the person views the product within their life. This includes the necessity and desire of the product, emotive attachment to brands, and how the product (or brand) relates to their passions in life. We could break out salsa customers based on meal planners, foodies, and social events. For example, meal planners and foodies can be intercepted on recipe sites, where they are searching for new recipes or meal ideas. If you choose to employ this tactic, you don't want to be a wallflower on the web page—your brand needs to be part of the editorial. Preferably, you would work with the site publisher to create native content that lives within the page and integrates your product into the overall editorial content. If banners are the solution, then think relevant context—the banners should be about an appetizing solution, either for meals or snacks.

The social event target comprises two mindsets: host and guest. The host is focused on throwing the perfect party and is looking for recognition from guests through compliments. The guest, keeping with social convention, intends to bring something to the event. The guest may be also looking for social recognition, especially if they are bringing an appetizer or dish to pass around.

Now take a step back and think about the following question: How would people react if a person came to the party with a store-brand product? In the case of salsa, how would people react differently to a private label salsa versus a fresh salsa?

In summary, there are two core mindsets for a shopper. The first mindset is based on the product relationship—their emotional desire in purchasing the product. Desire runs a spectrum from *all brands are pretty much the same* to *advocate for the brand*. Odds are that in any category there will be different proportions of people who view a product as a commodity and those who are passionate about a given product. It is important to isolate these different mindsets because you need to market to them differently.

The second mindset involves core shopper motivations—the DNA driving their retail decisions. Sometimes the brand is highly desirable, but the shopper DNA rejects the brand in favor of another product because it's a better deal or easier to purchase.

Isolating the mindset uncovers the core motivations that drive decisions—motivations that a brand must market to in order to convert customers. Comparing and contrasting those who bought and those who did not buy helps isolate different factors. Two critical points to analyze are *consideration* and *conversion*. By consideration I mean the list of brands a shopper considered at any point of their journey, while conversion encompasses the reasons the final product was in fact purchased.

THIRTY-NINE
Passion Platforms

Traverse City, Michigan is about a four-hour drive from any major city, tucked inside the Grand Traverse Bay on the Lake Michigan shoreline. The area is known for cherries, local wineries and lake-effect snow blanketing the nearby ski resorts. Truly a picturesque tourist destination, but hardly a film mecca. Yet it is—at least for one week during the summer.

How does a sleepy resort town on Lake Michigan create a film following? With three things: event persistence, passion, and a film-making celebrity in the person of Michael Moore, who founded the festival in 2005. Back then there were only a modest 31 films, 10 industry guests, and 50,000 paid admissions. Over the years the city built momentum. By 2016, the festival attracted over 200 films, 175 industry guests and sold over 123,000 tickets.

The festival is an example of how to build a "passion following" over time in an out-of-the-way destination. I talked about our Passion alter ego in a previous section, noting how our shopper motivation is often altered when we are passionate about a product or category. I am sure for every successful festival like the Traverse City Film Festival there are ten festivals that fail because the person marketing the event failed to understand traveler motivations and how to build momentum over time.

As I already mentioned, Traverse City is in wine country with numerous vineyards dotting the landscape. While the region is not a national destination like Napa or Sonoma, the local wineries compete for travelers in the Midwest, and there is indeed considerable competition. In the five-state Great Lakes area (Michigan, Ohio, Illinois, Indiana, and Illinois), there are hundreds of wineries. As you can imagine, attracting travelers is a challenge. Success lies in understanding why people go to wineries and then marketing to the passion or desire of the travel planner. Let me explain.

With the hundreds of Midwest wineries the diversity of wines is extensive. On the surface you might think the passion for wine is the primary driver for visitors. For some it probably is; however, for many there is a deeper motivation behind their vacation decision. If you were to audit social posts for Midwest wineries, several themes would emerge. There are two types of travelers: friends and couples. Friends toast each other to mark various occasions like bridal showers or just a girls' getaway. The couples may be toasting each other too, or romantically walking through the vineyard. Either way, at the core of the experience lies one key word: *intimacy*. Sure, wine is tasted and stories exchanged, but the core motivation for a wine getaway is to connect with someone else in a meaningful way.

At the core of a *passion platform* is a desire—the desire of the shopper/

planner. This desire does not change over the course of the shopping or planning journey. It is the guidepost or filter for the shopper's decisions. For most high-consideration purchases there is an overarching desire (or passion) driving the decision. In the case of the film festival, the passion for films drives people to come far and wide to Traverse City.

Sometimes there is limited competition in delivering on the desire, while in other categories there may be many brands that can deliver. Either way, the bottom line is that the product or experience purchased is the one that can make an emotional connection based on the shopper's desires.

Sticking with the wine example, if you were to look at marketing for the wineries in the Midwest you would mostly find the expected shots of wine cellars, grapes, wine bottles, and vineyards. What is marketed is a product-centric perspective on the winery. What's missing are the traveler's desires: the intimacy of how a particular winery caters to a girls' getaway, offering memorable activities to rehash over a glass of Merlot, or how the winery provides a picture-perfect backdrop (complete with couple activities) for a romantic weekend.

Passion platforms can apply to everyday products, too. Food is a cluttered category where many desires co-exist, ranging from an epicurious desire to create extravagant recipes to a pragmatic desire to create simple family meals throughout the week. There is no shortage of websites, cookbooks, magazines, and TV shows on the subject. Content is not an issue; however, if you look at the weekly shopping routine, very few grocery stores have cracked the code on helping the shopper.

Most grocery apps are focused on making a list. An app like Kroger's allows a user to create a list from all the products in the store. The user can type in the product or scan the bar code of an existing product in their pantry. A user can also clip digital coupons and save them to their card to be redeemed at checkout. Finally, the user can choose their store and the app will order the items by the aisle in which they're located. The Kroger app does a nice job of list management, but it does not meet the shopper's desire for recipe creation or meal planning. The burden is on the shopper to pre-plan meals and recipes before they even begin to type in a list.

A food passion platform takes into account the shopper's desire and designs ways to fulfill that desire through marketing content and/or experiences. Sure, grocery stores often offer recipe cards in the store, but this is too little, too late for many shoppers since the majority of planning is done at home. I would like to think as grocery apps mature they will go beyond functional list management and into actively assisting in meal creation.

As you can see from each of the passion platform examples, the target's desires are central. The brand experience must deliver on those desires. Doing so leads to purchase and engagement.

FORTY

It's About Time

During the dotcom era the consensus belief was that if you built a website people would come. Well, many sites were built, but few came. So, some companies changed their names, adding ".com" at the end, because then people would know how to find their sites (and make them look cool). The tactic didn't help their web traffic (or make them look cool).

Now let us fast forward to the rise of Facebook. Brands believed that if they built a page their multitude of fans would "like" them. Many pages were built and some brands' Facebook pages did attract fans. Other brands needed to bribe fans to "like" them, and some brands have yet to feel the love of their fans (or they realized they overestimated the size of their fandom).

Somewhere between the dotcom era and the social surge came the rise of YouTube and online video viewing. The catchphrase uttered by many clients was "viral videos." Just create a video and people will not only view it—they will share it. So, brands created videos and some of these went viral (less than 1 percent) while the majority of videos idled online awaiting viewers who never came.

I don't know about you, but there appears to be a pattern here. Many marketers hold a brand-centric view in which everyone loves their brand as much as they do. Hey, it's okay for a client to love their brand. They put a lot of effort into creating a great product and marketing. The missing perspective is that of their target. What do they love? What do they watch? What do they desire? Who do they connect with socially? In other words, how do they spend their time online?

This is the universal question: *Why would someone give up their time to engage in a brand experience?*

I touched on this in the last section in talking about the abysmal click-through rate for banners. The reality is not "build it and they will come"; rather, it is that there needs to be a compelling reason for people to give up some of their precious time. Some brands address this issue well, while many struggle with it.

To get a person to come to a brand experience, there needs to be a value exchange: if the person gives up their time, what do they get in return? The answer to this time question lies in six value propositions that are inherent in successful experiences. These value propositions are derived from an audit of over 1,200 online and offline experiences in eleven different industries. The value propositions are not mutually exclusive nor are they a checklist. Rather, they are thought-starters, intended to help marketers create a robust brand experience. In many respects the following section brings the various insights presented in this book together, encouraging you to think about how to apply them to create a "win-win" situation for both the brand and the shopper.

The six value propositions are Knowledge, Money, Simplicity, Social, Reward, and Entertainment. In the following pages I will explain each value proposition and give several examples of when and where they were executed correctly.

Knowledge: Consult the Shopper

There is no shortage of information on the internet. Search engines are a gateway to any type of information a shopper would need—or are they? Ironically, in the digital age there is plenty of information but very few answers. Think about a shopper's decision path. They are searching for *answers*, not information. You might think these are one and the same thing. They are not: let me explain.

Let's say a shopper is looking to purchase a new HDTV. They may have an idea about what they are looking for from past experience, but they could easily be overwhelmed because of the rapid evolution of TV tech. How many people truly know the difference between 2160p and 1080p? Or between a refresh rate of 60 hertz versus 120 hertz? And what the heck is Motionflow XR 960 and Clear Action 240? A shopper might surmise that in many cases the higher the number the better the television, and in general this is true, but is the higher number worth the added cost?

A few years back I stumbled upon an interesting approach from Samsung. On their brand site they had a seven-step process to help shoppers find the right television. Instead of focusing on product specifications, the experience focused on the shopper's needs. For example, in the first step the person provided the amount of space available on the wall. The next step asked the user to give the distance from television to the seating area. The consultative experience continued through the rest of the questions, from room lighting to primary usage (e.g., sports, gaming, movies) to budget. Upon completing the questions a list of recommended televisions based on the shopper's needs would be provided.

As you can see from the example, a shopper doesn't need to become a tech geek to figure out which HDTVs meet their needs. To build a knowledge experience, the brand needs to "*go shopper*"—to think shopper first. A brand should think about what decisions the shopper is trying to make and construct an experience to provide appropriate answers and advice.

Another example is the Lowe's video series on YouTube. You Tube has become the default go-to for DIY'ers, especially in home improvement. There are videos on how to fix appliances, landscape your yard, and remodel a kitchen. Lowe's smartly integrated their DIY content into the YouTube platform so they are right there on the site where DIY'ers are searching for answers.

Lowe's has a wide array of how-to videos to assist the shopper, everything from simple fixes like unclogging a sink to remodeling an entire kitchen. The kitchen remodeling videos range from inspirational ideas to help the homeowner envision their dream kitchen down to detailed how-to videos on replacing a countertop, refreshing kitchen cabinets, or putting in a tile floor. A recent addition to the Lowe's YouTube channel is a webisode series entitled *The Weekender*. Each video includes five simple projects a homeowner can do around their house.

The approach Lowe's takes is congruent with the Solution Shopper typology (Free Agent, Price Blind, Journey). This shopper is very much the home remodeler—their desire is to complete a project, whether it is fixing an appliance or sprucing up the back yard. Lowe's is offering free advice to create a brand connection and attempting to make the brand the solution center. The video series appears to be connecting with DIY'ers. The channel contains several hundred videos so far, with viewership of most over 100,000 and for some videos in excess of one million views.

Money: The Deal Equation

I spent a fair portion of this book talking about the Deal Seeker and their desire to save money. If a brand has many Deal Seeker customers, they need to consider how to increase the perceived deal the shopper is getting.

In the chapter "Feel the Deal," I discussed the deal equation and how a shopper interprets a deal. Fundamentally, this is the basis for how to increase the value of a brand through the experience. The trick to this is to sell a solution based on a desire, not a bunch of features. In fact, selling individual features of a product may backfire, in that it forces the shopper to think logically about whether all the features are in fact relevant and needed. If the majority of features are irrelevant to the shopper, then the brand is pretty much talking to itself.

If possible, a brand is better off selling based on the shopper's desire (think passion platform). Grocery brands can sell individual products or they can tantalize the shopper with a scrumptious meal at a great price. In fact, there are many sites posting meal plans based on a budgeted amount (e.g., "A Week of 5-Ingredient Dinners for Less than $50," "One Week $50 Meal Plan for a Family of Four"). A grocer can either sell individual products and let shoppers assess the value of each relative to the competition, or they can sell an entire meal solution.

Earlier I discussed different travel scenarios, and the same logic applies there. A hotel can battle the competition based on price and maybe throw in a few amenities. This left-brain approach is all about price, especially if the travel planner views hotels as pretty much all the same. However, if the hotel markets its brand based on the shopper's desires, it can increase the value it offers within the deal equation. This is the primary goal of passion platforms like those I discussed in the previous chapter.

Assume two different online hotel experiences. In the first, the hotel does the basics: price plus amenities. The second hotel takes the travel planner's desires into account. As an example, take a small resort called Lake 'n Pines Lodge in Interlochen, Michigan. The lodge is located near Traverse City, the Leelanau Wine Country, and several area ski resorts. The lodge maximizes the benefits provided by its surroundings by creating different packages based on different traveler desires. The following is a list of some of the packages the lodge is offering:

Desire	Packages
Romance Honeymoon Packages	• Northern Honeymoon Relax and Play Getaway • A Night of Romance • A Two-Night Interlude • Romantic Rendezvous
Food, Wine, Ale or Spirits Packages	• Brew & Moo for Two! (Traverse City Ale Trail) • Stillin' Away the Day (Tour local distilleries) • Vino Adventure (Grand Traverse Limo & Wine Tour)
Outdoor Nature Packages	• Pedal, Paddle, Pour (Combination of outdoor activity plus wine tasting) • Sleds 'n Treads (Trail riding on an ATV or snowmobile based on season)

As you can see, the lodge's packages are designed to attract adult travelers. The lodge combines its own amenities with local attractions to create a getaway of greater value. The package can either deliver on the travel planner's desires or be a source of inspiration for what to do on a getaway vacation.

The goal of a Money experience is to increase the deal or value of the brand offering. A cautionary note: there is rarely a "one desire fits all" approach. The brand needs to understand the desires of all their customers in order to design an experience that delivers on those desires and increases the value to the customers. Keep in mind that shoppers are willing to pay more for their dreams than for their needs.

Simplicity, Seamless, Serendipity

In 2006 Nike launched Nike Plus, creating an integrated running experience by combining shoe tech with the iPod. Nike Plus provided the competitive runner with accurate diagnostics on their run—their progress. The runner could keep track individually or share progress on playlists within an online community. I like to reference Nike Plus because it accentuated an existing experience with technology. The resulting brand combination (both Nike and Apple) created a new experience appealing to the competitive runner. The experience was easy to activate (simple), the iPod was already a part of many runners' routines (seamless) and, well, it felt like a natural extension (serendipity).

Simplicity experiences are designed from the customer out. Focusing on the customer means focusing on problems or opportunities.

A problem many grocers are trying to solve is appeasing the Mission shopper. This shopper views shopping as a chore and wants to limit their time in the retail environment. An early dotcom example of attempting to appease this motivation is Peapod, which is a grocery delivery service. In the spirit of Peapod, many grocers are delving more and more into ecommerce, including major players like Wal-mart, Kroger and Amazon.

One Amazon creation is the Dash button. The customer presses the button and the button automatically orders for them. Amazon offers over 200 different Dash buttons for products ranging from Tide laundry detergent to SmartWater to Ziploc bags.

Amazon is dabbling in many different ways to reinvent retail, from the Dash buttons to Prime Pantry to drone delivery to the checkout-line-free store. For the many shoppers exhibiting negative attitudes towards shopping, Amazon's effortless retail experience would be highly desirable.

As digital continues to integrate into our lives, I envision more seamless experiences. The technology is available in the home to automate many tasks such as creating a grocery list. A person could use Amazon's Alexa, Dash buttons, or a smart refrigerator to monitor food supplies and assist in drafting a grocery list. The issue is not the technology. The issue is adoption by enough people to make it viable from a marketing perspective.

From a brand perspective it is easier to build into an existing digital ecosystem than trying to introduce a new device into the mix. Device adoption takes time and is a burden on the brand if the device or technology is not adopted.

Social: Fuel the Advocate

Someone once said that attracting fans to Facebook is the easy part. Maintaining a conversation with fans is when the real work begins. This is an understatement. Keeping fans engaged takes commitment and resources. Many brands feel like tossing a topic out once a week is enough to fuel their fan base. They are missing the point of social and more importantly the power of social.

Fans (or advocates) are a critical part of brand marketing. Engagement is paramount in fueling the advocate to speak on behalf of the brand. There are four ways to think about engagement: Connect, Converse, Create, and Contribute.

Connecting is self-explanatory and most brands do this well. The goal is to connect fans with the brand and with each other. There are various social platforms to facilitate connection, with Facebook as the primary social channel. Connection is about belonging to a group, and it's an emotional connection which needs to be maintained over time.

This gets me to Converse, which is the conversation that fuels the passion. The conversation cannot be only on the brand's terms. It needs to be an interest shared by both parties (brand and fan). The topic also provides a reason for fans to talk to each other both online and offline. For many brands the conversation topics that fuel conversations are future-oriented—what's next. It could be insight into new products, services, or marketing. If the brand asks—and they have a vibrant fan base—they will get a reaction and conversation.

Contribute is the altruistic desire to pay it forward. One the best examples of this on the web is Wikipedia, where an online population crowd sources information every day. People feel the need to share their knowledge with the world. Sure, someone has to monitor it, but for the most part Wikipedia is self-policed by its contributors.

From a brand perspective Starbucks engages its fans through My Starbucks Idea (MyStarbucksIdea.com). The goal of the site is to encourage fans to create a better Starbucks. The site community brings together fans and Starbucks employees. Fans can add ideas for products, services, or philanthropic efforts. The community votes on the ideas and the more popular ones are activated. Since the site's inception in 2008, over 100,000 ideas have been submitted, commented and voted upon by the online community, with hundreds of them put into action. The site furnishes a great example of how a brand can fuel its fan base and also their marketing efforts.

Create is the final piece of fan engagement. Creation can fuel a brand. Take CIL, a Canadian paint company, as an example. CIL engaged their Facebook fans to solve a problem: most paint colors are feminine and not relatable to men. So the company created a campaign called Paint Chips for Men to garner a male perspective on colors. The company leveraged a Facebook app for fans to create their own paint chip names and then vote on their favorites. Instead of paint colors like Spice Island, Pansy Violet, and Almond Wisp, people submitted paint colors like Hockey Puck, Bacon, and British Teeth. The campaign generated 15,000 paint chip names, and most importantly the company saw a 10 percent increase in sales.

Reward: Recognize the Relationship

Sweepstakes. A tactic used by many brands to create attention for a campaign. If you go to Online-Sweepstakes.com you can find a list of active marketing sweepstakes. Last time I looked, there were over 4,000 active sweepstakes someone could enter. Sweepstakes range from food prizes to vacations to events to just cash. Sweepstakes reward people for entering the sweepstakes, and that is the problem—they don't drive brand engagement.

Think of sweepstakes as the icing on a cake. Icing makes a cake taste better, but if your cake tastes awful icing isn't going to save it. This goes for sweepstakes too. If a brand lacks any idea of how to engage people, then a sweepstakes isn't going to fix matters. I am not saying that holding a sweepstakes is a bad tactic. I *am* saying it needs to be a part of a bigger campaign to maximize its effect.

Rewards should be designed to reinforce the brand relationship. Loyalty programs are designed to reinforce loyalty. Many programs gamify shopping to motivate the shopper to buy at a higher frequency (or larger dollar amount). Grocery store fuel perks programs are one example. The idea is to get a larger portion of the shopper's grocery dollars by incentivizing them to spend more with the brand each month. The more a shopper spends, the higher the discount per gallon, and the more they feel rewarded for their loyalty.

Obviously loyalty programs are not restricted to one channel. This is an important point to remember when it comes to experience design. Always build the experience from the customer out. Define the value from the customer standpoint and then determine which customer touchpoints to include within the program. With loyalty programs there are many touchpoints to consider: brand website, mobile app, retail experience, direct marketing (e.g., email, direct mail). The key is to make the program accessible to the customer on their terms and to reinforce program participation through persistent reminders.

Entertainment: Brandvertainment

Remember the term "webisode"? I am probably dating myself a little, but there was a time when it was fashionable for brands to create serial content for their audiences' enjoyment. As was the case with other tactics discussed in this chapter, many brands dumped a lot of their marketing budget into production to produce their own branded content. Very few were successful in attracting views, and most failed to capture the interest of the masses.

The key to branded entertainment content is the ability to entertain an audience *and* build the brand. Dove's "Real Beauty Sketches" video is engaging content delivering on the brand's promise. Over 163 million people worldwide have watched the video. The video uses two perspectives: a first-person view of how a woman sees herself, and how a stranger perceives her. A forensic sketch artist draws both perspectives and then the sketches are presented to the various women who participated in the exercise. The reaction of the participants emotively draws in the viewer. Anyway, my description pales in comparison to the video, so if you haven't seen the video check it out.

Keep in mind that if you are designing a digital experience there are two modes: Lean Back and Lean Forward. Lean Back means having the user watch, listen or read content. This is not a bad thing, especially if the content is a benefit to the user and the brand. Lean Forward is about interacting with the target. Very few brand experiences online focus on Lean Forward. I believe this is a misstep by brands. They are not taking advantage of the medium.

Sure, some brands would argue their product does not lend itself to a Lean Forward experience. Don't tell that to OfficeMax. In 2006 they launched the classic experience Elf Yourself. The online experience allowed people to create and share an amusing elf experience by uploading faces of family members or co-workers onto elves. The elves would then do a holiday jig to the amusement of the person's social circle. I don't know why I am describing this to you, because you probably created a few elf vignettes yourself. During the six-week holiday period in 2007, the phenomenon generated 193 million visits and over 123 million elves were created.

There were several elements contributing to the success of Elf Yourself. One was a social reason—the ability for someone to "punk" another person. The ability to make light of another person provides share-ability not only between the creator and the other person, but also within their shared social circle. Secondly and more subtly, Elf Yourself allows a person to play. What I mean by play is the ability for a person to create something easily.

Lean Forward experiences are about interactivity, about play. Play creates engagement between the brand and person. It's better yet if the play can create a personal connection by allowing a person to make their own version. NikeID is a great example of play and personalization. NikeID is an online experience allowing customers to create their own versions of many different shoes including the Nike Zoom, Air Force 1, or the Jordan Super Fly as well as Converse shoes like the classic Chuck Taylors. In addition to shoes, the site has some basketball backpacks and duffel bags that can be personalized.

The customer can personalize every aspect of the shoe. They can change the color from the shoe tops to the soles, including the laces and the Nike Swoosh. You can save your designs and share them. The site even allows users to rate the shoes. The best part is that a customer can purchase their design right within the web experience.

Nike shoes are a premium product. The shoes on the NikeID site range from $110 to well over $300. By allowing a customer to personalize their shoe, the brand is creating a stronger connection between itself and the customer. Instead of just buying a pair of Nike Air Force 1's, the customer is buying their own version of the Air Force 1.

I would like to conclude this chapter by noting these value propositions are not mutually exclusive. In fact, a brand experience becomes more attractive to people the more value propositions it offers. Think about the CIL Paint Chips for Men example. The experience had multiple value propositions, including Social (integration into Facebook with the ability to share), Reward (recognition of people who created paint chip names) and Entertainment (both Lean Forward, allowing people to create new paint chip names, and Lean Back, where people could read the 15,000 names).

A cautionary note: while more value propositions create a more attractive experience, don't force it. Don't create a Franken-experience that feels disjointed to the user. The experience should engage the target on the basis of their desires, interests and motivations, and move them attitudinally and/or behaviorally closer to purchase.

FORTY-ONE
Decision Optimization

Many automotive websites attract more than a million visitors per month—some get around 10 million per month. An impressive amount of visitors, especially when you consider the majority came of their own volition. However, no automobile company sells more than a million vehicles per month. The question isn't how many people are coming to the site; instead, it is why some are converting and others are not. People come to the website purposefully—to research and buy a new vehicle. They did not click on a banner. They did not decide on a whim to check out the site for fun. They are interested in buying a vehicle in the future and are trying to find the right vehicle for them. Given the interest it seems like it should be easy to convert the person or at least move them closer to purchase.

Determining site conversion is relatively easy. It normally comes down to a simple survey question: Based on your website experience today, how much more likely are you to buy a vehicle? The respondent is given three choices: More Likely, About the Same, Less Likely. The question gives a marketer insight into how well the website is performing. I have run this survey many times over the years. In one instance about one-third of respondents stated they were more likely to purchase a vehicle based on the experience. The client was stunned. He exclaimed, "This is a 67 percent failure rate. Why did this happen?"

First off, the client was right about the failure rate. If shoppers come willingly to a brand website and the brand can only get one out of three closer to purchase, then the site is missing the mark for most people. The question of "why" lies in the decision path. In other words, what was the intent of the visit? What was the shopper trying to decide? And where did they go on the website to answer their questions?

In the early days of the internet we were lucky if we were able to pop a survey onto a site to learn about visitors' experiences. Today the survey solutions are more robust. With tech complexities and data integration, we are able to not only pop a survey, we can connect the survey to the site analytics tool and see where the person went on the site. The ability to combine a person's response with their behavior provides acute insight into a channel performance and the ability to optimize it. The key to understanding the reasons for success or failure is to ask the right questions, something which gets me back to the decision path.

The site survey asked many questions in addition to the conversion question. A core section of the survey focused on 22 macro decisions someone makes when purchasing a new car. The survey was set up to ask the respondent what decisions they had already made and, more importantly, the purpose of their site visit that day. For example, a person might say that they already decided on the brand and features and the primary purpose of their site visit was to determine how much they would pay for the vehicle. This person is nearing the end of their path to purchase. Conversely, a person earlier in their journey may be looking at what vehicles are available that meet their needs. They are not tied to one vehicle or brand and at this point are simply seeing what is out there.

The decision path helps a marketer focus on the intent, but it is only half the equation. The other aspect of interest is where visitors went on the site to answer their questions. In one analysis we compared visitors who were cross-shopping competing brand models. While there was a vehicle comparison tool on the brand website, the shopper did not go to this section (it didn't even make the top five). The number one section shoppers visited was the Build Your Own tool. The client was taken aback and immediately suggested that information on why the brand was better than the competition needed to be incorporated into the Build Your Own section.

Not so fast.

Many times selling is like dating, and a brand does not want to be a needy date. If a brand is constantly telling the shopper why they are better than the competition, they fail to convey why they are the right product for the shopper. The goal should be to connect with the shopper based on their desires in order to close the deal. No different than dating. A person will date a series of people until they find the one who is right for them.

Channel conversion is critical in understanding what brand touchpoint is working and for whom. Many times a marketer views their marketing efforts as a black box. They throw a bunch of marketing into the box and see what sales come out. Then based on macro-level insights they repeat the process—sometimes with the same results, sometimes with different ones. For many reasons this is a flawed approach. A major reason is that it treats all shoppers the same. We have different desires, different shopper motivations. As I have illustrated throughout this book, desires and motivations require different marketing and (possibly) different channels to convert a shopper to buying.

In optimizing channel conversion there are two focal points: source influence and decision influence. Source influence is nothing new. Many marketers run post-purchase surveys and have some idea of what source influenced their target; however, they probably do not know why. This is why decision influence is important.

In grocery shopping circulars still influence about one-third of shoppers. The number will vary by typology. Deal Seekers typologies will be influenced by circulars more than Price Blind typologies. As a point of clarification, when I am referring to circulars, they could be physically distributed (through newspapers or the mail) or accessed by the shopper online (through a website or app). There is little doubt about the influence. The real question is: What decision is the insert influencing?

In planning and carrying out their weekly shop, grocery shoppers face different questions, such as "What products should I buy?" and "How much will I pay?" However, for a grocery brand the number one question asked by customers is: *"What store do I go to?"* The circular influences about one in four shoppers on their choice of where to shop in a given week. Like the automotive example, the grocer needs to convert—they need to win the week.

By analyzing the persuasiveness of their circular relative to the competition, a grocer can increase the conversion rate. List relevance is key to conversion. If a grocer is promoting a majority of products that are on the shopper's list, they are more likely to convert the shopper that week.

This is easier said than done. Many grocers have two types of products: everyday and seasonal. Core products are offered on an ongoing basis, while seasonal products are offered for a limited time. Seasonal products may enhance a grocer's differentiation and timeliness; however, if a grocer promotes too many infrequently purchased products, then their list relevance will drop and they will likely lose the shopper that week.

So far I have been discussing channel conversion based on brand content and channels. I would like to shift the perspective and view the decision from the shopper's point of view and the sources that influence their decision. To illustrate, the diagram at the top of the next page displays the core vacation decisions (which I covered in the chapter on decision paths), with the addition of hotel-specific decisions.

The hotel's influence on the overall trip varies. Sometimes the hotel *is* the vacation, a common enough situation with all-inclusive resorts. Other times the hotel is just a bed—a place to sleep at night. The vacation decision of "Where do I stay?" can be extrapolated into six decisions that travel planners typically consider. These decisions are not mutually exclusive from the core vacation decision, which shouldn't be a surprise since the choice of hotel is a key decision in most vacation planning. The hotel decision could impact the vacation's location and activities, and definitely will impact the amount someone will pay for their vacation.

Once you hone in on the core decisions, you can determine which sources influenced those decisions. The diagram at the bottom of the next page links the sources of influence with the hotel decisions they affected. Note I only included sources with more than a 20 percent influence on a decision.

This represents an overall view of all respondents within the hotel study, and gives us an idea of the relative influence of different sources. Most sources are not brand-controlled. Still, a brand should be in tune with the content on these sites in order to understand the perception of their brand versus the competition. Often brands myopically focus on channels they control and lose sight of the bigger picture. A brand should be regularly (or constantly) surveying other sources to see how their brand is represented, both the good and the bad.

Driving the Trip Decision
Hotel Example

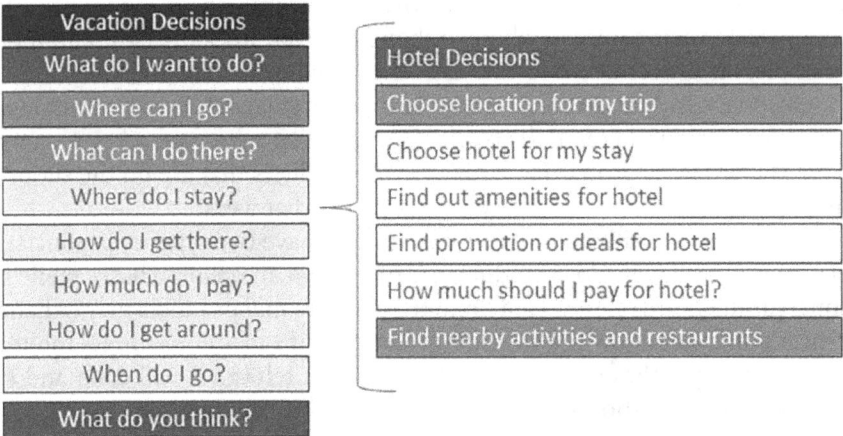

Vacation Decisions
What do I want to do?
Where can I go?
What can I do there?
Where do I stay?
How do I get there?
How much do I pay?
How do I get around?
When do I go?
What do you think?

Hotel Decisions
Choose location for my trip
Choose hotel for my stay
Find out amenities for hotel
Find promotion or deals for hotel
How much should I pay for hotel?
Find nearby activities and restaurants

Decision Sources
Hotel Example

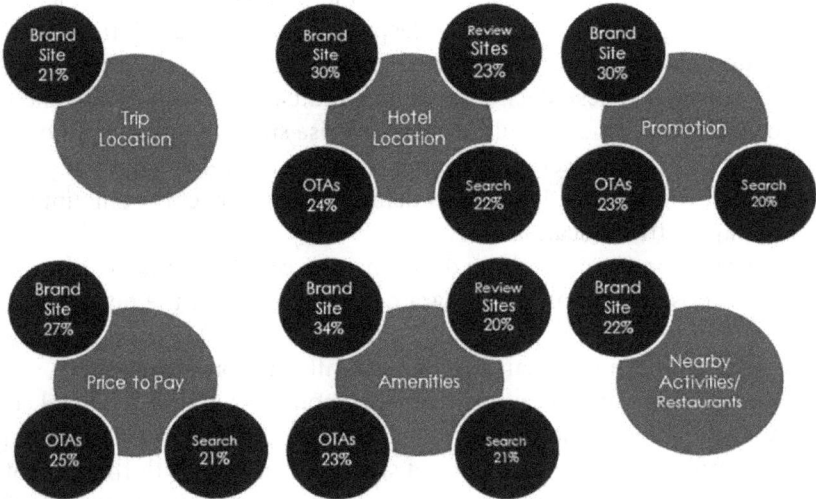

Trip Location
- Brand Site 21%

Hotel Location
- Brand Site 30%
- Review Sites 23%
- OTAs 24%
- Search 22%

Promotion
- Brand Site 30%
- OTAs 23%
- Search 20%

Price to Pay
- Brand Site 27%
- OTAs 25%
- Search 21%

Amenities
- Brand Site 34%
- Review Sites 20%
- OTAs 23%
- Search 21%

Nearby Activities/ Restaurants
- Brand Site 22%

Influential sources exceeding 20%.

200

The shopper sees no such restrictions. They tend to shop using sources they are comfortable with and based on their motivations. We know (from previous chapters) that different sources over-index based on different hotel typologies. One goal would be to look at the different sources by shopper motivation or typology. For example, 23 percent of respondents stated they were influenced by consumer review websites. If we look at this by typology, the results range from high-influence with 38 percent of Solution Shoppers (Free Agent, Price Blind, Journey) to a low of 4 percent for Loyalty Lasers (Brand Citizen, Price Blind, Mission).

The importance of identifying the influence of specific sources on a specific typology is to gain an empathetic perspective on the content—both relating to the brand and to the competition. For instance, looking at content through the lens of the Solution Shopper emphasizes the importance of the bigger picture: *How does the hotel accentuate the vacation?* Odds are the Solution Shopper is not looking for "just a bed"—they consider the hotel a critical part of the vacation. If the Solution Shopper is planning for a family trip, they are looking at what they can do during down-time, both at the hotel and nearby. If the Solution Shopper is planning a romantic getaway, the planner will be looking at the ambiance of the hotel itself along with nearby romantic activities.

Taking into account either of these Solution Shopper desires (family vacation or romantic vacation planner), the brand can look through consumer review websites to see what type of content exists. Is the content favorable, relative to the mindset of the travel planner? Or not? Knowing the likely positive or negative influence allows marketing efforts to either amplify the positive or combat the negative within the brand's own channels.

Optimizing the decision is a three-word summation of a lot of the learnings in this book. Decision optimization integrates the shopper's DNA with their decision path and takes into account how various sources influence the shopper's final purchase. I find this process provides a great deal of insight about why a shopper converts or doesn't. These insights contribute to creating better, more influential content—content which markets to the motivations of the shopper.

FORTY-TWO
The Shopper Sandbox

Swim lanes are popular in advertising today. Most agencies have an expertise: digital, social, traditional advertising, media. And many clients hire different agencies based on their expertise. To get an advertising campaign completed the client needs a coordinated approach among their roster of agencies. To ensure they get the best out of each agency they want each agency to stay in its swim lane—in its area of expertise. It seems logical: each agency focuses on its channel and therefore the client gets the most out of its roster of agencies.

But this channel-centric approach, while logical, has major flaws. The irony is that (sticking with aquatic metaphors) the client really needs to play water polo with its agencies. Creating marketing is a team sport—channels need to be integrated around the shopper to maximize conversion. This isn't about eight channels, each working in a silo; rather, it is about eight channels working together to move the ball (the shopper) to score (getting a sale).

The teamwork necessary to score is something that is missing for many clients—and for many agencies. There are different reasons why that teamwork is missing, but the most interesting one lies at the core of agency organizational behavior. I have talked throughout this book about shopper motivations and behaviors. To be successful in marketing to shoppers, it is just as important to understand organizational behavior and personal motivations.

My career has bounced around to a lot of different agencies. I have worked in traditional agencies, digital agencies, media groups, a tech company, and I co-owned a business for a bit. Each stop along the way gave me a unique perspective on advertising. One of the more interesting stops was my tour of duty at Team Detroit. I arrived shortly after WPP blended five agencies together to service the Ford business. The agencies—JWT, Y&R, Ogilvy, Wunderman, and Mindshare—were different in many ways: procedurally, culturally, and in their areas of expertise. My role was to actively work with the agencies to create integrated solutions, combining paid, earned and owned. No small task.

My background lent itself to the challenge. The experience I had gained from working at different types of agencies provided a unique, empathetic perspective to represent each area of expertise. I understood how to integrate channels and not to lose the integrity of each channel. During my three years at Team Detroit I worked on more than 20 major vehicle launches and campaigns. Were they all successful? God no, but based on this experience I would like to share with you a few observations on why some were successful, and, just as importantly, why others failed.

I could get into a lot of do's and don'ts; geez, that could be a book in and of itself. But for the sake of brevity I want to touch on three things which make or break integration: agency culture, channel expertise, and a sandbox.

Agency culture is a driving force in creation. Some agencies have a pronounced culture driving the creativity—the core purpose of the agency. There are many aspects to an agency's culture: its creative philosophy; its approach to cultivating talent; its recognized expertise; or its approach to creating a campaign. I could touch on different nuances; however, to make my point let's discuss the approach to creating a campaign.

Some agencies are more bureaucratic in their approach. They use a methodical process to uncover insights, create a campaign, and then produce the campaign. The antithesis of this is the entrepreneurial agency, which has a "get 'er done" mentality. They are far more chaotic. They may have a process document taped to the wall, but when it comes to getting work done their approach is far more fluid.

These divergent approaches also attract (and retain) different types of talent. A person who abhors structure will feel suffocated within a bureaucratic agency. Conversely, a person who prefers a highly structured world and work environment will have elevated anxiety within an entrepreneurial agency. So what happens over time is that each type of agency retains those people who are comfortable within its culture. This works well when an agency handles all (or the bulk of) a client's work. The challenges occur when a client asks two agencies with contrasting cultures to work together. Those challenges include sorting out who leads (and follows) and how to best work together. In a perfect world, the agencies (or the client) would decide at the outset how they will work together. In the real world, agencies stay in their own swim lanes.

I am not, by the way, advocating one culture over another. Whether bureaucratic or entrepreneurial, both types of agencies can be creative and create stellar work. This is not the problem. The problem is how they will work together. Unless someone intervenes and negotiates a way to work together effectively, it's not likely the client is going to get the most out of their agency roster.

One aspect of culture that is most divisive is channel agency. I saw this from the inside when I worked at digital agencies. Back in the dot-com days, digital agencies were all the rage. After all, digital was the new way of doing business, and the old rules of traditional advertising did not apply. We were creating a new marketing world order. And oh, by the way, anyone over the age of 40 didn't have a clue. Yep, there was a lot bravado back then (and even after the crash).

An interesting and disturbing unspoken belief also persisted within digital agencies. Since it was a new marketing world order, the belief was that traditional agencies must die. It seems drastic, but the prevailing opinion was that people who worked at a traditional agency didn't get digital, and therefore didn't understand the future of advertising. Some of this animosity arose from the fact the clients treated digital as a "below the line" marketing expenditure. This meant they funded traditional media first and below-the-line channels like direct marketing, collateral, and digital only afterward. Obviously this second-class citizen status didn't sit well with the ego of a digital agency.

Before anyone rushes to judgment, there was some truth in the bravado. In fact, traditional agencies at the time did not get digital. That is why digital agencies existed. Unfortunately, the animosity between the agencies blocked them from working together effectively. This deep-rooted animosity can still be found today, even beyond digital agencies. Let's face it, it doesn't matter if you are a digital, social, or direct marketing agency, no one wants to be treated like a second-class citizen—an afterthought.

As a result, many channel-expertise agencies began to expand their capabilities so they could be considered full-service agencies. They added production capabilities to do television and radio. They hired brand planners so they could work with clients to reposition their brands. They added media planners so they could integrate paid, earned, and owned all under one roof. Sometimes this worked. Other times, the "traditional" employees felt lost working in a channel agency pretending to be something that was contrary to its core culture.

You can see from this anecdote the difficulties of getting different disciplines to work together, even if they all work for the same agency. At Team Detroit we had all the disciplines under one roof. While we were affiliated with various sister agencies there was an overarching mandate to work together. The problem I encountered was not one of agency animosity or of second-class citizens; rather, issues with integration were rooted in human nature.

When brainstorming, human nature dictates that people want to contribute. They want to share their ideas and have them recognized by the group. A person wants the satisfaction of playing a part in creating a great campaign. The issue is not with the person; instead, it is when you brainstorm with a group of people all with different areas of channel expertise. Each person will want to pull the solution into their comfort zone—their channel expertise. Instead of building an integrated solution, the group will share disparate channel ideas.

There is an art to brainstorming. While there are different methods for coming up with ideas, it is important to understand group dynamics in order to get the most out of people. In my experience there are two types of thinkers: conceptual and literal.

The conceptual thinker does better in the abstract. They are comfortable building experiences that transcend any one channel. On the other hand, literal thinkers prefer to think tactically within a channel. They think in 30-second commercials, web pages, or social platforms. The reality of building successful marketing campaigns is that you need both types of thinkers—just not in the same room at the same time. Given this fact, brainstorming was closely choreographed to get the most out of the conceptual thinkers and literal thinkers. There was care to sequence brainstorming from channel-agnostic ideas to channel expertise.

The visual below depicts that brainstorming progression from conceptual to subject-matter expert. Note the number of arrows on the chart—this is intentional. The process is highly iterative to ensure the channels are appropriately integrated into the overall experience.

Two Step Ideation Approach

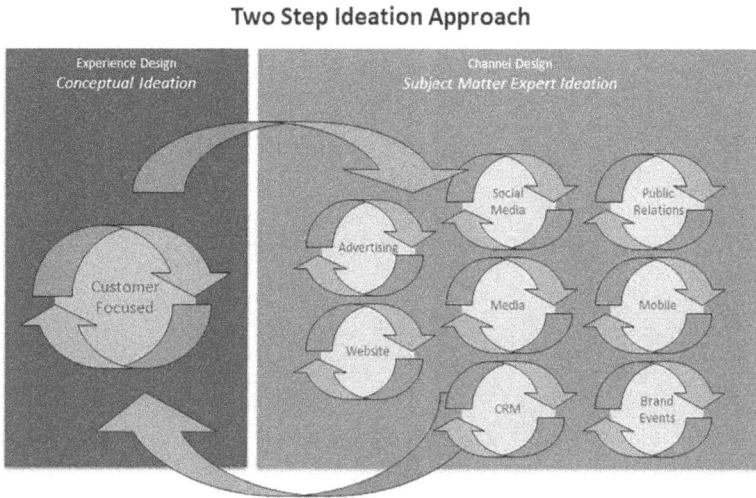

The brainstorming choreography began with channel agnostic ideation. The goal was to include six to eight individuals in these sessions. With fewer than six people you begin to lose diversity of thought and with more than eight some people shut down because of being in a larger group. There could be as few as two sessions or as many as eight or more. The purpose of the sessions was to architect the overarching campaign before turning it over to channel experts to build it out.

After the channel agnostic sessions came a series of channel expert sessions. Each session focused on a specific channel with six to eight channel experts brainstorming. Based on the nature of the campaign you could have eight or more channels involved in the brainstorming (e.g., traditional media, website, online advertising, social, mobile, CRM, retail environment, events). Each channel would build from the campaign blueprint defined in the conceptual sessions. As the channels were thought out, ideas and tactics were cross-pollinated from one channel to another, creating a tightly integrated campaign.

This is an intense approach to building out a campaign. In the course of a three-week period, we could easily have more than 20 two-hour brainstorming session. By focusing intensely on each channel, the campaign was deeply thought-out and participants were more satisfied because they had the chance to contribute on their terms within their fields of expertise.

Sounds great, right? It works. It really does. However, it doesn't work all the time. There are different ways brainstorming can be derailed, but number one is a lack of a centering point focusing all the channels. Some people refer to this centering point as a North Star (personally, I have heard that phrase too often and now cringe every time it is repeated). What I prefer to create is a shopper sandbox (see diagram). The sandbox provides focus. Without it, you find yourself in free-range ideation with many ideas and—guess what?—no wrong answers.

The Shopper Sandbox

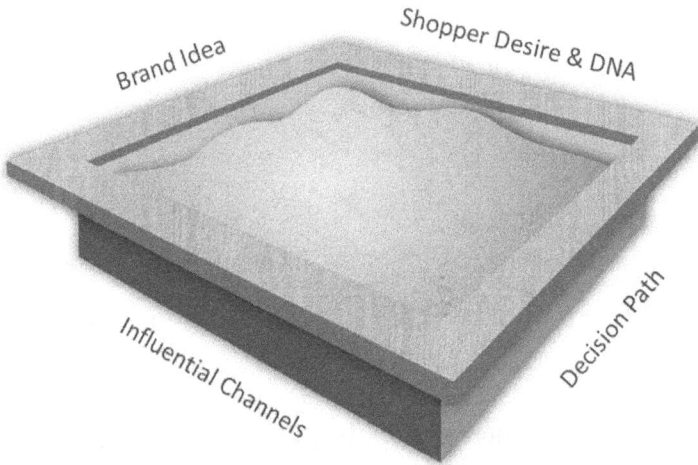

The sandbox focuses idea generation both within and between sessions. Four borders define the shopper sandbox: brand idea, shopper desire and DNA, influential channels, and decision path.

The borders should look familiar. The first one I want to talk about is the *brand idea*, which is the foundation of the brainstorming. Without it, the channel ideas could be about any brand. In the past I sometimes attempted to run brainstorming sessions without defining the brand idea. The resulting sessions were frustrating because it felt like we were going in a circle. Inevitably the group found itself trying to fill the gap and come up with a brand idea.

Shopper desire and *DNA* are the two mindsets influencing the purchase. Desire is the emotional connection to the product—the customer's product relationship. This can be highly functional and low emotion in nature, as is often the case for many high-frequency commodity products. Considered products are apt to be emotively more intense with shoppers demonstrating a stronger connection to the product.

Shopper DNA is critical in understanding the core typologies for the brand and product category. It is very different brainstorming for a Bargainista versus a Solution Shopper. The Bargainista is all about the find and social plays an active role. The Solution Shopper is driving to a solution, and brands that assist the shopper in finding that solution will more likely be considered.

The *decision path* is critical for considered purchases. By breaking down the shopper journey into key decisions, the brainstorming focuses on specific decisions where the brand may be suffering. Focusing the brainstorming on specific decisions will create content and experiences that increase conversion.

Finally, the *influential channels* are the catalysts for persuasion. Remember that there are two purposes for sources: to move the shopper both attitudinally and behaviorally. To move the shopper attitudinally, the brainstorming will focus on content and experiences that disrupt the shopper's current beliefs—beliefs preventing the shopper from considering the brand.

Coming up with ways to behaviorally influence a shopper will require participants to view content through the shopper's eyes, through the lens of the shopper's motivations. One way to get at this notion is to have participants *be* the shopper, pursuing the journey in the shopper's shoes. First, shopper personas are defined based on shopper desires and DNA, and then participants role play the persona. Session participants go to sources that will influence the shopper both online and offline. By walking together with the shopper through their journey, brainstorming is focused tightly on the shopper's preferences.

My purpose in this chapter has been to provide a general overview and sense of direction for creating an effective brainstorming process, not to be tightly prescriptive. Each brainstorming exercise will involve a different mix of channels and varying amounts of time to complete. Regardless of the dynamics of your brainstorming exercise, keep in mind three things and you will be fine:

1. Group like-minded people together as defined by type of thought process (conceptual versus literal) and area of channel expertise.
2. Create a shopper sandbox to focus the brainstorming.
3. Finally, invest in a facilitator. To this day I am amazed that many advertising agencies do not invest in a facilitator for brainstorming sessions. Instead, they default to someone on staff. It is worthwhile securing a facilitator who is well versed in advertising and who can inspire people to think differently.

FORTY-THREE
Final Thoughts

I used to oil paint quite a bit. I preferred oil because its flexibility as a medium allowed me to keep tweaking the painting. Days or weeks later, I could come back to the painting and pick up where I left off. In my view the painting was never done; eventually, however, I needed to put my brush down and resign myself to the fact that the painting was complete.

With this chapter I'm telling myself it is time to put the brush down, at least for now. However, let me leave you with a few parting thoughts.

First and most important, *put the shopper first*. In advertising currently, agencies proclaim they are a digital-first agency or a mobile-first agency. Don't do that. For a marketer, the shopper should always be first. First in understanding why they shop the way they do. First in uncovering insights driving their decisions for purchase. Begin with the shopper and then determine what channels and content will persuade them.

Don't settle for the *what*. The *what* is the weather outside. When working with strategists I always stress "Don't tell the client the weather!" The weather is an observation. The weather is not an insight. The weather is not actionable. Strive to tell them *why* it is raining. The best way to find the *why* is to get out of the channel and look at the problem from the shopper's perspective. Understand why the shopper acts the way they do. Why did they react (or not react) to a promotional stimulus?

Don't stop with what is contained in the pages of this book—I am not. I view learning as a series of building blocks. I'm building a tower of knowledge that will never be completed. Take what is in these pages and question it, debate it, and build on it. I believe there are truths about shopper motivations in this book. I also know for every one truth I have written about here, I can think of many more I want to research, prove (or disprove)—and then move onto the next one.

Finally, reach out to me. I would love to hear your stories about shopper behavior. I would be intrigued by the research and learnings you have uncovered in your career. I can be found at www.PrimalShopper.com or on Twitter at @egbowe.

Primal Shopper Surveys

The following four additional surveys are meant to give you an idea of different typologies by product category. I have included fast casual restaurants, mobile phones, hotels, and dog food. These surveys are abbreviated versions of the full surveys, but sufficient to gauge the base shopper typology. The typology results from the actual survey are provided at the end of each survey so you can compare them with your results.

Keep in mind the fact that these surveys are designed to be taken soon after the purchase in order to get the most accurate read on the shopper DNA.

Fast Casual Restaurant Survey

Please circle the answers for the following questions based on your most recent trip to a fast casual restaurant.

Brand		
1. When it comes to fast casual restaurants, I would describe myself as "brand loyal."	Agree	Disagree
2. When it comes to fast casual restaurants, I don't patronize brands, I just buy something to eat.	Agree	Disagree
3. When it comes to fast casual restaurants, I always choose the lower price over brand name.	Agree	Disagree
4. When purchasing fast casual, the restaurant name is:	Very important	Not very important
5. When I shop for fast casual, if a brand I prefer is unavailable, I:	Buy another brand	Wait and buy the brand I want at another time

Wallet		
1. When it comes to choosing a fast casual restaurant, I usually:	Spend time to save money	Spend money to save time
2. I often price out items or meals at more than one place, and then I buy it where it's cheapest.	Agree	Disagree

3.	I am not really satisfied with a fast casual restaurant purchase unless I feel I've gotten a good deal.	Agree	Disagree
4.	If I want to eat out at a fast casual restaurant, I usually look for a promotion.	Agree	Disagree
5.	When choosing fast casual, I actively use tools that save me money (e.g., coupons, deal websites, or pricing applications).	Agree	Disagree

Time			
1.	Choosing a fast casual restaurant is a task that I check off my "to-do" list.	Agree	Disagree
2.	I usually put off choosing a restaurant until I absolutely have to eat.	Agree	Disagree
3.	When I choose a restaurant, it is usually:	Like a mission—there is a very specific goal and plan of action	Like a journey—there is a process of discovery and evaluation
4.	When I choose a restaurant, I usually:	Want to spend as little time as possible	Enjoy it and like to browse around to see what's available
5.	When I choose a restaurant, I usually:	Have a plan for what I need and stick to it	Know what I need, but I'm open to other products and services

SCORING YOUR SURVEY

Based on your results above, give yourself a point for each of your answers that match the answers below:

Scoring for Brand		Answer	Score
1.	When it comes to fast casual restaurants, I would describe myself as "brand loyal."	Agree	
2.	When it comes to fast casual restaurants, I don't patronize brands, I just buy something to eat.	Disagree	

Scoring for Brand	Answer	Score
3. When it comes to fast casual restaurants, I always choose the lower price over brand name.	Disagree	
4. When purchasing fast casual, the restaurant name is:	Very important	
5. When I shop for fast casual, if a brand I prefer is unavailable, I:	Wait and buy the brand I want at another time.	
Total Score for Brand		

If you have three or more answers that match the above give yourself a "B" (meaning Brand Citizen) in the Brand typology box below; if you have less than three give yourself an "F" (meaning Free Agent).

Scoring for Wallet	Answer	Score
1. When it comes to choosing a fast casual restaurant, I usually:	Spend time to save money	
2. I often price out items or meals at more than one place, and then I buy it where it's cheapest.	Agree	
3. I am not really satisfied with a fast casual restaurant purchase unless I feel I've gotten a good deal.	Agree	
4. If I want to eat out at a fast casual restaurant, I usually look for a promotion.	Agree	
5. When choosing fast casual, I actively use tools that save me money (e.g., coupons, deal websites, or pricing applications).	Agree	
Total Score for Wallet		

If you have three or more answers that match the above give yourself a "D" (meaning Deal Seeker) in the Wallet typology box below; if you have less than three give yourself an "P" (meaning Price Blind).

Scoring for Time	Answer	Score
1. Choosing a fast casual restaurant is a task that I check off of my "to-do" list.	Agree	
2. I usually put off choosing a restaurant until I absolutely have to eat.	Agree	
3. When I choose a restaurant, it is usually:	Like a mission—there is a very specific goal and plan of action	
4. When I choose a restaurant, I usually:	Want to spend as little time as possible	
5. When I choose a restaurant, I usually:	Have a plan for what I need and stick to it	
Total Score for Time		

If you have three or more answers that match the above give yourself a "M" (meaning Mission) in the Time typology box below; if you have less than three give yourself an "J" (meaning Journey).

MY FAST CASUAL RESTAURANT TYPOLOGY

Brand	Wallet	Time

To determine your typology combine your three letters and find your typology in the table on the following page. I have included a brief description for each typology. For reference purposes I have also included the results of the Fast Casual Restaurant Survey.

COMPARE YOUR RESULTS FOR FAST CASUAL RESTAURANTS

Typology	Typology Name	% of Survey Respondents	Typology Description
BDM	Brand Tracker	4%	These shoppers know what they like, want a deal, and do not want to waste time shopping for it.
BPM	Loyalty Lasers	21%	Shopping is quick and easy for these people because they simply buy brands they know.
BDJ	Fanatical Finders	5%	These shoppers shop the same brands on a consistent basis; therefore they are knowledgeable about pricing and know when a brand is a deal.
BPJ	Comfort Zoners	35%	They limit their selection within a product category to brands they know and brands they have tried.
FDM	Deal Surgeon	3%	Saving money and efficiency are priorities. These shoppers identify what they need and which brands have the best deals.
FDJ	Bargainista	4%	Deal trumps brand, and these shoppers are willing to try different brands in order to save money.
FPM	Shopping Minimalists	12%	The goal for these shoppers is to spend the least amount of time shopping.
FPJ	Solution Shoppers	16%	These shoppers are goal-based and have a higher-level intent when they shop which supersedes brand and price.

Dog Food Survey

Please circle the answers for the following questions based on the last time you purchased dog food.

Brand		
1. When it comes to dog food, I would describe myself as "brand loyal."	Agree	Disagree
2. I don't buy brands, I buy dog food.	Agree	Disagree
3. When it comes to dog food, I always choose the lower price over brand name.	Agree	Disagree
4. When purchasing dog food, brand name is:	Very important	Not very important
5. When I shop for dog food, if a brand I prefer is unavailable, I:	Buy another brand	Wait and buy the brand I want at another time

Wallet		
1. When it comes to shopping for dog food, I usually:	Spend time to save money	Spend money to save time
2. I often price out dog food at more than one place, and then I buy it where it's cheapest.	Agree	Disagree
3. I am not really satisfied with a dog food purchase unless I feel I've gotten a good deal.	Agree	Disagree
4. If I want to buy dog food, I usually buy it on sale or wait for it to go on sale.	Agree	Disagree
5. When shopping for dog food, I actively use tools that save me money (e.g., coupons, deal websites, or pricing applications).	Agree	Disagree

Time		
1. Shopping for dog food is a task that I check off my "to-do" list.	Agree	Disagree
2. I usually put off shopping for dog food until I absolutely need to buy it.	Agree	Disagree

3.	When I shop for dog food, it is usually:	Like a mission—there is a very specific goal and plan of action	Like a journey—there is a process of discovery and evaluation
4.	When I shop for dog food, I usually:	Want to spend as little time as possible	Enjoy it and like to browse around to see what's available
5.	When I shop for dog food, I usually:	Have a plan for what I need and stick to it	Know what I need, but I'm open to other products and services

SCORING YOUR SURVEY

Based on your results above, give yourself a point for each of your answers that match the answers below:

Scoring for Brand	Answer	Score
1. When it comes to dog food, I would describe myself as "brand loyal."	Agree	
2. I don't buy brands, I buy dog food.	Disagree	
3. When it comes to dog food, I always choose the lower price over brand name.	Disagree	
4. When purchasing dog food, brand name is:	Very important	
5. When I shop for dog food, if a brand I prefer is unavailable, I:	Wait and buy the brand I want at another time.	
Total Score for Brand		

If you have three or more answers that match the above give yourself a "B" (meaning Brand Citizen) in the Brand typology box below; if you have less than three give yourself an "F" (meaning Free Agent).

Scoring for Wallet	Answer	Score
1. When it comes to shopping for dog food, I usually:	Spend time to save money	
2. I often price out dog food at more than one place, and then I buy it where it's cheapest.	Agree	
3. I am not really satisfied with a dog food purchase unless I feel I've gotten a good deal.	Agree	
4. If I want buy dog food, I usually buy it on sale or wait for it to go on sale.	Agree	
5. When shopping for dog food, I actively use tools that save me money (e.g., coupons, deal websites, or pricing applications).	Agree	
Total Score for Wallet		

If you have three or more answers that match the above give yourself a "D" (meaning Deal Seeker) in the Wallet typology box below; if you have less than three give yourself an "P" (meaning Price Blind).

Scoring for Time	Answer	Score
1. Shopping for dog food is a task that I check off my "to-do" list.	Agree	
2. I usually put off shopping for dog food until I absolutely need to buy it.	Agree	
3. When I shop for dog food, it is usually:	Like a mission—there is a very specific goal and plan of action	
4. When I shop for dog food, I usually:	Want to spend as little time as possible	
5. When I shop for dog food, I usually:	Have a plan for what I need and stick to it	
Total Score for Time		

If you have three or more answers that match the above give yourself a "M" (meaning Mission) in the Time typology box below; if you have less than three give yourself an "J" (meaning Journey).

MY DOG FOOD TYPOLOGY

Brand	Wallet	Time

To determine your typology combine your three letters and find your typology in the table below. I have included a brief description for each typology. For reference purposes I have also included the results of the Dog Food Survey.

COMPARE YOUR RESULTS TO THE DOG FOOD SURVEY

Typology	Typology Name	% of Survey Respondents	Typology Description
BDM	Brand Tracker	19%	These shoppers know what they like, want a deal, and do not want to waste time shopping for it.
BPM	Loyalty Lasers	32%	Shopping is quick and easy for these people because they simply buy brands they know.
BDJ	Fanatical Finders	7%	These shoppers shop the same brands on a consistent basis; therefore they are knowledgeable about pricing and know when a brand is a deal.
BPJ	Comfort Zoners	13%	They limit their selection within a product category to brands they know and brands they have tried.
FDM	Deal Surgeon	11%	Saving money and efficiency are priorities. These shoppers identify what they need and which brands have the best deals.

Typology	Typology Name	% of Survey Respondents	Typology Description
FDJ	Bargainista	7%	Deal trumps brand, and these shoppers are willing to try different brands in order to save money.
FPM	Shopping Minimalists	8%	The goal for these shoppers is to spend the least amount of time shopping.
FPJ	Solution Shoppers	3%	These shoppers are goal-based and have a higher-level intent when they shop which supersedes brand and price.

Mobile Phone Survey

Please circle the answers for the following questions based on your recent purchase of a mobile phone.

Brand		
1. When it comes to my mobile phone, I would describe myself as "brand loyal."	Agree	Disagree
2. I didn't buy a brand, I bought a mobile phone.	Agree	Disagree
3. When buying a mobile phone, I chose the lower price over brand name.	Agree	Disagree
4. When purchasing my mobile phone, brand name was:	Very important	Not very important
5. When I shopped for my mobile phone, if a brand I prefer was unavailable, I:	Bought another brand	Waited to buy the brand I wanted at another time

Wallet		
1. When shopping for my mobile phone, I:	Spent time to save money	Spent money to save time
2. I priced out mobile phones at more than one place, and then I bought it where it was cheapest.	Agree	Disagree

3.	I wouldn't have felt really satisfied with my purchase unless I felt I'd gotten a good deal.	Agree	Disagree
4.	I wanted a mobile phone earlier, but I waited for it to go on sale.	Agree	Disagree
5.	When shopping for my mobile phone, I actively used tools that saved me money (e.g., coupons, deal websites, or pricing applications).	Agree	Disagree

Time			
1.	Shopping for my mobile phone was a task that I checked off my "to-do" list.	Agree	Disagree
2.	I put off shopping for my mobile phone until I absolutely needed to buy it.	Agree	Disagree
3.	When I was shopping for my mobile phone, it was:	Like a mission—there was a very specific goal and plan of action	Like a journey—there was a process of discovery and evaluation
4.	When shopping for my mobile phone, I:	Wanted to spend as little time as possible	Enjoyed it and liked to browse around to see what was available
5.	When shopping for my mobile phone, I:	Had a plan for what I need and stuck to it	Knew what I needed, but I was open to other products and services

SCORING YOUR SURVEY

Based on your results above, give yourself a point for each of your answers that match the answers below:

Scoring for Brand	Answer	Score
1. When it comes to my mobile phone, I would describe myself as "brand loyal."	Agree	
2. I didn't buy a brand, I bought a mobile phone.	Disagree	

Scoring for Brand	Answer	Score
3. When buying a mobile phone, I chose the lower price over brand name.	Disagree	
4. When purchasing my mobile phone, brand name was:	Very important	
5. When I shopped for my mobile phone, if a brand I prefer was unavailable, I:	Waited to buy the brand I wanted at another time.	
Total Score for Brand		

If you have three or more answers that match the above give yourself a "B" (meaning Brand Citizen) in the Brand typology box below; if you have less than three give yourself an "F" (meaning Free Agent).

Scoring for Wallet	Answer	Score
1. When shopping for my mobile phone, I:	Spent time to save money	
2. I priced out mobile phones at more than one place, and then I bought it where it was cheapest.	Agree	
3. I wouldn't have felt really satisfied with my purchase unless I felt I'd gotten a good deal.	Agree	
4. I wanted a mobile phone earlier, but I waited for it to go on sale.	Agree	
5. When shopping for my mobile phone, I actively used tools that saved me money (e.g., coupons, deal websites, or pricing applications).	Agree	
Total Score for Wallet		

If you have three or more answers that match the above give yourself a "D" (meaning Deal Seeker) in the Wallet typology box below; if you have less than three give yourself an "P" (meaning Price Blind).

Scoring for Time		Answer	Score
1.	Shopping for my mobile phone was a task that I checked off my "to-do" list.	Agree	
2.	I put off shopping for my mobile phone until I absolutely needed to buy it.	Agree	
3.	When I was shopping for my mobile phone, it was:	Like a mission—there was a very specific goal and plan of action	
4.	When shopping for my mobile phone, I:	Wanted to spend as little time as possible	
5.	When shopping for my mobile phone, I:	Had a plan for what I need and stuck to it	
Total Score for Time			

If you have three or more answers that match the above give yourself a "M" (meaning Mission) in the Time typology box below; if you have less than three give yourself an "J" (meaning Journey).

MY MOBILE PHONE TYPOLOGY

Brand	Wallet	Time

To determine your typology combine your three letters and find your typology in the table below. I have included a brief description for each typology. For reference purposes I have also included the results of the Mobile Phone Survey.

COMPARE YOUR RESULTS TO THE MOBILE PHONE SURVEY

Typology	Typology Name	% of Survey Respondents	Typology Description
BDM	Brand Tracker	15%	These shoppers know what they like, want a deal, and do not want to waste time shopping for it.
BPM	Loyalty Lasers	5%	Shopping is quick and easy for these people because they simply buy brands they know.
BDJ	Fanatical Finders	16%	These shoppers shop the same brands on a consistent basis; therefore they are knowledgeable about pricing and know when a brand is a deal.
BPJ	Comfort Zoners	5%	They limit their selection within a product category to brands they know and brands they have tried.
FDM	Deal Surgeon	25%	Saving money and efficiency are priorities. These shoppers identify what they need and which brands have the best deals.
FDJ	Bargainista	26%	Deal trumps brand, and these shoppers are willing to try different brands in order to save money.
FPM	Shopping Minimalists	5%	The goal for these shoppers is to spend the least amount of time shopping.
FPJ	Solution Shoppers	3%	These shoppers are goal-based and have a higher-level intent when they shop which supersedes brand and price.

Hotel Survey

Please indicate whether you most often agree or disagree with each of the following statements specifically as it relates to your recent reservation and stay.

Brand		
1. When it comes to the last hotel where I stated, I would describe myself as "brand loyal."	Agree	Disagree
2. I didn't choose based on brand, I just needed a place to stay.	Agree	Disagree
3. When booking my hotel, I chose the lower price over brand name.	Agree	Disagree
4. When making my hotel reservation, brand name was:	Very important	Not very important
5. If when making my reservation the brand of hotel I preferred had no rooms available, I would have:	Looked for the same brand a bit farther from the location I was interested in	Just booked a room at another brand closest to the original location I was interested in

Wallet		
1. When it came to shopping for, researching, and booking my hotel, I:	Spent time to save money	Spent money to save time
2. I priced more than one location of the same brand of hotel in the area, and then I booked at the cheapest location.	Agree	Disagree
3. I wouldn't have felt satisfied with my reservation unless I felt I'd gotten a good deal.	Agree	Disagree
4. I wanted to travel at a different time, but I booked my hotel when I could get a better deal on it.	Agree	Disagree
5. When making my hotel reservation, I actively used tools that saved me money (e.g., price comparison websites, brokers).	Agree	Disagree

Time		
1. Booking the hotel was a task that I checked off my "to-do" list.	Agree	Disagree

2.	I avoided booking my hotel reservation until I absolutely needed to.	Agree	Disagree
3.	When I researched/shopped for my recent hotel reservation, it was:	Like a mission—there was a very specific goal and plan of action	Like a journey—there was a process of discovery and evaluation
4.	When I shopped for/researched my hotel reservation, I:	Wanted to spend as little time as possible	Enjoyed it and liked to browse around to see what was available
5.	When I shopped for/researched my hotel reservation, I:	Knew exactly where I wanted to stay and what type of options I was interested in	Had an idea what I wanted, but was open to different hotels and options

SCORING YOUR SURVEY

Based on your results above, give yourself a point for each of your answers that match the answers below:

Scoring for Brand		Answer	Score
1.	When it comes to the last hotel where I stated, I would describe myself as "brand loyal."	Agree	
2.	I didn't choose based on brand, I just needed a place to stay.	Disagree	
3.	When booking my hotel, I chose the lower price over brand name.	Disagree	
4.	When making my hotel reservation, brand name was:	Very important	
5.	If when making my reservation the brand of hotel I preferred had no rooms available, I would have:	Looked for the same brand a bit farther from the location I was interested in	
Total Score for Brand			

If you have three or more answers that match the above give yourself a "B" (meaning Brand Citizen) in the Brand typology box below; if you have less than three give yourself an "F" (meaning Free Agent).

Scoring for Wallet		Answer	Score
1.	When it came to shopping for, researching, and booking my hotel, I:	Spent time to save money	
2.	I priced more than one location of the same brand of hotel in the area, and then I booked at the cheapest location.	Agree	
3.	I wouldn't have felt satisfied with my reservation unless I felt I'd gotten a good deal.	Agree	
4.	I wanted to travel at a different time, but I booked my hotel when I could get a better deal on it.	Agree	
5.	When making my hotel reservation, I actively used tools that saved me money (e.g., price comparison websites, brokers).	Agree	
Total Score for Wallet			

If you have three or more answers that match the above give yourself a "D" (meaning Deal Seeker) in the Wallet typology box below; if you have less than three give yourself an "P" (meaning Price Blind).

Scoring for Time		Answer	Score
1.	Booking the hotel was a task that I checked off my "to-do" list.	Agree	
2.	I avoided booking my hotel reservation until I absolutely needed to.	Agree	
3.	When I researched/shopped for my recent hotel reservation, it was:	Like a mission—there was a very specific goal and plan of action	

Scoring for Time	Answer	Score
4. When I shopped for/researched my hotel reservation, I:	Wanted to spend as little time as possible	
5. When I shopped for/researched my hotel reservation, I:	Knew exactly where I wanted to stay and what type of options I was interested in	
Total Score for Time		

If you have three or more answers that match the above give yourself a "M" (meaning Mission) in the Time typology box below; if you have less than three give yourself an "J" (meaning Journey).

MY HOTEL TYPOLOGY

Brand	Wallet	Time

To determine your typology combine your three letters and find your typology in the table below. I have included a brief description for each typology. For reference purposes I have also included the results of the Hotel Survey.

COMPARE YOUR RESULTS TO THE HOTEL SURVEY

Typology	Typology Name	% of Survey Respondents	Typology Description
BDM	Brand Tracker	8%	These shoppers know what they like, want a deal, and do not want to waste time shopping for it.
BPM	Loyalty Lasers	15%	Shopping is quick and easy for these people because they simply buy brands they know.

Typology	Typology Name	% of Survey Respondents	Typology Description
BDJ	**Fanatical Finders**	15%	These shoppers shop the same brands on a consistent basis; therefore they are knowledgeable about pricing and know when a brand is a deal.
BPJ	**Comfort Zoners**	11%	They limit their selection within a product category to brands they know and brands they have tried.
FDM	**Deal Surgeon**	11%	Saving money and efficiency are priorities. These shoppers identify what they need and which brands have the best deals.
FDJ	**Bargainista**	18%	Deal trumps brand, and these shoppers are willing to try different brands in order to save money.
FPM	**Shopping Minimalists**	12%	The goal for these shoppers is to spend the least amount of time shopping.
FPJ	**Solution Shoppers**	10%	These shoppers are goal-based and have a higher-level intent when they shop which supersedes brand and price.

References

References are keyed by page number.

42–43   Beer and wine drinking habits: Neilsen, "Tried and true or adventurous: Do consumers stick to their favorite alcohol brands?" May 21, 2015; Wine Market Council, High Frequency Tracking Study, November 2015; Whole World Wines: U.S. Wine Industry Information; National Brewers Association, National Beer Sales and Production Data, 2017; "Here's why (and where) we're buying craft beer, according to Nielsen data," *Draft Magazine*, July 27, 2015.

43   "Getting a deal": Ipso, February 2015.

54   "According to J.D. Power": J.D. Power 2015 U.S. Insurance Shopper Study.

55   "Since 2014 Panera's mission": "Panera Cleans Up Its Act," *Advertising Age*, January 6, 2017.

71–72   "Many such shoppers rationalize": BigCommerce survey in concert with Kelton Global, March 2016.

72   "In 2013 Best Buy": "A New Move by Best Buy to Eliminate Showrooming Trap," *Forbes*, April 4, 2014.

75   "The five cities combined": Coupons.com.

84   "Consider the age-old question": Psych Central blog, "Why Men Don't Ask for Directions."

93   "Considerable work has been carried out on impulse buying": "What Motivates Impulse Buying?" *Psychology Today*, July 18, 2012.

97   "A study in the UK": "Nomophobia: A Rising Trend in Students," *Psychology Today*, September 18, 2014.

101   "Regardless of a person's perspective": "When Do US and UK Shoppers Shop Online?" *Digital Vision*, April 20, 2016.

102   Effect of weather on buying behaviors: "The weird ways the weather makes you buy things you didn't plan to," *Washington Post*, November 25, 2015; Google Food Trends, 2016; "The Mysterious Power of the Weather," *Psychology Today*, March 9, 2015.

104–5   "Think of the holiday shopper": "Three Out of Four Consumers Plagued With Holiday Gift Giving Stress," Market Wire, November 19, 2015.

105   "The next highest share": "Amazon grabbing the bulk of surging online sales this holiday," CNBC, December 23, 2016.

105   "As a reference point": National Retail Federation, 2016 Holiday Shopping Trends.

107   "Lastly, holidays are a time for sharing": "How The Holidays Change Consumer Behavior," *MediaPost*, October 3, 2016.

125   "As a teen in the late '70s": Pew Research, Teens, Social Media and Technology Overview, 2015; "Who needs a car? Smartphones are driving teens' social lives," *Los Angeles Times*, March 15, 2013.

130–1 *Advertising Age*'s Top 10 Super Bowl ads: Judann Pollack, "The Super Bowl Top 50 Ad Countdown: 10–1," *Advertising Age*, February 4, 2016.

132–3 Profound Brand Shift section: Chrysler— "The Super Bowl ad that changed the public's views of Chrysler," All Par. Domino's—CP&B website, http://www.cpbgroup.com/work/dominos/dominos-pizza-turnaround.

133   Breakthrough Brand Action section: CVS: "After CVS Stopped Cigarette Sales, Smokers Stopped Buying Elsewhere, Too," *Forbes*, February 20, 2017. Tom's: Tom's website.

135   "Past customers are an influential source": Invesp.

144   "But does this constant barrage": J.D. Power 2015 U.S. Insurance Shopping Study.

146–7 "The weekly circular": "Consumers want their printed circulars," *Retail Wire*, May 15, 2015.

148   "However, the average household": COLLOQUY Loyalty Census, February 2015.

150   "So are fast casual restaurants": Panera 2015 Fiscal Report.

141   "As of January 2017": DMR Stats.

158   "In fact, rewards that help consumers": Excentus 2015 Survey.

160   "The duality of the program": "Younger Consumers Visit C-stores Most Frequently," *Convenience Store News*, February 24, 2015.

160   "From a partner perspective": "Plenti Continues to Grow Loyalty Coalition," Pymnts.com, November 29, 2016.

171   "The first thing to think about": All Recipes 2015 Digital Grocery Shopping Trends.

172   "About 66 percent of Millennials": Food Marketing Institute U.S. Grocery Shopper Trends, 2016.

172   "The deal journey": "How Millennials Are Changing the Face of Marketing Forever," Boston Consulting Group, January 15, 2014; "Often Operating on Tight Budgets, Mothers Tend to Be Bargain Hunters," eMarketer, October 18, 2016; Food Marketing Institute U.S. Grocery Shopper Trends, 2016; Blackhawk Engagement Solutions.

186   "How does a sleepy resort town": Traverse City Film Festival web site.

190   "In fact, there are many sites": "Eating Well: A Week of 5-Ingredient Dinners for Less Than $50," http://www.eatingwell.com/healthy_cooking/budget_cooking/a_week_of_5_ingredient_dinners_for_less_than_50; "Don't Waste the Crumbs: One Week $50 Meal Plan for a Family of Four," http://dontwastethecrumbs.com/2015/06/one-week-50-meal-plan-for-a-family-of-four/.

191   "The lodge maximizes the benefits": To view package details, go to http://www.lakenpineslodge.com/.

192   "One Amazon creation is the Dash button": "Amazon Dash Button orders are through the roof," *Business Insider*, October 26, 2016.

193   "The campaign generated": See, for instance, "Connecting with Colour: CIL's Paint Chips for Men Campaign," at https://smbp.uwaterloo.ca/2013/11/connecting-with-colour-cils-paint-chips-for-men-campaign/.

194   "Over 163 million people": "Real Beauty Shines Through: Dove Wins Titanium Grand Prix, 163 Million Views on YouTube," *Think with Google*, June 2013.

195   "During the six-week holiday period": "OfficeMax Out Elfs Itself: A Case Study In Viral Marketing," *MediaPost*, January 21, 2008.

Index of Key Concepts

www.ingramcontent.com/pod-product-compliance
Lightning Source LLC
Chambersburg PA
CBHW071158210326
41597CB00016B/1588